Learning Resource Centre
Park Road, Uxbridge, Middlesex, UB8 1NQ
Renewals: 01895 853344

Please return this item to the LRC on or before the
last date stamped below:

		793. 01

The Aesthetic of Play

The Aesthetic of Play

Brian Upton

The MIT Press
Cambridge, Massachusetts
London, England

MIT Press books may be purchased at special quantity discounts for business or sales promotional use. For information, email special_sales@mitpress.mit.edu.

Set in Stone Sans and Stone Serif by Toppan Best-set Premedia Limited, Hong Kong. Printed and bound in the United States of America.

Library of Congress Cataloging-in-Publication Data are available

ISBN: 978-0-262-02851-6 (hardcover : alk. paper)

10 9 8 7 6 5 4 3 2 1

Everyone has some narrow talent. Mine happens to be the ability to explain complex subjects in clear language.

Howard Upton

This book is dedicated to my late father. He always had time to play.

Contents

Acknowledgments

I'd like to thank the following individuals who generously read earlier drafts of this manuscript and provided invaluable feedback: Andy Ashcraft, Kelsey Cowger, Noah Falstein, Diane Feldman, Thomas Grip, Nathan Kelber.

I'd like to thank the staff at the MIT Press and my editor, Douglas Sery, for their help in preparing the manuscript for publication. I'd also like to thank the staff members of the Starbucks at Olympic and Westwood in Los Angeles, who kept me supplied with coffee while I was writing the book, and my children, Sam and Rose, for being good-natured test cases.

But most of all I'd like to thank my wife and interlocutor, Elizabeth Randell Upton. The ideas contained in the book were developed during hundreds of hours of conversation between us. Many of the questions I've attempted to answer were first posed by Elizabeth. Without her collaboration, the book would not exist.

Introduction

When I was ten years old, I talked my mom into buying me my first war game. It was *Blitzkrieg*, by Avalon Hill. I can still remember stumbling upon it in the toy section of a department store in Tulsa. It looked oddly out of place among the mass-market family games such as *Monopoly* and *The Game of Life*. The cover art was a stark composition of purple and black and red, with barbed wire and tanks and fighter planes. "Realistic GAME of Lightning Warfare" it said, in large bold letters. And the box was *heavy*—two or three times as heavy as any game I'd ever held before—which seemed to suggest that there was something dense and important inside. I remember the weight of the box was actually one of the arguments that I used when convincing my mother to buy it. This wasn't going to be some flimsy trivial toy that I was going to get bored with in an afternoon. Something that heavy would clearly last a while.

When I got *Blitzkrieg* home, I discovered why it was so heavy. The board was huge—large enough to cover our kitchen table—and there were literally hundreds of pieces—little squares of pink and blue die-cut cardboard covered in numbers and cryptic symbols. The basic rules went on for pages, and the advanced rules were even longer. It took me more than an hour to punch out all the counters and lay them out neatly on the "order of battle" cards that showed the starting set-up. It took me even longer to figure out how the game was supposed to work. By the time I was ready to play, I'd already been fiddling with the game for the better part of a weekend.

That was when I discovered the heartbreak of the solitary board gamer. I had this amazing new game all laid out and ready to play, but no one to play it *with*. My parents and my sisters liked board games, but not if they took hours to learn. They took one look at the thick booklet of basic rules and refused. My friends wouldn't even look at the booklet. They wouldn't even let me try to explain the rules to them—they were too long, too complicated, too much work to understand. They preferred to play *Trouble*, or ride bikes, or run around in the back yard.

Eventually, a few years later, I would discover a group of fellow gamers. They met every Saturday at Tulsa's downtown library, and for eight hours every week I could hang out with people like me, people who didn't think there was anything strange about twenty-page rulebooks. We played *Imperium*, and *Cosmic Encounter*, and *Star Fleet Battles*, and *Ogre*, and dozens of others.

However, for three or four years at the beginning of my teens, my gaming experiences consisted mostly of me setting up a game and fiddling with it. *Blitzkrieg* was the first, but then came *Waterloo* (another Avalon Hill title) and *Anzio* and *Dungeons & Dragons* and *4000 A.D.* and *Divine Right.* I'd try out little experimental scenarios to see how the mechanics worked, and read through the rules over and over again, looking for odd nooks and crannies in the system that could be exploited in interesting ways. And as a result, I developed an odd relationship with games. Instead of approaching them as something to be *played*, I began to think of them as something to be *played with*. I discovered that *analyzing* the rules of a game could be just as much fun (for me at least) as following them.

Now, I admit, this is not normal. Most people don't approach games this way. But for me, this strange relationship with rule-based systems turned into a career. In my teens I began coding my own computer games, and in my twenties I began designing my own board games, and finally in my thirties I found myself, almost by accident, working as a professional videogame developer. I was the lead designer on the first *Rainbow Six* and the first *Ghost Recon*, among other titles. These days I'm employed for Sony in a capacity I like to describe as "a script doctor for games." I don't usually design an entire game from scratch anymore. Instead, I get called in to look at other people's games while they are in production to figure out how to make them better. Partially this involves playing them with a critical eye, but it also means crawling inside their rule systems and taking them apart, in exactly the same way that I did during those long summer afternoons in Tulsa thirty years ago.

It's a job that I'm lucky to have because, until relatively recently, no one thought about games as being *designed*. Games have always been with us, of course; archeologists have recovered 5,000-year-old board games from Egyptian tombs. But for most of human history, games were like folktales—invented by anonymous amateurs, and then incrementally tweaked and polished by the invisible hands of hundreds of different players. Because this process was so diffuse, people didn't even think of it *as* a process. Games just seemed to happen, spontaneously bubbling up out of nowhere. Their genesis was opaque—a mysterious conjunction of inspiration, intuition, and collaborative iteration. The idea that a game might have a *designer*— the way a novel has an author or a symphony has a composer—wasn't even considered.

As a result, while games have always been with us, no one gave any serious thought to the theory behind them. Games never developed the sort of critical language that we take for granted when we study art or literature or music. If I'm trying to understand how a story works, for example, I can draw on a 2,000-year-old tradition of literary criticism stretching from Barthes and Derrida back to Aristotle and Plato. Long-standing abstract concepts like character, plot, allusion, foreshadowing, irony, climax—these are all tools I can use to take a text apart and analyze how it generates (or fails to generate) an aesthetic effect. Music has melody, harmony, major keys and minor keys, chords and time signatures. Even film, a much newer medium, has a powerful theoretical framework of scenes, cuts, shots, and camera angles. The analytical methodologies that people working in other creative fields can take for granted are only just now being invented for games.

Greg Costikyan summed up the problem in his 1994 essay "I Have No Words & I Must Design":

As game designers, we need a way to analyze games, to try to understand them, and to understand what works and what makes them interesting. We need a critical language. And since this is basically a new form, despite its tremendous growth and staggering diversity, we need to invent one.[1]

We've made a lot of progress in the 20 years since Costikyan wrote those words. These days when I'm working with a team of designers I can refer to the cadence of an encounter, or talk about improving feedback cues, and I can be pretty sure that not only will everyone understand what I'm saying, they'll also understand why these factors are an important part of structuring player experience. We are no longer groping blindly in the dark, trying different mechanics at random to see what works and what doesn't. There is an emerging body of theory, both in the literature and in the minds of working designers, that allows us to analyze games and game designs and talk in specific ways about how they succeed or fail.

And yet we are really only at the very beginning of thinking critically about games. Most of our theoretical knowledge is very narrowly focused

---

1. Costikyan, "I Have No Words & I Must Design."

and practical. We are better at answering small questions ("Why is this boss battle boring?") than we are at answering big ones ("What does this game mean?"). We are better at designing experiences that are fun and addictive than we are at designing ones that are powerful or profound. We have learned a lot about the syntax of games, but we are still grappling with their semantics.

It is toward these larger questions that this book is addressed, although in the process of answering them I hope to answer a number of smaller questions as well. It's a book about the experience of play—how playful activities unfold from moment to moment as we participate in them, and how the rules we adopt constrain the shape of that unfolding. It describes a framework for thinking rigorously about play, for understanding why some play spaces work and others don't, and for understanding how play can be structured to deliver particular experiences for particular players. More important, it explores the broader epistemological implications of the existence of such a framework: What is the role of play in the construction of meaning? What does the existence of play say about the relationship between our thoughts and external reality? And, finally, this book investigates how meaning-making play is not merely a feature of games, but permeates virtually every aspect of human culture—how understanding the structure of play helps us to understand the structure of books, of music, of theater, of art, and even the structure of critical theory itself.

The rest of the book is divided into three parts. Part I, titled Games, lays out a basic framework for understanding the *experience* of play. It introduces a new set of critical tools and shows how they can be applied to analyzing the rule sets of various games. Part II, titled Minds, establishes a theoretical foundation for analyzing *meaning-making* during play. Pragmatic epistemology, neuroscience, and semiotics are used to construct a functional description of how meaning emerges through playful engagement. Part III, titled Stories, generalizes the model by extending it beyond games to other cultural artifacts. Specifically, it shows how play can explain particular aspects of narrative. It investigates how we assign meaning to texts, and describes how a play-based interpretative stance can even shed light on the process of critical engagement itself.

Though the ideas discussed in the book are framed in new ways, many of them are quite old. Various writers have been brushing up against this particular way of understanding the world for hundreds of years. This shouldn't be surprising. The impulse toward play is very ancient. Not only is play pre-cultural, it's pre-human. Zoologists have identified play behaviors in hundreds of different species ranging from chimpanzees to turtles.[2] Wherever there is a large enough brain and a rich enough environment, play seems to emerge as a natural consequence. So it would be very strange if the effect of play on culture had gone entirely unnoticed until now.

Books about new media often make a point of emphasizing how videogames represent a radical break from older forms of art. They are non-linear, procedural, interactive, ergodic. The purpose behind putting forth this idea of a radical break seems to be twofold: to carve out a unique critical space for discussing games that frees the discourse from the constraints of preexisting critical methodologies and to establish videogames as being on the vanguard of some sort of postmodern cultural revolution. I disagree with this approach. However personally satisfying it might be to those of us who make (or study) games to believe that we are doing something revolutionary, in fact videogames work only because they tap into something very fundamental and ancient within ourselves. The same impulse toward play that drives our behavior when we are playing a modern "first-person shooter" is present when we read a line from Homer or look at the paintings on the walls of the caves at Lascaux.

Furthermore, though the construction of a self-contained critical space for analyzing videogames might be useful within the game industry and the gamer community, the scope of such a game-specific critical discourse is necessarily limited. I'm interested not only in developing better ways to talk about games, but also in extending our tools for talking about games to other forms of culture. Thus, rather than trying to protect game studies from being *colonized* by literary studies I want to use game studies to *critique and inform* literary studies. And such a cross-media critical stance is impossible if you start from the position that videogames are radically different from other types of art.

This book is deliberately not radical. It is anchored firmly in much older critical and philosophical traditions. Yet, at the same time, it is very radical indeed. We all are born knowing how to play, but the very ubiquity of play in our cognitive landscape renders it invisible. We play all the time, not just when we are sitting at a game board or holding a controller, and the nature of our play in these non-game contexts is often far more ramified and subtle. The goals of this book are to illuminate the landscape of play that we inhabit, to make the invisible visible, and to explain how the shape of much of what we do is governed by the unconscious constraints of play's necessary structure.

2. Fagen, *Animal Play Behavior*.

And so, ultimately, this book is an invitation. It is an invitation to play a particular sort of game. It offers a set of rules designed to structure an open-ended critical play space that offers new creative moves and new interpretive strategies. The rules are long, I know, and I'll certainly understand if you don't want to read them; I'm all too well aware that not everyone likes complicated games. However, I hope that if you take the time to learn and understand them you'll discover what I've discovered: The experiences that this particular game delivers can be powerful and amazing. What I *really* want (ten-year-old that I still am) is not just for more people to play this particular game, but for more people to play this particular game *with me*.

I Games

1 Defining Play

Everyone plays.

From the pre-Columbian ball courts of Central America, to the board games of the Indian subcontinent, from the rope-skipping games of the Outback, to the pebble-and-pit games of Africa, from the chivalric tournaments of medieval Europe, to videogames in modern Japan—everywhere we look, in every era and every culture, we find games, and humans playing them.

More important, everywhere we look, *how we play* is the same. As long as I take a few minutes to learn the rules, I can play a game that originated in Germany, or Ghana, or Peru, or ancient Mesopotamia, and it will function properly for me *as a game*. It will contain the same mix of obstacles and affordances that all games do—the arbitrary restrictions that block easy progress, the obvious opportunities for meaningful action, the delicate balance between knowledge and uncertainty. As a beginner, I may not play well, but the experience of playing will nevertheless feel comfortable and familiar.

This is a remarkable thing. Most cultural practices aren't that portable. Most of the time when we encounter something from an unfamiliar culture our initial experience is a bit detached and awkward; we aren't able to jump right in and fully engage. For example, if I attend a performance of Chinese opera, I may be able to appreciate it on a superficial level as a vivid spectacle, but my lack of knowledge of Chinese culture will cut me off from the bulk of the performance. If I want to participate as an audience member, I need to learn a lot more about the context of what I'm looking at. I need to learn thousands of little details about Chinese history, etiquette, music, mythology, and family relations. This process of acculturation can take years, sometimes even a lifetime.

Games aren't like that. With games, the normal rules for cross-cultural experiences don't seem to apply. For example, the game of *go* was invented in China more than 2,000 years ago; its origins are far more remote than Chinese opera. Furthermore, until the nineteenth century it was virtually unknown outside of Asia, so its influence on Western culture has been vanishingly small. Yet a twenty-first-century American can learn to play *go* in about ten minutes. You don't need to be a historian to understand *go*. In fact, you don't need to know the first thing about ancient China. Translated into modern English, the old rules still make sense; they still structure an entertaining play experience. And if you follow those old rules, you aren't just pretending to play *go*, or going through the motions of playing *go*. You are really and truly playing *go*. In fact, if you continue playing, you can become very good at *go* without ever learning anything about Chinese culture. *Go's* ability to function as a game doesn't dependent on cultural context. *Go* is portable in a way that Chinese opera is not.

Now, this doesn't mean that the full experience of an American playing *go* in the twenty-first century will be identical to the full experience of a Chinese aristocrat playing it in the third century. Besides being a game, *go* is also a cultural practice, and so the wider significance of playing the game will be different when the game is played in different times or places. The *meaning* of playing the game will change depending on its cultural context. But the *mechanics* of the game, the obstacles and affordances that govern how the game unfolds, will function the same regardless of cultural context. The game doesn't feel broken, or unbalanced, or unplayable, even though it was invented in a culture very different from our own.

What is true of *go* is true of games in general. And I propose that the reason it is true is that there is a deep structure to play that transcends cultural boundaries. The mechanics of all games feel curiously familiar because in order for a game to function as a game it must meet certain universal conditions. There are rules for rules, as it were—a collection of meta-rules that must be followed if a rule set is going to structure a successful play space. Very simply, games that follow these meta-rules are playable, and games that don't follow them aren't. It doesn't matter if a game was invented 3,000 years ago in sub-Saharan Africa—in order for it to work as a game, its rules must conform to the deep structure of play. And if its rules conform to the deep structure of play, it will function properly as a play experience for anyone who tries to play it.

If we look closely at a wide variety of games, we can see the outlines of this deep structure. Furthermore, once we are aware of this structure, we can begin to observe how it exerts its influence on other types of play besides games. For example, the rules of narrative can be shown to be grounded in the meta-rules for successful play spaces; stories work as stories because they are structured to accommodate particular sorts of reader play. Music, theater, painting, or architecture (really, any activity that can be called "art") can be analyzed and understood within a play-based framework. And so, through the close study of games, we can arrive at a broadly applicable aesthetic theory that explains a number of different artistic experiences.

How this deep structure manifests itself in different cultural contexts will vary, of course. Just as the meaning of a game of *go* depends on who is playing it, so the way that play emerges in other artistic experiences will depend a great deal on the cultural work those experiences are doing. We can't always separate meaning and mechanics as neatly as we can with *go*. This is particularly true when we consider experiences in which it is meaning itself that is being played with.

This shouldn't be construed as a claim that "everything is a game." Games are a particular manifestation of play, not its totality. They happen to be a good starting point for an investigation of play because the formality of their rules makes the machinery of play easier to observe and analyze. But many traditional features of games don't translate well to other types of play spaces. For example, it doesn't make any sense to think of "winning" a Bach cantata, even though listening to a Bach cantata involves a great deal of play.

In fact, one of my motivations for inventing a cross-disciplinary framework for understanding play is that it highlights which elements of current game design practice are load-bearing and which aren't. For example, it is easy to fall in the trap of thinking that winning is an integral part of play. But, as Wil Wright has amply demonstrated with "software toys" such as *The Sims*, it is entirely possible to construct a successful play space without asking the player to work toward any specific victory condition. Understanding which features are essential and which are negotiable makes it possible to expand the sorts of aesthetic effects that games can produce.

In the next few chapters, I will develop a framework for understanding the deep structure of play. This framework will consist of a set of meta-rules for the construction of successful play spaces. But the first stage in the construction of this framework is simply spelling out exactly what I mean by the word 'play'.

The Problem with Definitions

Defining terms is tricky. There is an unspoken assumption behind the practice: that if a definition is *correct*—if it manages to capture the *essence* of the thing under discussion—then everything that logically follows from that definition will be correct too. And so scholars often take great pains to demonstrate that there is a strong correlation between their definitions and reality.

For example, Salen and Zimmerman, in their expansive book on game design, *Rules of Play*, spend nine pages surveying previous scholarship to arrive at their definition for the word 'game'. They construct a table of different characteristics attributed to games by different sources in an attempt to uncover a shared set of concepts that will encapsulate the essence of what makes a game a game. The definition they finally settle on—"A game is a system in which players engage in artificial conflict, defined by rules, that results in a quantifiable outcome"[1]—isn't a bad one. However, I'd argue that the process by which Salen and Zimmerman arrive at it is flawed. By searching for commonalities among previous definitions, they wind up with a definition that tells us a lot about how people have historically thought about games, but little about whether this way of thinking about games is useful.

Words are the tools we use to isolate particular aspects of reality from its totality. When we write a definition, we are designing a new tool. Thus, the question we should always ask ourselves is not "Is this definition correct?" or "Do a lot of people use this definition?" but "Does this definition allow us to say something useful or interesting?" The "goodness" of a definition is measured not by its popularity or how well it encapsulates the essence of a thing, but by its capacity to generate a productive discourse.

What this means is that trying to nail down "what a game *really* is" or "what play *really* is" is pointless. It's like trying to determine which coordinate system—polar or Cartesian—is the "correct" way to represent a position on a two-dimensional plane. The answer is that the "correctness" of a coordinate system is determined by the type of calculations you are attempting to perform with it. Some problems are easier to solve using Cartesian coordinates, and some problems are easier to solve using polar coordinates. The coordinate system we impose upon the plane (the framework for our mathematical discourse) isn't an expression of the essence of the plane; it is a computational convenience.

And so it is with definitions. A good definition is *computationally convenient*—in the sense that it structures a discursive field that makes it easier to say interesting or useful things. The "correctness" of a definition isn't a property of the relationship between the word and reality; it is a function

---

1. Salen and Zimmerman, *Rules of Play*, 81.

of the conversation that the definition facilitates. And, indeed, multiple contradictory definitions can all be equally "correct" if they each manage to independently structure a productive discourse.

Thus, in providing a definition of "play," I am not claiming that my way of thinking about play is the only correct way to think about play. I'm not claiming that it encapsulates the fundamental essence of play, and I'm not going to attempt to justify it through a convoluted preliminary argument. Rather, I'm claiming that my way of thinking about play structures an intriguing discursive field, one that allows us to say interesting and meaningful things about the practice of playing. The correctness of the definition doesn't justify the conclusions it leads us to; instead, the ease with which we reach useful conclusions justifies the appropriateness of the definition.

The process of intentionally designing a definition to structure a discourse is, in fact, identical to the process of intentionally designing a rule to structure a play space. As a game designer, I don't design games by collecting a set of "true" rules and seeing what happens when you play them. Rather, I begin with a particular experience I want for the player, then work backward toward a rule set that will evoke that experience indirectly. There is a particular conversation that I want to have about play, and so (since I tend to think of everything in terms of game design) I have deliberately chosen a definition that makes that conversation easy to have.

A Useful Definition of Play

In 1938, on the eve of World War II, Johan Huizinga, a Dutch cultural historian, wrote a book on how play manifests itself through human culture. That book—titled *Homo Ludens*, meaning "man the player"—has cast a long shadow in game studies. Huizinga has been cited over and over again in articles and books on game design.

Surprisingly, Huizinga says almost nothing about games themselves. The bulk of *Homo Ludens* is devoted to exploring how play manifests itself as a cultural force in a variety of different non-game activities, among them worship, war, art, and philosophy. Games themselves are dealt with as a rather trivial and obvious case in chapter 1. It is clear that Huizinga sees games as merely a jumping-off point for the larger cultural issues that he wants to address. Consequentially, for a game designer, *Homo Ludens* is a very short read. Almost all of the useful bits are located in the first few pages, where Huizinga lays out the foundation of his argument.

Here is how Huizinga defines play:

A voluntary activity or occupation executed within certain fixed limits of time and place, according to rules freely accepted but absolutely binding, having its aim in itself and accompanied by a feeling of tension, joy, and the consciousness that is different from ordinary life.[2]

Contained within this definition are four elements that Huizinga believes are fundamental to play: movement, freedom, rules, and boundaries. Play is a process, not a static state of affairs. Play can't be compelled or coerced—it is a state into which we enter freely. While we are playing, our choices are our own to make—we aren't following orders or executing a checklist. But, paradoxically, our freedom isn't complete. Instead, we allow our actions to be constrained by a set of arbitrary rules that structure and limit the experience. By submitting to the authority of these rules, we establish a boundary that temporarily divides the simplicity and clarity of the play space from the complexity and obscurity of the real world. We enter into this "magic circle"[3] for a while, explore it freely, then return to ordinary life when we are finished.

With a game such as chess, it is easy see how these criteria operate. Players freely choose moves within what the rules allow, and the action of the game is limited to the boundaries of the chessboard. Remove any one of the four elements and play collapses:

No movement   Staring at a static arrangement of chess pieces is not playing chess.
No freedom   Moving pieces in a predetermined order is not playing chess.
No rules   Moving pieces aimlessly around the board is not playing chess.
No boundaries   Freely executing a legal chess move at some random place and time is not playing chess. The moves have to occur within the context of an ongoing match.

Huizinga interpreted the boundary condition fairly strictly. He viewed all forms of play as standing separate and apart from "ordinary life":

Summing up the formal characteristics of play we might call it a free activity standing quite consciously outside "ordinary" life as being "not serious," but at the same time absorbing the player intensely and utterly. It is an activity connected with no material interest, and no profit can be gained by it.[4]

2. Huizinga, *Homo Ludens*, 13.
3. The term *magic circle*, which originated with Huizinga, has been popularized by Salen and Zimmerman. See *Rules of Play*, 95–98.
4. Huizinga, *Homo Ludens*, 13.

The obvious flaw in this strict approach is that it eliminates activities such as casino gambling and professional sports from the definition of play. In both cases, the outcome of a game may have a very large effect on the real-world fortunes of the players. The players certainly have a material interest in the outcome. But does this alter the experience so dramatically that it no longer can be considered playful? Is it true that a football game between two high schools is an entirely different sort of activity than one between two professional teams? And, in view of the social cachet of being a member of a winning high school football team, can it really be said that a high school player doesn't "profit" from his victory?

In fact, Huizinga undermines his own position in later chapters, particularly "Play and Law" and "Play and War." It is hard to imagine situations in which "players" have more "material interest" at stake than in a courtroom or a battlefield, yet Huizinga finds elements of play in both. Despite his early statement to the contrary, it is clear that he accepts the idea that play doesn't have to be strictly segregated from ordinary life. Rather, play is something embedded within ordinary life; something that can arise spontaneously even in situations that we wouldn't think of as inherently playful.

All that play requires is the construction of a system of rules and the freedom to move within them. It isn't surprising that in many cases this will create a sense of separation from the day-to-day world—if the rules are clearly arbitrary then they can't help but call attention to their artificial nature. The rules of chess are like this. They have only a faint resemblance to the realities of war, so the play space they create is very clearly separate from ordinary life. But many play spaces are more tightly intertwined with everyday existence, with the result that the line between play and non-play is more difficult to draw.

The definition of play that we will be using in this book is both a simplification and an amplification of Huizinga's definition:

Play is free movement within a system of constraints.

Play is a process, not a thing. It is a series of moves, either mental or physical, carried out by the player. These moves are free in the sense that the player has control over what he will do next, but this freedom is bound by a set of constraints. These constraints limit the moves available to the player at any moment to a relatively small number. Furthermore, these constraints aren't random; they are organized into a system that is structured to deliver a particular experience.

The definition given above is similar to the definition of "play" put forward by Salen and Zimmerman: "Play is free movement within a more rigid structure."[5] I prefer the term *system of constraints* for two reasons—primarily because it emphasizes the deliberate nature of the boundaries of a play space: Life is full of arbitrary "rigid structures" (the tax code, for example) that don't provide satisfying play experiences when we navigate them. In order for play to emerge from a set of rules, the various restrictions placed on the player must work together in a particular systematic way. My second reason is that the phrase "rigid structure" implies an element of permanence. It fails to capture the fluid, shifting nature of the restrictions that define a typical play space. As we will see as we dive deeper into the mechanics of play, a large part of what makes play fun is not just that our actions are constrained, but that the constraints fluctuate from moment to moment as play progresses.

The definition above is also similar to the definition of 'game' advanced by Bernard Suits: "Playing a game is the voluntary attempt to overcome unnecessary obstacles."[6] Unfortunately, Suits, who is a philosopher and not a game designer, fails to grasp the systematically structured nature of a well-functioning playfield, which leads him astray as he tries to explain why overcoming some obstacles doesn't feel playful. Aside from that, Suits ignores many types of play (make-believe, for example) that don't involve much struggle at all.

What the Definition Includes

Let's take a look at how different playful activities fit with the definition of play given above. With traditional board games, the fit is obvious. The rules of chess are a system of constraints. Players make literal moves on a physical board. Each is free to choose his or her next move within the limitations of the rules. And the rules have been selected specifically to shape the form that the play takes.

With videogames, the constraints are a bit more varied. Some are explicit rules, such as "If you shoot an innocent bystander, you lose the mission." But the physical geometry of a level, or the behavior of the enemy AI,[7] or the amount of damage that a hand grenade does—those are constraints too. Anything in the game that proscribes the player's actions is a constraint. The player is free to move around within the game world, to trigger actions, even to change the world's configuration, but always within limits laid down by the game itself.

5. Salen and Zimmerman, *Rules of Play*, 304.

6. Suits, *The Grasshopper*, 55.

7. 'AI' is a term of art for the computer-controlled enemies in a game. Historically it meant "Artificial Intelligence" (a separate field, entirely divorced from game AI).

Sports are similar to board games in that they have a set of explicit rules. But they also rely on the real-world behavior of physical objects for part of their system of constraints.[8] The physical properties of a chess piece have little bearing on a game of chess, but the physical properties of a soccer ball are central to how the game is played. The physical properties of a pair of dice determine how they roll, but we could replace the dice in a game of *Monopoly* with a set of numbered chits drawn from a cup without changing how the game is played. However, we can't replace a baseball with a croquet ball without dramatically altering the experience. This is a crucial distinction between games and sports.

When we set out to construct a game, we don't have to start from scratch in designing a system. It is possible to take an existing constraint from the world around us—the physical behavior of an inflated ball, for example—and assemble other rules around it to create an opportunity for play. Furthermore, the same ball can be used in a variety of different games, depending on the supplementary rules we choose to apply to it. There is nothing intrinsic in the ball that compels us to use it only to play soccer. If we choose to do so, we can use it for kickball instead, or volleyball, or an entirely original game of our own invention. It all depends on the additional constraints that we decide to apply.

In board games, in videogames, and in sports, the rules tend to be clear-cut and formal. In order to score a run in baseball, the runner must touch all three bases in turn before returning to home plate, and must do so while remaining within the base paths and avoiding being tagged. There isn't much fuzziness in the system. It doesn't matter if the runner came *very, very close* to touching second base or the shortstop *very nearly almost dropped* the ball during the tag; the runner is still out.

But it is possible to have play without defining the rules so strictly. Most of the play that children engage in is governed by much looser and more flexible systems of rules. In a game of make-believe, for example, the participants take on roles and are expected to limit their actions accordingly. When my children were small, I often found myself assigned the role of "monster." Appropriate behavior for a monster was to stomp around, make growling noises, act scary, and die dramatically when hit over the head with a foam sword. At the same time, a wide range of other actions were disallowed: Monsters don't pick flowers, or offer to be friends with the hero,

8. "The main difference between the rules of a video game and the rules of a sport is that sports use the preexisting systems of the physical world in the game." Juul, *Half-Real*, 59.

or sing funny songs while they are dying. Doing any of these things would be met with cries of "You're doing it wrong!" or "You're ruining it!" However, there were always gray areas. The constraint of "monster" implied that some actions were mandatory and others were forbidden, but many others fell somewhere in the fuzzy middle. Was it permissible for the monster to fall asleep, for example? Maybe, and maybe not, depending on the dynamic flow of play at that particular moment.

When we hear the word 'rule', we think of the formal rules that dominate the structures of board games and sports. They are rigid and inviolate, with clear-cut meanings and little room for ambiguity or flexible interpretation. The word 'constraint' is more open-ended. It encompasses formal rules, but it also includes guidelines, suggestions, and inclinations. *Anything that privileges one line of action over another is a constraint.*[9] Sometimes this is done by explicitly allowing some things and forbidding others; other times the process is more fuzzy and informal.

We can see an intersection of these formal and informal constraints at work when we look at tabletop role-playing games such as *Dungeons & Dragons*. Most such games use formal rule-based systems to govern certain aspects of play—combat, for example. But they also encourage the players to simultaneously participate in a game of make-believe. The actions a player takes during a game session aren't limited only by the formal rules; they also are limited by the constraints imposed by the personality of the character he is playing and the narrative context of the adventure. For example, even though it may be to a player's advantage to ambush an enemy and stab him in the back, he may refuse to do so because "Sir Percival would never strike such an underhanded blow!"

What the Definition Excludes

The utility of a definition lies in its capacity to illuminate difference. If we articulate what something *is*, we do so because we are interested in distinguishing it from other things that it *isn't*. A definition that is too vague or too broad is useless. Our definition of play is intentionally very broad. But is it too broad? Does it make a meaningful distinction between things that are play and things that aren't? Or is it so vague that virtually any human activity can be considered "playful"? In order to answer these questions, let's look at what the definition excludes.

9. "Constraints—limitations on human behavior—may be expressed as anything from gentle suggestions to stringent rules, or they may by only subconsciously sensed as intrinsic aspects of the thing that a person is trying to do or be or create." Laurel, *Computers as Theater*, 99.

First, work isn't play. A job may present a set of constraints that must be navigated, but the movement within those constraints isn't free. As was discussed above, one of the essential criteria for play is that it can't be coerced or compelled. Play is an end unto itself. Workers may make decisions and perform actions as part of their jobs, but those tasks aren't ends unto themselves. Rather, they are done in the service of some external mandate or directive.

Consider the job of a game tester. A typical videogame undergoes thousands of hours of testing before it is released to the public. The goal is to flush out bugs and to provide feedback to the designers to help with play balance. Testers sit down with a game and methodically work through every conceivable variation of player interaction to track down gaps and flaws. Superficially, what they are doing resembles playing a game, but instead of feeling fun the experience of testing is often tedious drudgery. The primary difference is the tester's lack of freedom to choose his own path through the play space.

Furthermore, the constraints that most jobs impose aren't organized systematically. One of the primary features of the constraints that define play spaces is the way they interrelate with each other. The rules of chess aren't a random assortment of dos and don'ts. Each serves a specific function in structuring the overall experience—a function that is significant only within the context of the entire system. If we look at the various examples of play listed above, it is easy to see the systematic nature of their constraints. The rules of games and sports are designed to function together as an integrated whole.

For example, in the videogame *Portal* the player periodically passes through a "material emancipation grid" that vaporizes any object he happens to be carrying. The purpose of the grid in the system of constraints that defines *Portal*'s play space is to control the resources available to the player as he moves from puzzle to puzzle. By not allowing objects to be carried over from one puzzle to the next, the game makes it clear to the player that he will always have all the tools he needs to complete the current level. He need not worry that he is stuck because he forgot to pick up a crate when he left the previous level. The purpose of the material emancipation grid isn't to forbid possession of certain objects, but to enforce tight bounds on the scope of the puzzles.

Compare the structural function of the material emancipation grid with an analogous real-world situation: an airport security checkpoint. When you pass through a security checkpoint, the guards will "emancipate" certain objects (scissors, knives, bottles of shampoo) that are believed to pose a threat to your upcoming flight. The constraints enforced at the checkpoint aren't intended to be part of a larger system that structures your travel experience in interesting ways; rather, they serve a specific utilitarian purpose. Engaging with these rules will certainly affect your overall travel experience, but the effect is unintentional; it's merely an accidental by-product of their primary function.

Everyday life presents numerous constraints. The laws of physics and human physiology limit our physical capabilities, and the laws and customs of society limit what we are legally and morally allowed to do. To live life is to navigate these constraints on a daily basis. But in most cases this everyday action isn't playful—sometimes because we are coerced or compelled to take a particular course, but more often because the constraints we face aren't organized in a meaningful way. Play demands both the freedom to move and a systematically organized framework to move within.[10]

None of this should be surprising. For most people, play is something they use to escape the drudgery of work and the mundane tasks that make up day-to-day life. If our definition didn't recognize this distinction, it would be badly broken.

But people seek diversion in a wide variety of ways. They play chess and soccer, but they also ride roller coasters, have sex, eat steak dinners, and take long walks on beaches at sunset. All these activities have the potential to be diverting and entertaining, but are they all play?

Sometimes they are and sometimes they aren't. Play is often a source of pleasure, but not all things that provide pleasure are play. Play is movement, and movement takes time. In order for play to occur, there must be a sense that the player has traveled from one configuration of the play space to another—the pieces have shifted on the chessboard, the ball has moved down the field, or the first level has been cleared and the next one is beginning. But it is also possible to take enjoyment in the immediate sensory experience of the moment. When we take a bite out of a fresh, crisp apple, our pleasure is instantaneous and experiential. The taste is pleasurable in and of itself, not in relation to how it functions within a system of constraints.

10. "It is important, however, to understand how and why game structures do shape player behavior; indeed, understanding this is fundamental to mastering the craft of game design. You cannot simply throw together a bunch of different game elements, and expect them to cohere; you must consciously set out to decide what kind of experiences you want to impart to your players, and create systems that enable those experiences." Costikyan, "I Have No Words & I Must Design."

Thus, we should add sensation to the list of things that are not play. A sensation is enjoyable on its own terms. It isn't part of an evolving process; instead it occurs spontaneously in response to a particular constellation of stimuli. In his book *Man, Play and Games*, Roger Caillois constructs an entire category of play (which he dubs "ilinx") around the pursuit of the sensation of vertigo.[11] Vertigo certainly fits as a form of play within Caillois' interpretation of Huizinga, but its inclusion is problematic. It isn't clear why the pursuit of one particular physical sensation (the thrill of disorienting movement) should count as play but the pursuit of other sensations— visual, aural, tactile—should not. If spinning around to induce dizziness counts as a form of play, then so should taking a bite of sushi or having a massage.

Sensations can certainly add to the experience of play. They can be used as limits on players' behavior, or as rewards, or as means of supporting the atmosphere of make-believe, or even just as a parallel form of entertainment. Part of the pleasure of playing baseball is the satisfying smack the ball makes when it lands squarely in the pocket of one's glove. The rules of baseball don't require that catching the ball be sensually satisfying, but that sensual satisfaction is an important part of the experience. It is interesting to reflect on the battles that have been fought by baseball fans over the use of aluminum bats. As a physical constraint to define baseball's play space, an aluminum bat is just as good as a wooden one. But the player's sensation of using an aluminum bat is quite different. If you view baseball as pure play—free movement within a system of constraints—the composition of the bat is largely immaterial. But if you view baseball as comprising both play *and* a collection of specific sensations, the elimination of the crack of a wooden bat from the experience is a significant change.

Play stands in contrast to work, to everyday life, and to sensation. Play is not a thing, but a process. It is a way of moving within and engaging with a particular sort of system—a system that has been constructed according to a universal set of organizing principles. In the pages that follow, we will gradually build up a conceptual framework that will allow us to articulate what these organizing principles are.

11. Caillois, *Man, Play, and Games*, 23–26.

2 Interactivity

It is taken as a given within the game industry that the major difference between games and other forms of popular entertainment is interactivity. To play is to engage in a dialogue—information flows back and forth between player and game. With film, literature, theater—pretty much everything else—the flow of information is one way only. When you watch a movie or read a book, you aren't engaging in a dialogue; you are listening to a monologue.

This critical stance is very deeply ingrained. Every year the Academy of Interactive Arts and Sciences gives out the Interactive Achievement Awards to deserving game developers. There are game companies named Take-Two Interactive and Disney Interactive. Numerous digressions on videogames begin with a quick nod to their special interactive nature and how much they differ from traditional linear media.

Typically, non-electronic games and sports are also included under the umbrella of interactivity. When you play tennis, there is clearly a back-and-forth between you and your opponent. Information is flowing in both directions. The "interactive" label isn't intended to distinguish videogames from other games and sports. Rather, it is intended to draw a sharp distinction between games of all sorts and other more "passive" forms of entertainment.

Interactivity is, by definition, active. It's the give-and-take between player and rule system. I press a button on my controller and information is communicated to the game. The game updates the image on the screen, feeding information back to me. This new information provides the context for my next move. My actions influence the game and the game influences my actions in an ongoing chain of cause and effect (figure 2.1).

Although this way of representing interactivity may be accurate, it is trivial. It doesn't provide much insight into how games actually function

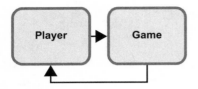

Figure 2.1
A very simple model of interactivity.

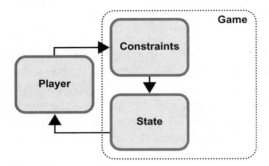

Figure 2.2
A slightly more complicated model of interactivity.

as play experiences. After all, even dull games usually do *something* when you press a button; interaction alone isn't enough to make a game interesting to play. For a game to be interesting, it must respond to our actions in certain very particular ways. And if we are going to understand what those ways are, we need to construct a more complicated conceptual framework of interactivity.

Let's begin by breaking the game down into two sub-components: constraints and state (figure 2.2). The constraints determine which moves are permitted; the state is an evolving record of the player's movement within the system. The constraints are fixed; the state is fluid. This fits nicely with our definition of play ("Free movement within a system of constraints"); it is also a very natural way to think about all sorts of games. Consider chess, for example. The rules of chess are a fixed set of constraints. (In fact, they have remained constant across millions of games played over hundreds of years.) However, the state of a game of chess—the arrangement of pieces on the board—changes with every move.

We can make a similar distinction with videogames. The contents of a game disk are fixed. All copies of the game that emerges from the manufacturing plant are identical. Every time I insert a disk into a game console, the same code and data—the same fixed constraints—are loaded. But as I play the game, things change. I move around. My health fluctuates. My character learns new skills. In addition to the fixed constraints I've loaded off the disk, there is a fluid state that changes from moment to moment. And if I'm forced to interrupt my game, I can copy this state to a save file so I can continue playing later.

Dividing games into constraints and state allows us to make a valuable distinction between the framework that structures a play experience and the play experience itself. A game isn't just a system of rules considered in isolation; it is also the pattern of movement that emerges within the play-field that the rules define.

Furthermore, although the set of constraints defining a play space may be fixed, their individual relevance varies during play. Every constraint doesn't structure every move. Depending on the state of the game, some constraints will play a large part in structuring our current actions and some constraints will play no part at all. For example, in chess the rules for castling apply only when the king and the rook are in particular positions. If that configuration of the board isn't an element of the current state, the rule for castling can be ignored. Similarly, when we play a videogame, our constraints change dramatically every time we advance to a new level. The constraints that defined level 2 don't affect our actions after we move on to level 3.

We can think of the set of constraints for a play space as divided into *active constraints* and *potential constraints*. An active constraint affects our actions right now; a potential constraint may affect us at some time in the future, or may have affected us at some time at some time in the past (figure 2.3).

During the course of play, changes in the state can cause potential constraints to become active, and can cause active constraints to recede back into mere potentiality. In fact, it is possible for some potential constraints to never become active. Think of a chess match in which neither player advances a pawn to the far side of the board, and the rule for pawn promotion thus never comes into play. Or think of a videogame that has a secret level that you never unlock. Similarly, particularly important active constraints may remain active through the entire game. The high-level constraint "stay on the road" structures every action we take during a racing game, even while the transient constraints provided by the geometry of the track and the positions of the other cars continually flicker in and out of potentiality.

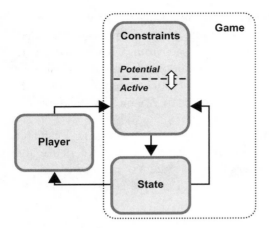

Figure 2.3
An even more complicated model of interactivity.

Constraints act as a filter on intent. They determine what changes to the state are allowed. But at the same time, the state determines which rules are active. This reciprocal relationship between constraints and state creates a situation in which both our position within the overall system and the immediate restrictions on our moment-to-moment actions are continually shifting and evolving.

What is useful about this way of thinking about play is that it focuses analysis of the play experience squarely on the evolving active constraints. It is easy for a game designer to get caught up in the global architecture of a rule set, and to conceptualize the entire play space as a static structure with certain affordances and restrictions. But from the player's perspective, the large-scale structure of the rules is invisible. From the player's perspective, the play experience consists of an unfolding encounter with a small but variable set of active constraints. And the quality of that experience is determined largely by the game's capacity to vary those active constraints in interesting or even seductive ways.

Deconstructing Interactivity

Now let's ask what seems to be a simple question: When we're playing a game of chess, where are the rules?

The location of the state is obvious. The board is on the table in front of us. The pieces are arranged in their proper positions. If we are using a chess clock, it is sitting next to the board. But where are the rules?

If we are novice players, the rules may be written on the back of the box the chess set came in. Or they might be in a book on a bookshelf behind us. Or they might be displayed on a computer screen nearby. The interesting thing, though, is that unless we are novice players the rules will not be consulted during the game. The rules of chess are written down in millions of locations around the world, but when you are actually playing a game of chess those physical manifestations of the rules aren't a part of the process. When you are actually playing a game of chess, the only rules that matter are the rules in your head.

As the game historian David Parlett writes,

There is a widespread assumption that all games have official rules that are recorded in writing. But it is mistaken. For one thing, most games are not book games but folk games, being transmitted by word of mouth, example and practice. For another, even where written rules *do* exist, probably no folk games and certainly very few book games can lay claim to a widely recognised governing body responsible for authorizing them. ... The most basic level of experience suggests that the rules of a game are something inherent in the game itself—or, more accurately (since a game is essentially a mode of behavior), an abstraction existing in the minds of all its players.[1]

The importance of this is hard to overstate. It is customary to think of players and games as distinct and separate entities. But when we take a hard look at a game such as chess, we discover that this distinction is illusory. The rules are clearly an essential part of the overall system of the game, but for all practical purposes they exist only in the heads of the players. The game isn't a separate entity that stands in isolation from the players; it is a hybrid of external components (the board, the pieces) and internal mental states.

Every game has constraints and a state. But those constraints and that state may not necessarily have a separate physical existence from the player. It is possible for a game to exist partially, or even wholly, inside the minds of its players (figure 2.4).

Some constraints are outside the player's head. These *external constraints* are imposed upon the player by some outside force—a baseball umpire, for example. And some constraints are inside the player's head. These *internal constraints* are, like the rules of bridge, imposed by the player on himself.

Similarly, some elements of the state are outside the player's head. A chessboard and chess pieces are an example of *external state*. But at the same time there are elements of *internal state* that exist only inside the player's

1. Parlett, "Rules OK or Hoyle on Troubled Waters."

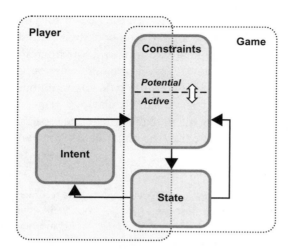

Figure 2.4
Blurring the line between player and game.

head—whose turn it is, for example.[2] In fact, if you are a good enough chess player, you can do away with the board and the pieces and hold the entire state of the game in your mind. Grandmasters sometimes play blindfolded as a stunt. The externality of the state of a game of chess is really just a notational convenience. The game plays the same even if the state is entirely internal and players make moves by calling them out to each other.

Different games draw the boundary between internal and external in different ways. For example, in a game of soccer the constraints have a large internal component. The players themselves know what is allowed and what is forbidden and tailor their actions accordingly. However, professional soccer games are played with a referee, who provides additional external reinforcement of the rules. On top of that, soccer has a number of physical constraints—the shape of the pitch, the natural capabilities of the human body, the dynamic properties of the ball, and the laws of physics themselves. These are obviously external.

Most traditional games rely heavily on internal constraints. Even when a referee is present, most players are self-policing. Videogames make much

2. Often games require that players maintain consensus about elements of their internal state. If I am playing chess with you, we must agree on whose turn it is in order for the game to proceed. However, maintaining this internal state generally doesn't require any communication between us. We track it independently, and talk about it only if one of us makes a mistake or attempts to cheat.

greater use of external constraints—the player doesn't participate in enforcing them. The contrast is obvious if we compare the computer version of a game with its real-world counterpart. When I play real-world solitaire, I make a conscious decision not to peek at the hidden cards. But when I play solitaire on my laptop, peeking isn't possible. Enforcing that constraint has been taken out of my hands.[3]

Because videogames depend heavily on the externality of their constraints, it is tempting to assume that they don't have an internal component at all. When I play a videogame, it is easy to imagine that all the obstacles I'm pushing against are all out there, in the outside world. What is in my head doesn't matter. But is that really true? Consider a sewer level in a typical action game. The slime-covered walls are a system of constraints that limit free movement through the space. If you run up against a wall, you stop. The game will not allow you to move further. But players rarely collide with the walls. The walls form a system of constraints, but players don't interact directly with it. Instead, they move through the space in such a way that they avoid obstacles before they collide with them. They have created an internal representation of the level inside their heads. They are aware of what the external constraints are, and they limit their actions accordingly. The external constraints still exist, but they are encountered only rarely. For the most part, when a player moves through a level, his actions are governed by the knowledge accumulated inside his brain—a set of internal constraints.

Learning how to play a game is often a matter of internalizing a set of external constraints. With chess, this process is explicit—we read the rules and memorize them. But with a videogame, we learn the rules mostly by experimentation. We jiggle the joystick and observe how our character responds. We collide with things to discover what blocks movement and what doesn't. We pick up a gun and shoot it to see how powerful it is. Step by step, we build an internal model of how the game world functions. As time goes by, our actions are structured less and less by the rules of the game and more and more by our understanding of those rules.

From this perspective, the entire notion of interactivity becomes suspect. Rather than treating play as a reciprocal exchange between player and game, it often makes more sense to view it as a player-centric activity that is sustained by occasional corrective nudges from an external system of

3. "Computer games *impose* the rules: they are not subject to discussion. Computer game rules are insurmountable laws the player has to acknowledge and surrender to in order to enjoy the game." Sicart, *The Ethics of Computer Games*, 27.

constraints. Game design then becomes less about building a system that responds in interesting ways and more about encouraging the formation of an interesting set of internal constraints in the mind of the player. Sometimes the former can result in the latter, but not inevitably.

Any theoretical framework that fails to take the role of internal constraints into account will necessarily exclude large swathes of the play experience from critical analysis. For example, the first major commercial game I designed was a first-person shooter—*Tom Clancy's Rainbow Six*, a tactical combat game about the actions of an international hostage rescue team. Most of its missions are rescue operations: sneaking into a barricaded building, killing (or avoiding) the terrorists inside, freeing their captives, and bringing them back out to safety.

Rainbow Six differs from other shooters in several important ways. For one thing, it has a targeting mechanic that penalizes the player for moving and shooting at the same time. Unlike other shooters that emphasize a "run and gun" style of play, the most effective tactic in *Rainbow Six* is to move through the levels carefully and methodically, much as a real hostage-rescue team does. A second important difference is a "one-shot kill" damage model. In contrast with games in which a character can safely absorb dozens of bullets, each of the characters in *Rainbow Six* can be killed by a single well-placed shot.

The result is an experience I have described as "entertaining claustrophobia." As you move through a level in *Rainbow Six*, your lines of sight are severely restricted. You never know where the next threat will come from, so even basic actions, such as turning a corner or stepping through a doorway, become fraught with danger. And because the combat mechanic restricts your ability to blast your way out of a bad situation, a lot of the gameplay revolves around anticipating danger and avoiding it. Thus, even an area entirely devoid of enemies can be packed with interesting gameplay. Moving down a corridor with doors on both sides is an exciting experience in *Rainbow Six*—not because the game is providing loads of feedback, but because the threat represented by the doors shapes the player's response to the space. In fact, during development we realized that even standing still and observing what is around you could be fun in the right circumstances, a discovery we put to use in the design of the follow-on titles *Rogue Spear* and *Ghost Recon*. In both of those games, the level-design team paid particular attention to how they structured the approach to threat zones, deliberately creating overlooks and cover locations where the player could safely pause and study the more dangerous terrain ahead.

Equating interactivity with play makes it difficult to understand the appeal of a game such as *Rainbow Six*. Because of the "one-shot kill" mechanic, the firefights in *Rainbow Six* tend to be over quickly, and so the amount of time the player spends actually interacting with the dynamic game system tends to be relatively low. Instead, the bulk of the gameplay in *Rainbow Six* is derived from the game's non-interactive moments: observing, anticipating, analyzing, planning. The abrupt and bloody gun battles serve primarily as exciting punctuation for the tactical game that plays out almost entirely inside the player's head.

Strategy as Internal Constraint

Sometimes it is hard to learn everything we need to know about a game through trial and error. More complicated games often begin with tutorials to make sure we internalize a minimal set of constraints before we begin to play. Or, if we get stuck further on, we can download a fan-created walkthrough to provide us with even more internal constraints, such as "Always use the grenade launcher when you're going up against large groups of enemies," "When you enter the warehouse level, take the door on the left," and "Don't go on the offensive until you have researched gunpowder."

Whereas tutorials teach basic rules, walkthroughs focus on strategies. Strategies are still constraints—they privilege certain lines of actions over others—but they are general guidelines, not hard-and-fast rules. Rather than telling us what we *can* do, strategies suggest what we *should* do.

Sometimes learning a minimal set of basic strategies is an important part of learning to play a game. For example, small children, when playing soccer, tend to congregate in a tight pack around the ball, kicking frantically. Nothing in the rules of soccer forbids playing the game that way, but it is more effective (and more fun) to spread players evenly across the field and assign them different roles. If you are coaching a children's soccer team, your job isn't just to teach them the rules of soccer, but also to teach them a collection of strategies that will structure their play experience in particular ways.

A few pages ago I noted that learning how to play is often a matter of internalizing external constraints. But that was an oversimplification. Learning how to play is a matter of constructing a minimal workable set of internal constraints. Sometimes that means memorizing rules, or discovering them through trial and error. But sometimes it means learning strategies—figuring out (or being told) effective ways to play within the rules. The effectiveness of a strategy is determined by how it interacts with the rules, but a strategy is not contained within the rules. The rules of chess never say "try to control the center of the board," even though controlling the center of the board is an effective strategy.

Besides learned rules and invented strategies, there are other types of internal constraints that structure our play experiences. Many games contain depictions of real-world situations. The characters we play often walk through simulated landscapes, or drive on simulated roads, or shoot simulated guns. In all these cases, the system of constraints that structures our play experience contains a large number of real-world expectations. When we run through a forest level in a videogame, we tend to follow simulated trails because we know from real-world experience that trails tend to be easier to traverse than crashing through the underbrush. We tend to skirt hills because we know that climbing up and down real hills is tiring. The fact that most games don't simulate these aspects of the real world is immaterial. Our set of internal constraints for navigating real terrain is so deeply ingrained that we unconsciously incorporate it into our strategies for navigating the simulation. In driving games, we unconsciously follow the rules of the road even if those rules are never enforced. In sports games, we avoid strategies that have little chance of success in the real world, regardless of how likely they are to work in the videogame world. In first-person shooters, we imbue computer-controlled enemies with human motivations and intentions, which leads us to overestimate or underestimate their capabilities.

In fact, the design of many videogames is predicated on the assumption that players will bring their real-world knowledge to bear in the construction of the play space. Nolan Bushnell stumbled upon this technique after his first game, *Computer Space*, was a commercial flop:

You had to read the instructions before you could play[.] [P]eople didn't want to read instructions. To be successful, I had to come up with a game people already knew how to play; something so simple that any drunk in any bar could play.[4]

The result was *Pong*, the first commercially successful videogame. Although the goal of the simple back-and-forth tennis game was obvious, Bushnell did include one instruction to the player to help him construct the appropriate internal constraint: "Avoid missing ball for high score." Most modern games don't even go that far. Golf games assume you that you already know

4. Cohen, *Zap! The Rise and Fall of Atari*, 70–75.

that you're are supposed to put the ball in the hole, first-person shooters assume that you already know that you're supposed to shoot at the bad guys, and so on.

In addition to borrowing constraints from the real world, we also borrow constraints from other games. When I play a new racing game, I don't have to learn every nuance from scratch. I already have a large body of internal constraints that I've built up from years of playing other racing games. When I start up a game of *Split/Second,* my experience is partially structured by strategies I learned when I played *Burnout* years before, just as my experience with *Burnout* was partially structured by strategies I learned from *Ridge Racer,* and my experience with *Ridge Racer* was partially structured by strategies I learned from *Pole Position,* and my experience with *Pole Position* was partially structured by strategies I learned from *Night Driver.* Each new iteration of the genre is similar enough to its immediate predecessor that my existing body of internal constraints is still largely applicable. I already know how to drift, how to find the line, and how the AI-driven cars racing with me are likely to behave. New racing games are designed with the expectation that many players, like me, will already possess a particular body of constraints before they even begin to play.

From the player's perspective, it doesn't make much difference if an internal constraint is a learned rule, an invented strategy, or a distillation of real-world knowledge. If it privileges one line of action over another, it is a meaningful constraint. And if it's a meaningful constraint, then we should take it into account as part of our analysis of the play experience. If we are trying to understand how a game works, it isn't enough to just look at what the rules allow. We also have to look at what the player *thinks* the rules allow, the strategies the player invents on the fly, and the player's knowledge of similar games and similar situations in real life. All of these structuring elements are present in the active internal constraints, and each of them plays an important part in the unfolding of the play experience.

The Challenge of Design

We can group a game's constraints into four broad categories (figure 2.5):

The Game as Designed The static system of constraints that exists before the play experience begins—the rules written in the rulebook, or the software stored on the disk.

The Game as Encountered The active external constraints that influence the player's immediate actions—the rules that matter right now.

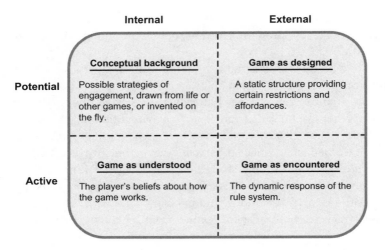

Figure 2.5
Varieties of constraints.

The Game as Understood   The set of active constraints in the player's head—a mixture of internalized rules, invented strategies, and real-world knowledge.

The Conceptual Background   The broad collection of potential ways that a player *might* engage with a game. How a player understands a game depends a great deal on the conceptual background the player starts with.

A game developer has direct control over only the game as designed—the external potential constraints. When I design a game, I am constructing a static framework of restrictions and affordances. But I don't have direct control over the dynamic response of this framework—the game as encountered. As the player moves freely through the game, his experience is shaped not by the rules as a whole, but by a fluctuating subset of active constraints.

Designers sometimes get caught up in the elegance of their rule system without thinking about how those rules translate into player experience. Years ago, I sat through a pitch for a space combat game. The designer went into great detail about an economic simulation his team was planning to create. The game universe would have dozens of planets, each with cities, farms, factories, and mines. AI-controlled merchant ships would shuttle raw materials and goods back and forth between the planets. Which cargos these ships carried would be determined by supply and demand, and commodity prices would fluctuate naturally in response to events such as natural disasters and political crises. It was a beautiful and well-thought-out rule system. However, the player played a space pirate. The action revolved entirely around raiding merchant ships and dodging naval vessels. Not only couldn't the player influence the overall economy, he didn't even have enough information about what was happening to understand it. A famine on the far side of the galaxy might change shipping patterns across half of the game's universe, but the player had no way of knowing that. From the player's perspective, the game's entire complex and subtle economic simulation was *experienced* as nothing more than a sequence of cryptic fluctuations in prices and cargoes. The entire economic model could have been replaced by a simple random number generator without changing the player's experience. The problem was that the designer was thinking about the economic system as an end unto itself rather than as an engine for generating player experience. If you are playing as a space pirate, the ships you attack should contain an interesting mix of cargo. Some planets should appear to be prosperous trading hubs, others impoverished backwaters. But the game need not simulate an entire economy to provide those sorts of external constraints. In fact, a complicated simulation can get in the way of constructing an interesting experience by generating constraints that are arbitrary or baffling. Salen and Zimmerman put it this way:

> The challenge ... is that the experience of play is not something that a game designer directly creates. Instead, play is an emergent property that arises from the game as a play engages with the system. The game designer creates a set of rules, which the players inhabit, explore and manipulate. ... The game designer only *indirectly* designs the player's experience by *directly* designing the rules.[5]

An important skill for any game designer is the ability to "see through" a set of rules—to be able to glance at a set of static rules and extrapolate the sorts of dynamic constraints they will generate during actual play. At the same time, a designer should be able to reverse the process—to reason backward from a desired player experience to arrive at a simple rule set that is capable of evoking it. Learning to roam easily back and forth across the conceptual gap between the game as designed and the game as encountered is an important step toward becoming a professional designer.

Another design challenge is bridging the gap between the game as encountered and the game as understood. Usually the existence of this gap is ignored; designers simply assume that, for purposes of analysis, the player is playing the game they designed. If the gap is acknowledged, it is

5. Salen and Zimmerman, *Rules of Play*, 316.

treated as a problem to be solved. If a player doesn't understand a game, it's because the game didn't do a good enough job of teaching him—the rules were too complicated, there wasn't enough feedback, the tutorials were inadequate, the learning curve was too steep.

I approach design somewhat differently. Rather than trying to eliminate gap between the game as understood and the game as encountered, I'm interested in *exploiting* it. I'm less interested in teaching the player the rules than in structuring an experience that will coax the player into constructing an interesting set of internal constraints. Some of these constraints may mimic the actual rules of the game, but most of them will not. The goal isn't for the player to play the game as designed or even the game as encountered, but rather for these two external systems to work together to guide the player toward a successful internal play space—the game as understood.

Here is a simple example. An important internal constraint in many games is "Don't let them see you." "They" may be palace guards, zombies, terrorists, or orcs—the fiction doesn't matter. In games to which this constraint applies, the player gains some advantage from hiding—he can sneak past enemies that are too tough to fight, or gain an edge in combat by setting up an ambush. "Don't let them see you" strongly favors some actions over others. It has a profound effect on how a player moves through the space, and can even generate long stretches of gameplay in which the player doesn't move at all.

The first thing to note about "Don't let them see you" is that it is a strategy, not a rule. The game software doesn't contain a single line of code that specifies "Don't let them see you" as a limit on the player's actions. Rather, "Don't let them see you" is an off-the cuff improvisation in response to a particular constellation of AI behaviors that *are* coded into the game's software.

Furthermore, the AI characters to whom the player is responding aren't capable of "seeing" anything. Their behavior is triggered by a series of line-of-sight checks; the game draws a line segment between the player and the AI character and tests to see if it intersects any world geometry. If it doesn't, then the AI can "see" the player. However, this form of "seeing" is very different from what happens when we see someone in the real world. In the real world, becoming aware of an object within our visual field is a complicated problem in pattern recognition. It can be confounded by motion, camouflage, lighting, fog, distractions, or simple lack of attention. It isn't a simple line-of-sight check.

If you pay close attention while playing a game, you can usually spot the gap between seeing and "seeing." You can "hide" behind a slender tree even though parts of your body are still visible. You can be "seen" even when you are in deep shadow. However, even when we are aware that this gap in our understanding, we don't play the game as designed. We don't move through the level thinking "If I stand here, that AI's line-of-sight check will fail." We still think in terms of *not being seen*.

The game is performing a clever bit of misdirection. We have years of experience with seeing things and being aware that other people are seeing us. Peek-a-boo is one of the first games we learn as babies. We play hide and seek, and cops and robbers. We learn how to drive, and how to flirt. Our conceptual background contains a wide assortment of different strategies for interpreting visual information and interpreting the intentions of others on the basis of the visual information we believe they possess.

Thus, the line-of-sight checks in a typical stealth game aren't set up as a rule system for us to learn. Rather, they are part of a collection of cues intended to coax us into borrowing a pre-existing strategic constraint from our conceptual background. We don't need a tutorial to teach us how to play the "Don't let them see you" game—we have been learning how to play that game since we were able to crawl. We just need a few hints to nudge us in the right direction.

The rules for AI behavior certainly play an important role in guiding us toward adopting "Don't let them see you" as an active strategy, but a number of less formal elements contribute: Does the enemy turn his head toward us when he sees us? Do our character's animations suggest that we are trying to be sneaky? Does the lighting of the level, or even the mood of the music imply that stealth would be fruitful?

Designers often draw a hard line between the rules of a game and its fantasy. Gameplay is seen as a product of the rules—the game's inner framework of restrictions and affordances. The fantasy is merely a pleasing "wrapper" that serves no gameplay purpose. How a character looks, how he is animated, how the world is lit, how it sounds—these things may be parts of the *overall* experience of the game, but they don't affect how the game *plays*. This is a mistake. A game's fantasy is as much a constraint on player action as its rules are. Seemingly inconsequential details, such as the sound of a footfall or the flutter of a piece of fabric, can have a profound effect on the strategies we adopt toward the situation that faces us. Game design is more than just inventing an interesting set of rules; it is structuring a total experience (both rules and fantasy) that will coax the player toward adopting an interesting set of internal constraints.

What internal constraints a player adopts will depend heavily on his conceptual background. Most players will stumble onto a strategy such as "Don't let them see you" relatively easily because "Don't let them see you" leverages basic intuitions about vision and intent that most of us developed in childhood. But we can't be sure whether less-universal strategies will be in the player's conceptual toolbox or not. "Control the high ground" isn't a strategy that most people learn as babies. Even more interesting, some players may know or invent strategies that the designer doesn't or didn't. The set of internal constraints that a player constructs in response to a game may not only be something that the designer didn't intend; it may be something that the designer didn't even imagine.

3   Play Spaces

The quality of a play space is determined by how its active constraints structure our immediate actions. Thus, if we want to understand how a play space works, we need to develop a set of tools that we can use to analyze these active constraints. A particularly useful abstraction for this purpose is the mathematical concept of a *phase space*. A phase space is a hypothetical space representing all possible states of a system, such that any particular state corresponds to a unique location within the space (figure 3.1). For example, an important element of the state of a game of ping-pong is the position of the ball. At any moment the position of the ball can specified by three numbers: its location from side to side, its distance from the net, and its height off the table. If we want to record the position of the ball, we can plot these three numbers as a point within a three-dimensional phase space. As the ball is batted back and forth, this point moves around in the phase space along a trajectory that mimics its path through real space.

However, if we really want to capture the state of a game of ping-pong, just specifying the position of the ball isn't enough. We also need to account for its velocity. After all, there is a big difference (in gameplay terms) between a ball that is moving left over the net and one that is moving right, even if they are both momentarily in exactly the same spot. Completely representing the speed and direction of the ball requires three more numbers. And if the players are putting "English" on the ball (as good ping-pong players do), the ball's spin is also an important part of the state of the game. Accurately representing the spin requires three more numbers.

Thus, the state of a ping-pong ball can be represented as a set of nine numbers. As the ball is batted back and forth, all nine of these numbers will be constantly fluctuating. We can think of the ball as tracing out a trajectory within a *nine-dimensional* phase space, each point within the nine-dimensional space representing a specific unique combination of location, velocity, and spin.

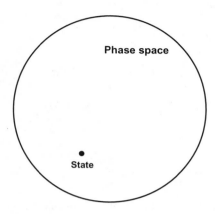

Figure 3.1
Phase space and a state within it.

It isn't possible to draw a nine-dimensional phase space on a two-dimensional page. But we can still use it as a conceptual tool. Phase spaces allow us to visualize every quantity that varies during a game as *movement from one location to another*. For human beings, this is a particularly powerful cognitive frame. Since early childhood we have constructed a number of strategies for understanding and influencing the movement of objects (including ourselves) from one location to another. Even though there are other types of change besides movement, *treating* all types of change *as* movement allows us to use these strategies. A phase space is an external constraint that coaxes us toward borrowing a typical set of internal constraints from our conceptual backgrounds. It is a way of structuring our discursive field to make it easier to say certain interesting and useful things about systems that change over time.[1]

When we talk about the phase space of a game, we aren't talking about a direct representation of the physical playfield. We are talking about a conceptual space with hundreds or even thousands of dimensions. Some of these dimensions may correspond to actual locations in our normal three-dimensional world, but most of them represent abstract quantities, such as the spin of a ball, how much grain your farmers have grown, or how many houses you have built on a property in *Monopoly*.

Depending on the game, the number of locations within the phase space can range from relatively small to unimaginably huge. On the simple end of the spectrum is tic-tac-toe. There are 765 unique arrangements of X's and

---

1. For more information on the use of spatial metaphors in cognition, see Johnson, *The Body in the Mind*.

O's that can occur during a game of tic-tac-toe. Every "move" will always result in one of those 765 states, so the phase space for tic-tac-toe has 765 locations. The phase space for chess, on the other hand, is considerably larger—it has been estimated to consist of roughly 10^{50} unique board positions.[2] And in games (such as basketball) in which the action isn't broken down into discrete moves, the phase space is effectively infinite.

The current state of a game is represented by a single point within its phase space. When you play a game, the state evolves over time, and that evolution can be represented by a line tracing a trajectory through the phase space. Points on the line are states that *did* occur; points off the line are states that *could have* occurred had you made different choices.

Once we are comfortable with the idea of a phase space, we can use it to help us understand the large-scale structure of different games (figure 3.2). Soccer, for example, has a fairly open structure. The players can roam freely around the field, and similar configurations of offense and defense can recur in the course of a match. The same rules and physical constraints apply throughout. A simple bubble with a wandering trajectory that crosses and re-crosses itself is a reasonably adequate model of this sort of homogenous gameplay.

Chess is a different matter. Because the number of pieces dwindles as the match progresses, the phase space of chess has *directionality*. Some states are accessible only at the beginning of a match, others only at the end. The origin of the trajectory is a single point. Every game of chess begins with the same configuration of pieces on the board. As the match progresses, the trajectory gradually wanders away from the origin and toward states that

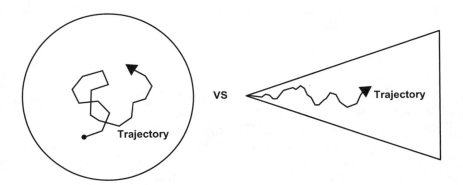

Figure 3.2
The trajectory of play in soccer vs. that in chess.

2. Allis, *Searching for Solutions in Games and Artificial Intelligence*, 171.

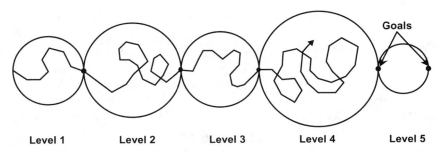

Level 1   **Level 2**   **Level 3**   **Level 4**   **Level 5**

Figure 3.3
The phase space of a typical videogame.

contain fewer and fewer pieces. Previous configurations are rarely revisited, and moves at the end of the game are very different from the moves at the beginning.

Goals

Videogames often combine free-form and directional phase spaces. Many of them have multiple levels. Within each level, the player is free to explore, but the transitions between levels impose rigid gates between the free-form bubbles (figure 3.3).

A diagram of a videogame's phase space helps to illustrate an important point—the idea of *goals*. A goal is simply a privileged configuration of the game's state. It is a particular arrangement of playing pieces (either real or abstract) that is afforded some special status. Examples include putting a ball in a net, placing the opposing king in checkmate, and navigating to the end of a level.

If we look at our diagram for the phase space of a level-based videogame, we see that the action within each level terminates with a goal. What this goal is will differ from game to game. It may be reaching the end of the level alive, killing a particular enemy, or clearing away all the blocks in *Tetris*. In each case, reaching the goal means that the player has succeeded in putting the state in a particular desirable configuration.

A goal functions as a constraint. By privileging a particular configuration of the play space, the goal focuses the players' actions. Movement within the other constraints is then directed toward bringing about the desired configuration. For example, the goal in *go* is to control more territory than your opponent, so on every turn the players tend to pick moves that are likely to maximize their territorial gains.

A goal can exert either a positive or a negative influence. Rolling your bowling ball into the gutter, landing on a property owned by another player, dying in a videogame—these are goals too. But rather than configurations that the player is working to achieve, they are configurations the player is working to *avoid*.

Goals tend to be very powerful constraints.[3] Many rules exert their influence only in certain contexts. For example, baseball has rules governing how runners may behave while rounding the bases (they must stay within the base paths, they must not interfere with the ball while it is in play, and so on), but these constraints are active only when there are men on base. When the bases are empty, the rules governing base runners recede into potentiality. But the overall goal of baseball—to score more runs than the other team—is active throughout the entire game. Every action taken on the field is shaped and directed by this particular overarching constraint.

Failing to respect the goals of a game often triggers the same negative response as failing to honor any of the other rules. "You're letting me win!" carries the same level of disapproval as "You're cheating!" even though the transgression is to the benefit of the aggrieved party. This suggests that the feelings of outrage we feel when we think we have been cheated are less about the loss of relative advantage than about transgression of the play space.

In order for the choices we make within a system of constraints to feel as if they matter, there must be different degrees of desirability assigned to different locations in the phase space. Some outcomes must be good, others bad. Most commercial games accomplish this through brute force. Their formal rules simply present players with explicit goals. However, not all play spaces work this way. For example, when children play make-believe, they aren't working toward one specific outcome; rather, new goals are improvised on the fly in response to the flow of the fantasy—for example, "Now goblins are attacking the fort! We have to defend it!" Similarly, you can have fun in an open-world videogame, such as *Grand Theft Auto* or *Red Dead Redemption*, without working toward any particular mission or objective. Weaving in and out of traffic for the hell of it and sitting on a hilltop idly taking potshots at crows are fun in these games, even though the self-imposed goals that drive them don't figure in the formal reward structure.

3. "Games have a lot of rules—how to move and what you can and cannot do—but there is one rule at the foundation of all the others: The Object of the Game." Schell, *The Art of Game Design*, 148.

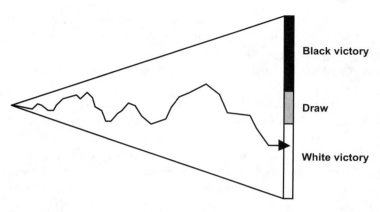

Figure 3.4
Goals in the phase space of chess.

In the absence of formal victory conditions (and sometimes in defiance of them), players often invent their own constraints to privilege certain locations within a game's phase space. Years ago, I spent several enjoyable hours with a group of friends building human pyramids in a session of *Quake*. We certainly had a goal—maximizing the number of characters we could stack on top of each other (I think we managed six). But it was a goal of our own invention, entirely distinct from the normal objective of racking up the most kills.

Figure 3.4 illustrates the phase space of chess with goals added in. There are multiple configurations that result in victory for one side or the other. And there are also some configurations that result in a draw—victory for neither side. In a competitive game, the positive goals for one player are the negative goals for the other. In the figure, black is working toward checkmating the white king, white toward preventing it.

In chess, a draw is less desirable that a victory but more desirable than an outright loss. Thus, a configuration that results in a draw can be either a positive or a negative outcome, depending on the current state of the game. If you are close to victory, a draw is a negative goal—something to be avoided. But if you are close to defeat, a draw becomes a positive goal—something to work toward.

As was discussed in chapter 2, when a player formulates a strategy we can think of that strategy as just another form of constraint. These constraints are often expressed as goals—interim configurations of the state that are either desirable or undesirable. Consider the strategy "Make sure you have full ammo and health before you start the final boss battle." Achieving full ammo and health then becomes an interim goal that exerts a strong tug on the trajectory of play immediately before the boss battle.

One major difference between a novice player and an expert is the expert's knowledge of interim goals. The expert knows that certain configurations of the game state are advantageous and works to achieve them, whereas the novice is capable only of responding to the immediate challenges of the moment. The expert's knowledge imposes an additional set of constraints on his trajectory through the phase space. He may avoid certain actions not because the game forbids him from doing them, but because he knows from experience that they are worthless or counterproductive—they lead to undesirable locations in the game's phase space. Similarly, an expert may pursue certain lines of action even though they appear to be disadvantageous in the short run, because he knows that in the long run they are likely to lead to desirable outcomes.

The Horizon of Action

Each point within a game's phase space represents a particular configuration of the game's state. But because the game's active constraints are determined by the game's state, we can think of each point in the phase space as also representing a particular set of active constraints. As play proceeds along a trajectory through the phase space, these active constraints will shift and change.

Furthermore, the active constraints at any point in the phase space determine where the trajectory of play can go next. The player can't just hop to any configuration of the state he wants. The rules constrain which future configurations are allowed. And the player's beliefs and strategies constrain which future configurations are desirable.

We can think of every point in the phase space as having a *horizon of action* (figure 3.5). The horizon of action is the set of all states attainable by the player within the near future. And this horizon is determined, not surprisingly, by the set of active external constraints associated with the current state.[4]

4. The "horizon of action" is related to Jauss' "horizon of expectation." In Jauss' reception theory, a "horizon of expectation" is the cultural context of a reader's interpretive acts. The relationship between these two concepts will become more apparent later in this book. However, readers who are familiar with Jauss' work should be aware that they aren't equivalent. The horizon of action operates on a shorter time scale than Jauss' horizon of expectation, and encompasses more possible constraints. For more on the horizon of expectation, see Jauss, *Toward an Aesthetic of Reception*.

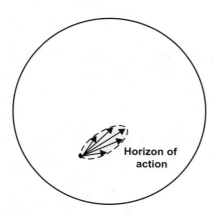

Figure 3.5
The horizon of action.

Suppose you are playing a classic two-dimensional "platformer," such as *Donkey Kong*. The current level consists of a set of platforms that you can reach by jumping. As you move around within the level, you are tracing a path within the game's phase space. At any moment there will be some platforms that you can reach in the near future and others that are inaccessible to you. Whether a particular platform is accessible or not is governed by the architecture of the level and the jumping abilities of your character—these are the external active constraints that define your horizon of action.

Note that your horizon changes as you move around within the level. Depending on your location, the level geometry will constrain your movement in different ways. Sometimes you will be presented with a very narrow range of potential actions; sometimes your range of options will be very wide. Each different point in the phase space has its own horizon. Typically, however, states that are similar to each other will tend to have similar horizons. If you shift your character a few pixels to the left you will occupy a slightly different point in the phase space, but your horizon of action will remain virtually unchanged.

Thus, we can think of the player's trajectory through the play space not merely as a series of different configurations of the state, but as a series of different opportunities for action. As the player moves through the game, his horizon of action shifts and changes. At any moment, he is offered a range of potentially achievable outcomes. On the basis of his actions, one of those potential outcomes becomes the new state. That new state defines a new horizon—a new range of potentially achievable outcomes. The cycle of gameplay continues, each evolution of the state defining a new horizon and each horizon constraining the next evolution of the state (figure 3.6).

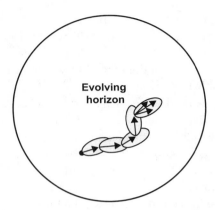

Figure 3.6
The evolving horizon of action.

Some states within a game may be unstable—that is, may change even if the player does nothing at all. Picture a soccer ball rolling down the field. Even if the players stand completely still, the state of the game is still changing. And as the state changes, the horizon of action—the set of possible states that a player can achieve in the near future—also changes.

Unstable states are important in many videogames. The current state of the game is used by the rules to determine what the state of the game should be in the near future, and that new state leads to another and another in an ongoing chain. This evolution of the state occurs continuously, even if the player puts his controller down and walks out of the room. This property is particularly obvious in simulation games, such as *SimCity*. It is possible to "play" *SimCity* without providing any inputs at all for long stretches of time. The rules are set up so that the state will evolve in interesting ways even without a player's intervention. Even a relatively minor input from a player can trigger an unfolding cascade that may take many minutes to play out. Most real-time videogames have such internal loops, though they may not be as obvious as those in *SimCity*. When you put down the controller, the state of the game continues to change (usually in ways that lead to losing). The *Tetris* blocks continue to fall. Your car stops while the others roar around the track. Your knight stands with his sword by his side while the battle swirls around him.

The Horizon of Intent

The term *horizon of action* describes the set of all the things a player can do at a particular moment. But often the set of things we *believe* we can do is more important for analyzing gameplay that the set of things we *can* do. For example, if I believe that a platform is too far away, I will not try to jump to it even if in fact it lies within my horizon of action. Similarly, if I believe that a platform is close enough to jump to, then I might try to jump to it even though in fact I will not be able to reach it.

Thus, each point in the phase space, in addition to having a horizon of action, also has a *horizon of intent*. The horizon of intent is the set of all states that the player believes to be valid, attainable, and desirable in the near future. It is defined by the player's current set of active internal constraints. The horizon of intent is a product of the game as understood, whereas the horizon of action is a product of the game as encountered.

Some of the constraints defining the horizon of intent will be internalized approximations of external constraints. For example, if I am playing baseball there is no physical barrier preventing me from running directly from home plate to second base when I get a hit. But my knowledge of the rules blocks that particular action. Similarly, my knowledge of a videogame's level geometry means that I will avoid obstacles before I collide with them. I know that the obstacles exclude certain locations in the level from my horizon of action, and I adjust my horizon of intent to match.

But other constraints in the horizon of intent have no external analogues. I may avoid doing certain things not because they aren't possible or because they are against the rules, but because I know that they are tactically unwise. I could stand still in the batter's box after getting a hit in baseball; however, I don't, because that would make it easier for an opposing player to tag me out. I could run straight into the maw of a boss during a boss battle; however, I don't, because I know that would get my character killed. My horizon of intent is defined not just by what I believe I *can* do, but also by what I believe I *should* do—my internal strategic constraints.

The internal constraints defining my horizon of intent will also include any goals I have adopted. These may be internalized versions of external objectives supplied by the rules of the game, they may be interim goals constructed on the fly as part of some strategy, or they may even be purely idiosyncratic inventions that run counter to the grain of the designer's intent for the play space.

The horizons of action and intent have to overlap at least a little for a game to be playable (figure 3.7). You can't play a platformer if you aren't aware that you can jump. At least a few of your apparent choices must correspond to valid actions. However, for gameplay purposes, it turns out that it's also a good thing if your apparent choices don't match valid actions too closely. In fact, one of the reasons why many games have unstable states

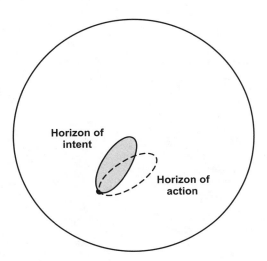

Figure 3.7
The overlapping horizons of intent and action.

is that they encourage the divergence of the two horizons. If your opportunities for action are constantly changing, your awareness of what those opportunities are (and their relative worth) will necessarily lag a bit behind. This may seem counterintuitive at first. Shouldn't one goal of game design be to ensure that the player understands the rules of the game clearly? The answer is "Yes and no." It turns out that some degree of uncertainty about the consequences of our actions is necessary if a system of constraints is going to function as a successful play space. We will explore why this should be so in much greater detail in the next chapter. For present purposes, it is sufficient to keep in mind that what the player believes he can or should do in a game (the player's horizon of intent) will almost always differ somewhat from what the rules of the game actually allow (his horizon of action).

Narrowing our focus to the horizons of intent and action gives us a way to grapple with the tremendous complexity of a game's full phase space. There may be 10^{50} unique positions within the play space of chess, but at any moment during a game only a few dozen lie within the horizon of action. And since many of these will be rejected as tactically unwise by expert players, the typical horizon of intent in a game of chess contains only a few moves. If we are interested in analyzing gameplay, these two horizons give us a way to talk about the moment-to-moment texture of the encounter while allowing us to ignore huge chunks of the play space that don't affect a player's immediate experience.

4   Heuristics

Some play spaces are better than others. On a purely personal level, we enjoy some games and don't enjoy others. On a societal level, some games are wildly popular and endure for years; others find only a tiny audience and are quickly forgotten. If a play space is defined by its system of constraints, there must be something about how those constraints are organized that determines the quality of the space. What sorts of constraints yield good play spaces, and what sorts of constraints yield bad ones?

The horizon of intent is a particularly useful tool for attacking this question. It forms a bridge between the rules of a game and the experience of playing it. It gives us a way to talk about what the player is doing from moment to moment, and to observe how particular constraints work to produce particular gameplay effects. More important, it gives us a way to factor the player's own strategies and attitudes into our analysis.

We can think of a game as an engine for generating horizons of intent. A good game is one that consistently generates interesting horizons. But what does it mean for a horizon to be "interesting"? What specific properties distinguish a good horizon from a bad one? In this chapter, we will try to answer these questions. Step by step, we will build up a framework of six general heuristics that describe the characteristics of a good horizon of intent:

Choice   Horizons offer a range of possible actions.
Variety   Horizons aren't repeated.
Consequence   Actions have outcomes.
Predictability   Outcomes can be anticipated.
Uncertainty   Outcomes aren't predetermined.
Satisfaction   Desirable outcomes are attainable.

Designing a play space that meets these criteria is a tricky business. You can't just assemble an arbitrary set of rules and expect them to provide an interesting play experience. For example, when I'm at the Department of Motor Vehicles to renew my driver's license, I'm unquestionably navigating a system of constraints—there are rules for where I must wait, and what information I must provide, and what I'm supposed to do when my number is called—but these rules don't structure a successful play space. Often I have no choice at all about what to do next, and when I can make a decision ("Hmmm; which pen should I use?") it has little effect on what happens in the future. There is very little uncertainty to how to the experience will unfold—I can see the next hour monotonously stretching out ahead of me with no pleasant surprises or challenging twists. And although I probably will experience satisfaction when the experience is over, there isn't a lot to be had while it is in progress.

Play spaces that consistently generate horizons of intent that meet these criteria are interesting; play spaces that consistently fail to do so aren't. By exploring these heuristics in detail, we can articulate a detailed catalogue of the specific ways in which a play experience can succeed or fail.

Choice

The most obvious factor in determining the quality of a horizon of intent is simply the number of possible moves that it offers. Too few choices are undesirable, but so are too many. There is very little play in shifting chess pieces through a predetermined sequence of moves, and there is also very little play in moving them aimlessly about with no rules at all. Good play requires that we have enough choice that we are challenged, but not so much that we are overwhelmed.

But how much choice is the right amount? That question is difficult to answer. Game design would be much simpler if there were a magic number of choices that inevitably yielded maximum play value. Play spaces could then be constructed so that players were always faced with exactly three, or nine, or fourteen possible moves to pick from, guaranteeing maximum enjoyment.

Reality is more complicated. Not all actions are created equal. Three moves that result in three very different outcomes will feel like more choice than fourteen moves that yield virtually the same result. And many games don't offer us a well-defined set of moves at all; rather, they present us with a fuzzy continuum of opportunities for action. For example, when we play an arcade driving game we choose how far to turn the steering wheel, but there is no way to meaningfully map that continuous range of motion onto "picking a move."

Figure 4.1
Boredom vs. confusion.

Instead of trying to nail down the optimal amount of choice that will yield the ideal experience, a more fruitful approach is to look at how the play experience breaks down at two ends of the continuum. As we reduce the number of actions within the horizon of intent, our range of free movement gets smaller and smaller. We have fewer and fewer opportunities to affect our trajectory through the game's phase space. Eventually we feel as if we are being forced to execute a fixed sequence of moves. We plod through a predetermined experience, step by step, and boredom sets in.

But if we increase the amount of choice, the opposite happens. As we are presented with more and more opportunities for action, the range of free movement grows. Eventually the number of moves can grow so large that we can no longer meaningfully assess their relative worth. Confusion is the result (figure 4.1).

Novice players can easily be overwhelmed by horizons that appear unmanageably large. For example, making the first move in a game of *go* involves placing a stone somewhere on a 19 × 19 grid. Even if you account for identical positions produced by mirroring and rotating the board, the horizon of action still consists of 55 different unique moves. However, expert players know that most of those moves are strategically worthless. Because it is important to control the corners of the board early in a game of *go*, there are only three opening moves that make tactical sense—a much more manageable horizon of intent.

Similarly, expert players can become bored with horizons that have become excessively constricted through the accumulation of internal strategic constraints. For example, tic-tac-toe appears at first glance to provide an acceptable number of moves each turn. Accounting for mirroring and rotations, there are three openings—the same number as in *go*. However, once you have played a few games of tic-tac-toe you discover that there is an ideal opening strategy that you should follow: putting an X in the center square. Following this strategy narrows your horizon of intent to a single move, and the game becomes boring.

In practice, underconstrained systems tend to have more play value than overconstrained ones. When players encounter a system with too few constraints, they often compensate by inventing their own on the fly.

If a game offers too many options to choose from, a player may respond by simply ignoring some of them and concentrating on a manageable subset. For example, a beginner in a complex strategy game may ignore resource gathering and focus entirely on combat. This keeps the number of choices within his horizon down to a manageable number. A player in a pen-and-paper role-playing game may theoretically be able to do virtually anything—for example burglarizing a local nobleman's house, getting drunk in the local tavern, and dancing in the street in a bear costume—but in practice his actions will be constrained by self-imposed ideas about who his character is and what will move the adventure forward. It is easier to add new constraints than to ignore existing ones.

All this is pretty obvious. It's really just a reformulation of our original definition of play—free movement through a system of constraints. In any good play space there is always some tension between freedom and constraint. Too much constraint means your horizons are too narrow and the game becomes boring. Too much freedom means your horizons are too broad and the game becomes confusing. Good play requires the right number of choices—neither too many nor too few.

But good play is more than that. Imagine a game in which you are asked to choose a number from 1 to 10, then to do it again, and again, and again. Your horizon contains a moderate number of "moves" (about as many as you would have if you were playing chess), but this sort of open-ended guessing game becomes dull very quickly. And varying the number of moves doesn't help. The game isn't any better if you are picking a number from 1 to 3 or a number from 1 to 1,000. We can tighten or loosen the constraints all we want, but the resulting experience will still feel empty and pointless.

Something more complicated is happening in the horizon than just a simple tug-of-war between too many moves and too few. Good play isn't just about the *number* of moves; it is also about the *kinds* of moves. Thus, if we really want to understand how play operates, we need some additional heuristics.

Variety

Imagine playing a first-person shooter that is set entirely in a sewer. Each level consists of the same narrow corridors repeated over and over again. At each moment, your horizon offers a reasonable range of potential actions (move forward, move back, pull the trigger, take cover), but there is little novelty. You often find yourself in situations that closely resemble encounters from earlier in the game. You are confronted by the same ravenous monsters charging toward you down the same slime-covered hallways. After a while, it gets boring. A situation that is fun the first time it is encountered becomes less entertaining when it is repeated. With each successive repetition, the situation becomes duller and duller.

It isn't just that players enjoy a change of scenery. You can play chess for years on the same board and each new game will still feel fascinating and challenging. Some of the boredom of our hypothetical sewer shooter is certainly attributable to seeing the same visuals, but most of it is attributable to the repetition of similar configurations within the game's phase space.

Each encounter is defined by a set of active constraints—among them the layout of the sewer, the behavior of the monsters, and the capabilities of the hero character. These constraints create opportunities for action. Choosing from this range of opportunities gives us the feeling that we are moving freely through the game's framework.

But we *remember* our previous choices. When we encounter a similar configuration again, the knowledge of what we did before imposes an additional internal constraint on the situation, reducing the range of potential actions. If we did something that turned out particularly well, we are more likely to do it again, ignoring other untried avenues of play. On the other hand, if we did something that turned out poorly, we are likely to avoid doing it again. Our growing set of internal constraints gradually pares away most of the original opportunities for action and focuses our attention on a small number of dominant strategies. When only one dominant strategy remains, the horizon is exhausted or "played out." There is no freedom left in it, only an opportunity to execute a rote move that will carry us along a predetermined trajectory.

Good play spaces address this problem by continuously varying the horizon of action, and by extension, the horizon of intent. As we exhaust the potential of the current horizon, a new one takes its place, giving us a new range of opportunities to explore. Each individual horizon is unique. Horizons seldom, if ever, repeat.

There are several techniques that can be used to guarantee that players always have fresh horizons to explore. The simplest is the brute-force approach: hand-crafting new horizons one by one. This is how a game such as *Myst* works. The player is confronted by a series of puzzles, each with its own unique solution. Each puzzle is a single horizon of intent, or, at most, a short chain of horizons. Solving these puzzles usually requires an "aha" moment of insight when the correct sequence of moves becomes obvious.

Games based on puzzles are very labor-intensive to create. Each puzzle is a specialized set of constraints that is active only for a short period of time. The construction of a puzzle-based game requires the designer to meticulously craft dozens (or even hundreds) of these little one-off constraint sets. Each individual puzzle may be relatively simple to design, but the sheer number required to keep the player supplied with fresh challenges can be daunting. And because each puzzle is exhausted as a play experience as soon as it has been solved, there isn't much replay value in a puzzle-based game.[1] Many hours may be required to craft an experience that provides only a few minutes, or only a few seconds, of entertainment.

This is not to say that there is no replay at all in puzzle games. Puzzles such as Rubik's Cube vary their starting position; thus, even if the form of the puzzle itself is the same each time, we have to make quite different choices to arrive at the solution. Even if a puzzle has a fixed solution we can still replay it if we let enough time elapse between plays for us to forget what the solution was. And some puzzles are part of larger play experiences that offer other pleasures—I might replay an adventure game simply because I love the story, even though solving the puzzles is trivial the second time.

Because creating one-off puzzles is so labor-intensive, many games are designed so that their constraints are *modular*—that is, they can be reused in a variety of situations instead of having to be individually crafted for each challenge. With a modular set of constraints, a designer can build interesting horizons by combining different off-the-shelf components in different ways. For example, in a first-person shooter, the level geometry is one constraint, the behavior of a monster is another, and the player's current weapon is a third. When the player is in a particular location in the level, facing off against a particular monster, and armed with a particular weapon, the result is a unique horizon of action that presents the player with a fresh set of choices and challenges. Merely by swapping out monsters or moving the encounter to a different location, the designer can alter the horizon without having to craft an entire new set of constraints from scratch.

By the same token, many games are designed so that their constraints can evolve *procedurally*. An action taken in response to one set of active constraints automatically leads to activation of a different set of active

---

1. "Puzzlemaster Scott Kim once said that 'A puzzle is fun, and has a right answer.' The irony of that is that once you find the right answer, the puzzle ceases to be fun. … The thing that really seems to bother people about calling puzzles games is that they are not replayable. Once you figure out the best strategy, you can solve the puzzle every time and it is no longer fun." Schell, *The Art of Game Design*, 209.

constraints through a cascade of unstable states. For example, in most first-person shooters the enemies are designed to react to the player. As we move and shoot, we set in motion processes that alter the configuration of the constraints within which we are operating. The new states that emerge as the game procedurally evolves will generate a wide variety of different horizons over a relatively short period of time.[2]

Game designers often characterize rule sets as *elegant* or *robust*. These two adjectives are closely related to the procedural generation of interesting horizons. A rule set is elegant if only a small number of constraints are needed to generate a large number of horizons. It is robust if it can generate a large number of horizons without the addition of extra one-off constraints to handle special cases. Crafting a rule set that is both elegant and robust is often a major goal in game design. The incentive for this is partially economic. It requires fewer man-hours to create one set of rules that works in a hundred different situations than it requires to create a hundred different sets each of which works in only one situation. But elegant and robust systems are also easier for a player to navigate. It is easier to internalize a small, consistent set of rules with few exceptions that to internalize a large and complicated set of rules with many exceptions.

While the external constraints of a game can evolve procedurally over time, players' internal constraints can also change. Players can figure out how various game systems work and invent their own interpretations and strategies. Typically, this leads to gradual constriction of the play space as the player's new internal constraints prune away unrewarding avenues of action. But if the rules are designed to accommodate this progression, the opposite can occur. A novice player may overlook non-obvious opportunities for action in the welter of possibilities that are open to him. But as his range of choices narrows, he may discover that those overlooked actions lead to previously unexplored areas of the game's phase space that provide new horizons of gameplay for him to experience.

When a rule set adapts smoothly to a player's growing set of internal constraints, we say that it is *deep*. In a deep game, mastering the basics doesn't lead to the game's becoming exhausted. Instead, it exposes new

2. The potential for a simple set of rules to procedurally generate interesting horizons is sometimes called *emergence*: "Playing a game is synonymous with exploring a game's space of possibility. If a system is fixed, periodic, or chaotic, it does not provide a space of possibility large or flexible enough for players to inhabit and explore through meaningful play. On the other hand, if a system is emergent, exploring possible relationships among game elements is continually engaging." Salen and Zimmerman, *Rules of Play*, 165.

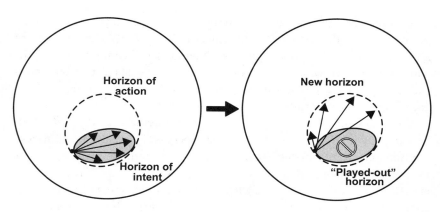

Figure 4.2
A player's evolving horizon of intent.

territory in the game's phase space for potential exploration. For example, a novice playing a driving game will spend most of his time concentrating on merely staying on the road. But an expert playing the same game will hardly think about staying on the road at all; instead, his attention will be focused on how his actions play off the behaviors of the other drivers. The play space experienced by the expert player is invisible to the novice until he builds up an internal framework that will allow him to see it. (figure 4.2).

The horizon of intent can also shift as a result of the actions of other players. Some of the fun experienced in a soccer match comes from manipulating the ball within the natural limitations of physics and the self-imposed constraints of the rules, but most of the fun comes from responding from the horizons constructed by the other players as they move around the field. In a well-designed multi-player game, the actions taken by other players reshape my horizons in interesting ways and vice versa. This is why multi-player games often supply many more hours of gameplay than single-player ones. Even if you are playing on a map you have played a thousand times before, a fresh group of opponents can still provide a fresh experience.

Most videogames draw on a combination of these techniques. Long stretches of algorithmically generated play alternate with brief handcrafted puzzle moments. Elegant and robust external constraints are quickly internalized, encouraging the power to invent new internal constraints to eliminate poor lines of play. Open-ended systems that support deep strategies are further extended by incorporating unexpected constraints from other players. The goal is always the continuous construction of fresh horizons so that the player never feels as though he is making a decision that he remembers making before.

Consequence

Imagine that you are playing a racing game in which your only control is a steering wheel. The screen shows your car zooming down the track. As the first curve approaches, you ease the wheel to the right. The car doesn't respond. Surprised, you wiggle the wheel back and forth. The car executes a perfect turn on its own and continues on down the course. You realize that the steering wheel is just for show; it doesn't actually have any effect on the car's path. There are certainly choices for you to make, but these choices don't have any consequences. No matter what you to do, the outcome is still the same.

In videogame arcades, one sometimes see a forlorn child, who has run out of tokens, pretending to play a game that is in "attract mode" (a pre-recorded loop of gameplay designed to entice passers-by to play the game). The child moves the controls to mimic the canned action, but that doesn't influence anything. No matter what choices he makes, the events on the screen always play out in exactly the same way. There is some meager fun to be gleaned from participating in this simulacrum of play, but it's thin gruel in comparison with the experience you get when you drop a token in the slot.

In order for an action to feel playful, it must produce a change in the game's state. It must transport us to a new location within the play space, and that new location must offer us fresh opportunities for future action (figure 4.3). If our actions don't affect the state, or every action has the same effect, the game feels pointless. We are no longer freely navigating a system of constraints; we're merely performing a sequence of empty gestures.

Sometimes the consequences of an action are obvious. If I'm playing a platformer and I jump from one platform to another, the state of the game clearly has changed. My character is here rather than there, and the new platform offers opportunities for future action that the old platform didn't offer. But at other times the consequences of my actions are subtler and less direct. If I'm playing a first-person shooter and I shoot at a monster, how do I know that the game's state has changed? The monster's health has decreased—somewhere in the game code, a number has been decremented—but how do I, as the player, know that?

Most shooters display an animated blood splash whenever the player shoots an enemy. On one level this little bit of gore can be read as a

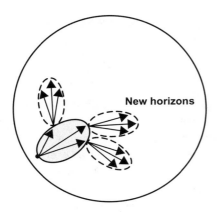

Figure 4.3
A horizon with meaningful consequences.

gratuitous thrill—a bit of heightened violence to pump up the excitement of the moment. But from a gameplay perspective, the blood splash serves an important purpose. It's a hint that the shot has hit its target. It lets us know that our actions have altered the state of the game in a meaningful way. The target previously had more health, and now it has less, and that knowledge induces a shift in our horizon of intent.

Cuing consequence is particularly important when the effects of an action play out over longer time frames. Sometimes it can take minutes or even hours for the full significance of a choice to become apparent. Perhaps I wasted all my rockets on the sewer rats and now don't have any left for the big boss battle with the rat king, or I made my main road too narrow and now my city has horrible traffic jams, or I put all my upgrade points into close-range attacks and now I'm getting shot by enemy archers. Because the effects of my decisions aren't reflected in immediate changes to my horizon of action (that is, what I'm *allowed* to do), the game must provide me with enough information to alter my immediate horizon of intent (what I believe I *should* do) in order for these choices to feel playful.

The value of an outcome is determined by considering it in relation to the game's goals. Does this action move me closer to a preferred location within the game's phase space, or further away? The most interesting decisions are those in which we choose between different desirable outcomes—between different ways to advance toward our goals. If one action is obviously superior, deciding to perform it isn't much of a decision. Deciding which of two platforms to jump to is interesting; deciding whether to jump to a platform or to jump into a pit of spikes isn't.

There are several ways to create tension between different outcomes within the same horizon. One of the most common is to set up consequences that play out over different time frames. Do I choose the small short-term reward, or the larger long-term one? If the time frames were identical, the large reward would clearly be superior to the smaller one. Similarly, if the rewards were equally valuable, the one that came sooner would clearly be superior to the one that came later. Splitting the desirability of the consequences across two orthogonal axes (small/large vs. now/later) makes deciding between them considerably more complicated.

Sometimes, rather than creating tension between time frames, games create tension between probabilities. Do I choose the small reward that is likely, or the large reward that is unlikely? All things being equal, a likely reward is more desirable than an unlikely one; if the unlikely reward is significantly larger, deciding between them is more interesting. There isn't one course of action that is obviously superior, so whatever decision we make feels significant and meaningful.

Play spaces often are designed to have multiple, conflicting goals. For example, in the card game hearts, players earn points by taking tricks. During each round of play, one player leads by playing a card of a particular suit. The other players must play a card of the same suit if they have one, or a card from a different suit if they don't. You take the trick if the card you play is the highest in the current round that follows the suit that was led. The goal is to take as few tricks as possible and minimize your point gain. However, if you manage to take *every* trick in a hand (a feat called "shooting the moon") then you don't receive *any* points; every other player gets points instead. The tension between the primary goal (taking as few tricks as is possible) and the alternate goal of shooting the moon (taking all the tricks) creates numerous opportunities for interesting decisions during play.

Sometimes conflicting goals are explicit in a game's rule set, but sometimes they are supplied by the players. For example, some players are explorers. They like to discover hidden locations and secret treasures, even if doing so doesn't contribute in any meaningful way to winning the game. A horizon that offers a choice between an interesting opportunity for exploration and a chance for the player to advance directly toward victory may or may not feel playful, depending on the player's internal system of constraints. Whatever techniques are employed, the effect is the same. Playful horizons offer a range of actions whose consequences are clear but whose value is ambiguous. Different actions produce distinctly different outcomes, but the relative worth of those outcomes varies, depending on which criteria we use to assess them. Interesting choices result from tension between these competing valuation strategies.

In practice, real games draw on all these techniques mentioned above to create interesting choices for the player. In a racing game there is constant tension between being in first place and avoiding a crash; an action that increases the probability of the former usually reduces the probability of the latter. Similarly, taking advantage of a short-term opportunity to swing wide around a competitor may have longer-term consequences for negotiating an upcoming turn. Navigating the racetrack requires us to grapple with a constant stream of non-trivial decisions, and to quickly analyze situations in which the best course of action isn't always obvious. We are continually weighing and sifting our actions in relation to a variety of competing (and sometimes contradictory) criteria.

Predictability

Imagine a racing game in which the car on the screen responds randomly when we turn the wheel. When we spin the wheel to the right, sometimes the car turns right. But sometimes it turns left, sometimes it comes to a dead stop, and sometimes it explodes. Our actions have consequences, but the consequences aren't predictable. When we perform an action, we are never quite sure what the outcome will be. Such a game will not be boring—anything involving lots of explosions rarely is—but it will not be very interesting either. In order for a play space to function properly, our actions have to be linked to consequences in a clear cause-and-effect relationship. We need to know that doing A probably will result in B or C and probably will not result in X, Y, or Z.

The importance of predictability is closely tied to the existence of goals. If every configuration of a game's state is equally desirable, we may be satisfied with executing a random walk through the phase space. But if some configurations are more desirable than others, then our sense of having freedom of movement depends on our ability to steer our trajectory toward the more positive outcomes. In order to do that, we need to be able to connect cause and effect. We can't work toward a goal if we don't have a clear sense of which actions will move us closer and which will move us farther away.

In the real world, the fact that two things occur in close proximity to each other doesn't automatically prove that one causes the other. Correlation may be a hint that a causal relationship may exist, but it isn't proof. In classical logic, this is referred to as *post hoc ergo propter hoc*, or the *post hoc fallacy*. That the rooster crowed before dawn doesn't prove that the rooster caused the sun to rise.

But in a well-constructed play space, correlation *does* imply causation. Not only do play spaces tend to include cues to help us to make correct connections between cause and effect, they also tend to avoid cues that would lead us to make incorrect ones. If a skeleton guard outside the temple of evil falls down, we can be sure it's because we smacked him with our sword, not because he tripped over a tree root.[3] This *overloaded causality* helps us to anticipate the outcomes of our actions within the game and, as a result, influences our trajectory through the play space.

How are cause and effect cued within a play space? How do we distinguish things that happen at random from things that happen because of our actions? Sometimes it takes minutes or even hours for the consequences of an action within a game to become apparent. How do we form a mental link between a particular event and the action that caused it?

There are four primary techniques for cuing causality:

Familiarity   From our experiences with the real world and with other games, we already know that many things have causal links. If you shoot someone, he falls over. If you damage your car, it doesn't drive as well. When we assess whether or not a particular evolution of the state has been triggered by a particular action, we are strongly biased toward correlations that match up with our existing understanding of the world and of other games.

Proximity   When things happen in close proximity to each other in time and space, we tend to assume they are related. In *Tetris*, when a row of blocks vanishes the moment the last block drops into place, that is a strong cue that some sort of correlation exists between the two events. It is reasonable for us to assume that dropping the last block *caused* the row to vanish.

Continuity   Once we have established a causal link between an action and a particular object within a game, that link will persist as long as the object does. When we press a button to throw a grenade in a first-person shooter, the instantaneous appearance of the grenade in the world establishes a

---

3. "People commonly assume that coincidences in noncomic representations *have causes that will be revealed*; that is, they are more than 'random' accidents. In fact, seeming coincidences stimulate people to look for causal connections. If a sword shows up just at the moment when I need it in the enchanted castle, is the wizard protecting me? Fortuitous events imply agency, and that is essentially what they are good for—implying the involvement of characters or forces in the action." Laurel, *Computers as Theater*, 80.

causal link. But because the grenade persists, the link persists too. When the grenade blows up 10 seconds later, we make a causal connection. Even though we may have performed dozens of other actions in the interim, we still connect the explosion back to the original triggering button press.

Repetition   Even in the absence of other cues, we can still make a connection between cause and effect if they repeat often enough. However, without proximity or continuity to help us, it can take a long time for us to notice a correlation through repetition alone. Repetition usually works to magnify the effects of the other cues. The more times we notice that one thing follows another, the more likely we are to establish a causal link between them.

A play space that behaves predictably allows us to chain together horizons of intent. If I know the outcome of an action, I can use that information to project what will happen in the future: If I make a certain move, what will my new horizon be? And if I make a move within that horizon, what will my next horizon be after that? By thinking forward along different hypothetical lines of action, I can assess the relative worth of different moves not merely by their immediate outcomes, but also by the part they play in long causal chains directed toward specific goals.

Predictability is essential to the architecture of choice. Good play spaces consistently offer us non-trivial choices to make. But in order for a choice to feel non-trivial, we need to be able to weigh the relative worth of different outcomes in relation to our goals. If we can't predict the consequences of our actions, deciding between them becomes meaningless. If every action is a blind leap into the unknown, there is no reason to prefer one over the other. Our decisions don't feel like decisions, and the play space collapses.

Uncertainty

In view of the importance of predictability in the construction of a successful play space, we might be led to assume that more predictability in a game is always better. If we want the player to be able to direct himself toward specific goals, the best approach seemingly would be to structure his moment-to-moment horizons of intent so that the outcome of each "move" is obvious and unambiguous.

But if we look at actual games, we discover that this is almost universally not the case. Virtually all games include mechanisms to introduce uncertainty into the outcome of our actions. In *Monopoly* we roll dice to determine how far we can move. In *Super Mario Bros.* we execute jumps under time pressure, increasing the chance of making a mistake. In baseball the trajectory of a line drive is the product of a complicated and unpredictable physical interaction between ball and bat. Even in a game in which the immediate outcome of a move is unambiguous (e.g., chess), the unforeseen countermoves of our opponent cast a veil over the more distant future.

Why should this be? If play is a function of our capacity to freely navigate a play space, why should we enjoy experiences that contain much potential for our intentions to be thwarted?

A few pages ago, in the section on variety, we looked at how the horizon of intent is shaped not only by the external constraints imposed by the game but also by the internal constraints that the player supplies. If the same situation is repeated over and over, it gradually becomes played out as we construct more and more internal constraints that limit our actions.

Something similar happens in a play space in which the outcomes of our actions are completely predictable. If we know exactly what the result of a particular move will be, we can accurately anticipate the horizon of action that we will occupy after the move occurs. And if the outcomes of various actions in that horizon are similarly predictable, we can anticipate the next horizon, and so on, and so on.

In short, if the outcome of every action in a play space is always obvious and unambiguous, it becomes possible for us to anticipate long chains of moves extending far into the future. We can see exactly how the evolution of the state will unfold. But the knowledge gained from this process is carried forward as a new set of internal constraints. As we arrive at each new horizon, there are now no longer any meaningful choices to make. We weighed our options and decided what we were going to do back when we originally imagined the sequence of moves lying before us. Each horizon is already exhausted by the time we arrive at it.[4]

Long-term uncertainty about future horizons is a fundamental feature of most play spaces. And there are a variety of different techniques that can be used to achieve it:

Hidden information If some of the constraints that will be used to construct future horizons are kept secret from us, we can't fully anticipate the consequences of our actions. In a game of bridge, for example, we can't

4. "One way to understand why games need uncertainty is that if the outcome of a game is predetermined, the experience cannot provide meaningful play. If a game has no uncertainty—if the outcome of the game is completely predetermined—then any choices a player makes are meaningless, because they do not impact the way the game plays out. Meaningful play arises from meaningful choices. If a player's choices have no meaning in the game, there really is no reason to play." Salen and Zimmerman, *Rules of Play*, 174.

see the cards held by the other players. Over the course of the game, their hands are gradually revealed, continuously reshaping our horizons.

Random chance   Many games use overt random number generators, such as dice, to scramble our ability to anticipate the future. When we roll the dice in *Monopoly*, we are randomly selecting one out of eleven different horizons to engage with.

Real-world physics   Most sports are built around physical systems whose behavior is extremely sensitive to initial conditions—in mathematical terms, chaotic. Very small variations in the initial velocity and rotation of a bowling ball will translate to very large differences in the number of pins knocked down.

Motor skills   This is closely related to real-world physics. Slight variations in the timing or degree of an action will produce very different outcomes. In one-on-one fighting videogames, the difference between landing a blow and missing often comes down to differences of a few milliseconds or pixels.

Other players   These are ultimate form of hidden information. Not only are some of the future constraints of the system hidden from us, but other players have the capacity to construct new constraints that may not have even been imagined by the original creator of the system.

The point here isn't to exhaustively list all the ways perfect anticipation can be thwarted. Rather, it is to point out that all good play experiences use some mechanism to introduce a sense of uncertainty into our trajectory through the play space.[5]

Satisfaction

Sometimes a game is just too hard. We have a goal, a particular configuration of the state we would like to achieve, but the constraints we face are too tight. No matter what actions we attempt, we aren't able to steer our trajectory through phase space to achieve the desired result.

Most games aren't designed to be completely unwinnable. Usually even with the hardest game, the rules are set up so that some combination of moves results in victory, or at least a prolongation of the play experience. But when we combine the rules with our capabilities as players, we sometimes find ourselves in situations in which winning becomes impossible. Maybe our reflexes are too slow. Maybe we don't have the necessary endurance. Maybe our grasp of strategy is weak. Maybe we misunderstand what

5. For a much more detailed exploration of various mechanisms that can be used to introduce uncertainty into game, see Costikyan, *Uncertainty in Games*.

the actual goals of the game really are. Regardless of the reason, we repeatedly find ourselves encountering horizons within which all our actions lead to negative outcomes.

We may tolerate temporary setbacks, but if a game repeatedly demonstrates that desirable outcomes are unattainable, we quickly become frustrated and disillusioned. At the same time, we like it when things go our way, particularly when we have the impression that the victory is the result of our own skill and not just random chance.

An expert player's knowledge of future outcomes can lend satisfaction even in situations in which there doesn't seem to be an immediate reward. For example, a player who is very familiar with a particular map in a real-time strategy game may begin by working through a fixed pattern of harvesting resources and constructing units and buildings. Each of these individual actions may provide very little in the way of direct positive feedback, but because the player can anticipate how they build toward a desirable result, stepping through the series can still be fun. A novice executing the same sequence of rote actions without the knowledge of what each step represents would not experience the same feelings of satisfaction. Satisfaction isn't merely a matter of achieving a desirable outcome. It's a matter of achieving an outcome we have anticipated will be desirable.

Sometimes winning and losing have ramifications that extend beyond the game. If I beat my buddies at poker, the fruits of my victory (money and status) persist after the game ends. Thus, it is tempting to frame winning solely in terms of the rewards that it brings. Viewed from this perspective, playing a game is primarily a social activity whose purpose is to grant the player increased wealth or stature. It is an algorithm for generating a dominance hierarchy.

However, if we look closely at how games are actually played, we notice that people enjoy winning even when no external reward is attached. Many videogames are played solo. It's fun to beat them even if we never share the knowledge of our victory with anyone else. *Asteroids* and other early videogames quantified winning by assigning the player a score. A high score was a type of reward—it gave the player bragging rights, social currency that he could spend after the game was over. But as videogames have evolved as a medium, designers have discovered that scores are superfluous. Most players don't need a reward to enjoy winning. The feeling of satisfaction that we feel when a game goes our way is sufficient.

At the beginning this chapter, I laid out a simple model of play based on Huizinga's ideas of freedom and constraint. Too little choice is boring, and too much choice is confusing; good play lies in the tension between the two. As we have worked our way through other heuristics, we have seen that they can also be understood as questions of player choice. When there is a lack of variety from one horizon to the next, our memories of past actions create new internal constraints, and the result is boredom. Similarly, when the outcome of every action is certain, our too-perfect anticipation of future opportunities creates a similar reduction in meaningful decisions; again the result is boredom. And if the consequences of our actions aren't clear—if there are numerous moves that we can make, but there is no way to winnow our choices down to a manageable number—the game will feel confusing.

Winning and losing don't fit neatly into this pattern. It isn't enough that we have the right number of choices. Those choices also need to provide us with the opportunity to work toward desirable destinations within the game's phase space. The satisfaction of achieving a desired goal isn't a function of the amount of moment-to-moment freedom afforded by the game system. The loser in a racing game makes just as many meaningful decisions as the winner, even though he experiences significantly more frustration.

In addition to our primary axis determined by the strength of the constraints on the player's actions, we need to construct a secondary axis that spans the desirability of the *outcomes* of those actions. Play exists not only in the tension between freedom and constraint, but also in the tension between success and failure.

The two axes in figure 4.4 are largely independent of each other. Play experiences can fall in any of the four quadrants. For example, simple, repetitious gameplay that consistently rewards the player can be both boring *and* satisfying. Most gamers have experienced the mindless pleasure of replaying an old favorite. We may know all the levels backward and forward, and we are making very few meaningful decisions, but executing the right moves over and over again is enjoyable in its own right.

A play space can also be simultaneously confusing and satisfying. When we encounter a game for the first time, we haven't yet constructed a system of internal constraints to limit our potential actions to a manageable subset. The game's world seems wide open. Anything is possible. We choose our early moves almost at random, without much sense as to the ramifications of our choices. But if our floundering leads to positive outcomes, we still feel satisfied by the experience. This is why tutorial sections at the beginning of games tend to be easy and forgiving. We may be confused and uncertain, but we are willing to temporarily overlook our excess of freedom if the outcomes of our actions are almost universally positive.

The same is true on the other side of the axis. A frustrating game may be boring, or confusing, or neither boring nor confusing. If you are playing

Figure 4.4
Satisfaction vs. frustration.

chess against a much stronger opponent, you may consistently have an interesting range of moves to choose from, but because every choice takes you another step further down the road to your inevitable defeat, the experience will nevertheless prove highly frustrating.

Within our two-axis diagram, we can construct a triangle that encompasses the range of acceptable play experiences for most players (figure 4.5). We are more willing to put up with systems that are overconstrained or underconstrained if they allow us frequent opportunities to succeed. Similarly, as the likelihood of failure increases, our tolerance for boredom and confusion plummets. In the extreme case, even a game that strikes the perfect balance between freedom and constraint may still be not much fun to play, simply because its demands exceed our skills.

If players enjoy winning, why not design all games to be trivially easy? To answer this question we have to return to the notion of consequences. In order for an action to feel like a real choice, it must have a meaningful effect on altering the game's state. The resulting new horizon of action should be different from the horizons that might have emerged from other potential actions. But if every action in a game leads us inevitably toward victory, the notion of having made a meaningful choice collapses. If all horizons are equally worthwhile, then arriving at one is as good as arriving at another. In order to create a feeling of play in a goal-oriented space, it is essential that we be presented with the opportunity to choose poorly. The possibility of failure is central to our experience of play.

Several caveats should be added to the preceding observation. First, the games we have analyzed so far have had clearly defined victory states, but

Figure 4.5
The triangle of acceptable play experiences.

trying to achieve victory isn't the only way to play. In games of make-believe, for example, players often have little concern for winning or losing. They may have goals they are trying to accomplish ("Quick, rescue the dolly from the burning building!"), but successfully accomplishing these goals isn't the primary source of satisfaction. Nevertheless, satisfaction and frustration are important parts of playing make-believe. There is still a distinction between a "right" move and a "wrong" move in a game of pretend, even if "rightness" and "wrongness" aren't tied to a predetermined victory condition. Later in the book, we will examine how coherence and closure can replace winning as mechanisms for assigning worth to different moves.

Second, how satisfaction applies to "abusive game design" is worth mentioning. Abusive games, as identified by Douglas Wilson and Miguel Sicart, are games that are deliberately designed to frustrate the player. Games such as *Super Meat Boy* or *Kaizo Mario* are punishingly hard, filled with near-impossible challenges and unfair perversities. Playing these games is often an exercise in repeated failure. Wilson and Sicart correctly point out that such games walk a very fine line.[6] They must go right up to the edge of what the player will tolerate without pushing them into quitting in anger. What

6. "The trick is to push players right up to the breaking point, but not beyond; after all, you can't abuse your players if they stop playing your game. In this sense, an abusive game designer is like a virus—one which avoids killing the host in order to better propagate throughout the population." Wilson and Sicart, "Now It's Personal: On Abusive Game Design."

this means is that abusive game design depends heavily on the player's own conceptual background. What does the player think the game is trying to accomplish? What sort of thoughts does it trigger? In other words, the player of an abusive experience is willing to tolerate frustration in low-level moment-to-moment play if that frustration is essential to the construction of an interesting high-level interpretive play space. A similar approach is required for the analysis of experiential games such as *Dear Esther* or *Proteus*. The challenges such games offer are so minimal that successful progression is almost automatic. However, the vacuity of their moment-to-moment play is overshadowed by a compensatory complexity in the interpretive play spaces that they construct. Indeed, the very absence of immediate challenge is an important constraint in the construction of these higher-level play spaces.

The topic of interpretive play (and how the heuristics apply to it) is covered in much greater detail in the final chapters of this book. For the moment, it's enough to keep in mind that we want to succeed when we play, and in a typical goal-directed game success is any move that advances us toward victory.

These six elements—choice, variety, consequence, predictability, uncertainty, satisfaction—are at the core of every play experience. Back in chapter 1, I noted the curious universality of game mechanics. Even though hundreds of years and thousands of miles separate us from the culture that invented *Nine Men's Morris*, we can still sit down and navigate its mechanics without experiencing any sense of cultural dislocation. Like all games, it offers several moves to choose from. These moves vary from turn to turn, and which move we pick determines what moves are available in the future. The regularity of the rules allows us to plan several moves ahead, but the choices of our opponent sometimes thwart our plans. Nevertheless, the game is winnable. If we pick the right moves, eventually we will meet the game's victory conditions and the game will end. Despite its dislocation and time and place, *Nine Men's Morris* feels familiar because its structure conforms to the universal meta-rules that govern all play spaces.

In fact, the six heuristics should feel strangely familiar. We all know intuitively how play spaces are supposed to work, even if we have never articulated that knowledge explicitly. We can feel it in our guts when a game is going wrong, and we are good at tweaking the rules on the fly when play deviates too far from the norm. Handicaps, mulligans, house rules, do-overs, walkthroughs, and cheat codes all are techniques that we naturally and intuitively slip into when a game stops working the way it is supposed to.

For example, players don't peek at the cards in a game of solitaire when they are winning. They only do it when their frustration with losing becomes too great. They do it when they want to reduce the uncertainty and increase the predictability of their current horizon, so as to more easily construct an anticipatory chain toward a desired location in the phase space. Furthermore, players inevitably cheat in ways that make a game more interesting, not simply in ways that make a game easier (although often there is a significant overlap between the two). After all, it would be trivial to "win" a game of solitaire by flipping over all the cards over and moving them to their final positions. But even though it would guarantee a win, players don't cheat in that way. That sort of cheat isn't any fun. It doesn't produce interesting horizons of action or structure new meaningful choices. Cheating isn't a random or arbitrary act. It is a deliberate move to shift the constraints in a play space that has ceased to be entertaining.

Similarly, we know that it's a good idea to go easy on a much weaker opponent. Trouncing someone may be satisfying, but it's also boring. If the constraints supplied by the other players don't generate interesting horizons for us to navigate, we intuitively add new constraints to change the shape of the play space. We remove one of our pawns from the board, or limit ourselves to the weakest gun, or give our opponent a head start. Giving each side a fair chance doesn't just make the game more fun for the weaker player; it also benefits the stronger player. When play drifts too far outside the triangle of acceptable play experiences, we intuitively try to steer it back on track by tweaking the constraints.

5 Anticipation

Why are turn-based games fun? In our model, play is free movement within a system of constraints. However, when you play a turn-based game, you spend most of your time not moving. In a game such as *go*, at least half of your time is spent waiting for the other player to make his move. And when it's your turn, you spend more time deciding where you want to place your next stone. The physical movements that actually change the state of the game may add up to only a few minutes spread over a play session lasting several hours. Most of the time, when you are playing a turn-based game, you aren't moving; you're sitting and thinking.

Why, then, don't we experience turn-based games as punctuated enjoyment? Shouldn't the moments of fun that accompany making a move alternate with long stretches of boredom when we aren't moving? Why do we experience a feeling of continuous, ongoing play, even though our trajectory through the game's phase space consists of a series of intermittent jumps?

A turn-based game feels like a continuous play experience because thinking about our next move is itself a form of play. When we play *go*, the fun isn't merely in placing the stones; it's also in mentally exploring the ramifications of different placements. When it isn't our turn, we aren't just idly waiting; we're actively sifting through potentialities.

If you have ever played a board game against a very slow opponent, you probably have witnessed how this feeling of continuity can break down. If the other player takes a very long time to make his moves, you may exhaust all your opportunities for interesting strategizing. Once you have a good idea what you are going to do next, all we can do wait for your turn to come around. The result is an annoying, staccato experience.

This element of turn-based gameplay puts an upper bound on the number of players who can participate in many games. As each new player is added, the gap between moves increases. If the gap becomes too long, we run out of options to consider for our next move and the game becomes boring.

Because of this, many turn-based multi-player games function better as frameworks for social interaction than as pure gameplay experiences. For example, the large amount of randomness in a game of *Monopoly* discourages deep strategizing. It prevents you from thinking too far ahead, leaving you plenty of time to talk with the other players sitting around the table. Contrast this style of play with a more deterministic game, such as chess. The strategic depth of chess makes it better at delivering a continuous play experience, even if a lot of time passes between moves. However, this strategic depth can interfere with social interaction; the cognitive challenge of planning one's next move can easily crowd out casual conversation.

When I originally explored the idea of internal game states, I used the example of two chess grandmasters calling out moves on a board that exists entirely in their imaginations. But a similar process takes place even when players with less skill play on a physical board. The physical board may represent the current state of the game, but the players spend most of their time concentrating on the hypothetical boards in their heads and considering the consequences of different lines of attack. We can represent this by adding a thought bubble to our play flow diagram (figure 5.1). When we play a game, we construct an internal model of the game system and use this model to plan out a variety of scenarios, imagining different actions

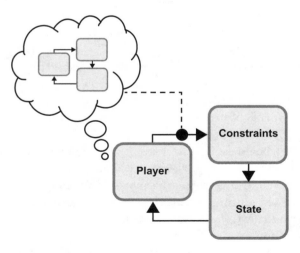

Figure 5.1
Anticipation influences action.

and their potential outcomes. In this way, we develop a sense of which actions probably will produce desirable results. And this new information will then be used to shape our decisions about which actions to perform in the actual game. This is *anticipation*. We take our knowledge of the rules, the current state, our capabilities, the knowledge and capabilities of our opponents, and we use that information to imagine how the game will unfold in the future. And when we use our imaginations in this way, we are *moving freely within a system of constraints*. We are wandering within an envelope of potentialities extrapolated from the current horizon of intent. Anticipation is itself a way to play.

We examined anticipation in turn-based games first because it is easy to see in that context. The continuity of the play experience between discontinuous moves is a strong clue that the players are doing something interesting while waiting for their next opportunity to act. But anticipatory play is an important feature of all play spaces—even ones in which the action is rapid and continuous.

It is possible to play a typical first-person shooter as a simple exercise in stimulus and response. A monster appears somewhere on the screen, we aim our gun, and we pull the trigger. But as we play more and more, we gradually internalize the game's rules. We learn how the monsters behave and how they interact with the layout of the levels. So now, as we move through the corridors of the alien spaceship, we begin to anticipate the form that future threats will take. Instead of blundering mindlessly forward and blasting away when monsters appear, we adjust our actions to give ourselves a tactical advantage: We move from cover point to cover point to give ourselves protection if we are ambushed. We circle-strafe around corners to keep our weapon pointed toward where new threats will be revealed. If we spot a monster, we hold our fire until it makes itself vulnerable.

As our aiming skills improve, we may even discover that our experience gradually shifts away from the shooting-gallery gameplay of the earlier levels toward a more tactical challenge built around our ability to anticipate. Satisfying play is no longer just about aiming and pulling the trigger. Instead, it's also about moving through space and controlling encounters so they will resolve to our advantage. The killing shot, when it finally comes, is more than just an immediate gameplay moment. It is also confirmation that our earlier game of anticipation was played successfully.

Once we make the shift from immediate to anticipatory gameplay, we can even have fun in an area of the map with no enemies at all. If the level layout convinces us that there is the possibility of danger ahead we can have fun moving and guarding against it even if no real threat ever

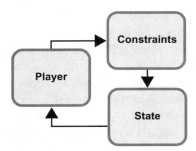

Figure 5.2
The cycle of play.

materializes. Anticipatory play gives us a model for talking about the non-interactive beats of a game such as *Rainbow Six*—those moments when the player stops, looks, and thinks about what he is doing. Instead of defining a play experience entirely by what the player is allowed to do, anticipatory play allows us to focus instead on what opportunities any play experience provides for elaborated analysis, contemplation, and reflection. With this in mind, we can eliminate the thought bubble we just added to our game-flow diagram (figure 5.2). Anticipation isn't a mental state that sits *outside* the structure of play, directing and informing it. It's merely another manifestation of play, another way of moving freely within constraints. We still cycle around the diagram, but many of the loops occur entirely within our minds. The state we are updating on those internal loops isn't the position of physical pieces on a physical board; it's a collection of possible future positions existing entirely inside our heads.

Structuring Anticipatory Play Spaces

All games offer some anticipatory play, but there are conditions that make such play more likely. For example, the more stable a game's active constraints are, the more opportunity there is for anticipatory play. In a so-called twitch shooter, where most horizons resolve over the course of a few seconds, the foreseeable causal chains will be relatively short. We must make quick tactical decisions and act upon them immediately before the situation changes. Bursts of anticipatory play may only span a few fractions of a second before the demands of the procedurally evolving constraints force us into choosing a course of action. But in a strategy game, such as chess, the constraints defining the play space remain largely the same throughout the entire game. The rules are the rules, and although our strategies may slowly evolve as we study our opponent's play style, we are never surprised by an unexpected level layout or the introduction of a new playing piece that moves in unexpected ways. As a result, our foreseeable causal chains can grow very long indeed. We may find ourselves exploring a landscape of potential board configurations that stretches a dozen moves in the future or more. Anticipatory play occurs not as a flurry of short bursts, but as a series of extended ruminations that are only occasionally punctuated by a change in the physical state of the game.

If anticipatory play is to occur, it is also important that the constraints defining the play space be easy to internalize. The more complicated an external simulation or a rule set is, the more difficult it is for the player to construct an internal analogue of it. If every goblin in the dungeon displays a small set of consistent behaviors, we can learn what to expect from them in a battle and plan accordingly. But if the goblins are programmed to have dozens of unique behaviors, each triggered by a wide range of different conditions, the complexity of the simulation will defeat us. We can't internalize the external constraints. Though the goblins may still present interesting moment-to-moment challenges when we encounter them in the game, they will not be a source of anticipatory play.

In chapter 4, we touched on the linked notions of elegance and robustness. A small set of rules that generates a large number of horizons is elegant; if it can do so without *ad hoc* additions, it is also robust. Elegant and robust rules are particularly good for anticipatory play because they are easier to learn.[1] Furthermore, not only must the rules be easy to learn, but players must also be given the opportunity to learn them. They need breathing room to observe the evolution of the game and to grasp the significance of what they have observed. If things happen too quickly, or the player isn't given enough time to consider the significance of events, anticipation collapses and play becomes entirely about reacting in the moment.

Not only does it take time to internalize anticipatory constraints, it also takes time to navigate them. We may be able to consider potential moves much faster than we can make them, but the act of consideration isn't instantaneous. Furthermore, the longer the anticipatory chain, the more time it takes to adequately explore it. Thus, if a game is going to support anticipatory play, it must provide the necessary time for anticipation to occur. This means providing lulls in the action—intervals in which the

1. "Elegance is one of the most desirable qualities in any game, because it means you have a game that is simple to learn and understand, but is full of interesting emergent complexity." Schell, *The Art of Game Design*, 197.

evolving state of the game temporarily stalls to supply us with a stable anticipatory playground. Paradoxically, this means sometimes the most entertaining thing a game can do is hold still. One of the drawbacks of associating games so closely with interactivity is that it biases design away from stillness. It encourages the construction of games that are action-packed, with lots of short-term business for the player to attend to. But if the moment-to-moment demands of immediate play are too pressing, we may never have the mental space for longer arcs of internal play. It's hard to plan your getaway in the middle of a gunfight, even if planning your getaway would be fun. And it's hard to think about the deeper meaning of a play experience if your entire attention is required merely to sustain it.

As a type of play, anticipation obeys the same heuristics as other play spaces. An interesting anticipatory moment is one in which there are a small number of alternatives to consider and the alternatives are different from the alternatives we have seen before. Considering an alternative creates new opportunities for additional anticipation, and different alternatives lead us to different imaginary futures. We need to be able to predict roughly where various alternatives will lead us, but never be exactly sure. Finally, the process of anticipation should lead us to some satisfactory conclusion—at least one imagined future should feel superior to our present state.

Anticipatory play and immediate play often are closely bound together, so the sort of constraints that are fun to play through are similarly fun to imagine playing through. However, there are situations in which the two types of play are decoupled. For example, if you are playing a shooter, a blank corridor is less exciting than a corridor with an open door on one side, even if there are no enemies beyond the door. The anticipatory chain triggered by the open door ("Is there an ambush ahead? I have to move carefully. I can't see anything. Can I peek around the corner?") is an interesting experience even though the play is taking place entirely inside your head.

Espen Aarseth touches on the power of anticipation in his work on cybertexts. Aarseth refers to these interactive works as "ergodic," meaning that, as narrative experiences, cybertexts require a non-trivial amount of effort to traverse. At first glance this seems a strange definition. How is the effort required to turn a page in a book substantially different from the effort to click on a hyperlink? However, Aarseth clarifies what he means:

[W]hen you read from a cybertext, you are constantly reminded of inaccessible strategies and paths not taken, voices not heard. Each decision will make some parts of the text more, and others less, accessible, and you may never know the exact results of your choices; that is, exactly what you missed. This is very different from the ambiguities of a linear text. And inaccessibility, it must be noted, does not imply ambiguity but, rather, an absence of possibility—an aporia.[2]

The effort in engaging with a cybertext is not the physical effort of turning a page or pressing a button, but the mental effort of making a meaningful decision. And the decisions you make within a cybertext are meaningful because they open up some pathways in the text and close off others.

However, why should the existence of unexplored pathways in a cybertext matter so much? Whatever choices I make within a work of interactive fiction, my own path through the narrative will always be linear. Why should the knowledge that alternative unexplored storylines exist affect my experience within the particular storyline I have chosen? It's as though all the books left unpicked on a library shelf had the power to change the book I'm actually reading.

The answer lies in anticipation. By explicitly calling out moments of narrative divergence, cybertexts encourage anticipatory play. Although our actual path through the work is still linear, our attention flickers out from that linear path along ramified filaments, sifting through various imagined possibilities implied by various choices. What story will I get if I walk through the blue door? How will that differ from the story I get if I walk through the red one? Even though you can only pick one door to walk through, the anticipation of the road not taken is a significant part of the experience.

I disagree with Aarseth that cybertexts are entirely different from traditional linear texts in this regard. Traditional texts provide their own moments of anticipatory play, and their own sense of diverging paths. However, the divergence of traditional texts lies less at the level of narrative ("What will happen next?") than at the level of interpretation ("What does this mean?"). We will explore this idea in more detail at the end of the book. For the moment, it is sufficient to keep in mind that anticipation works at different levels in different works, and that even if our path through a play space appears to be linear, our experience along that path is often profoundly shaped by our fleeting consideration of unexplored branches.

Gambling and Grinding

Anticipation also helps to explain the play value of certain experiences that, at first glance, seem to violate the heuristics. The most obvious example

2. Aarseth, *Cybertext: Perspectives on Ergodic Literature*, 1–3.

is gambling. In most casino games, the player's choices are limited and repetitive and have no effect on the player's future horizons. In roulette, for example, the player chooses a number and lays his money down, but because where the ball lands is completely random; the choice has no predictable consequences. With many casino games, it isn't possible to plan out a series of moves that will lead to victory.

But even though games of chance block us from accurately predicting the future, they are extremely good at fostering the illusion that we can. They supply a series of independent events that appear to be parts of a causal chain, even though they aren't. Within this sequence of random consequences, we perceive imaginary patterns. Our minds construct a framework of winning and losing streaks, lucky numbers, gambling "systems," and all the other imaginary baggage that goes with the gambling experience.[3]

The anticipatory play of casino games is almost completely disconnected from their immediate mechanics. The fun in these experiences doesn't come from our physical actions; rather, the play takes place entirely within an imaginary framework of cause and effect—a framework in which arbitrary events are imbued with consequence, and pure randomness is tamed and rendered comprehensible.[4]

There are various techniques that can be deployed to encourage players to construct causal relationships where none actually exist. Slot machines are designed so that near misses of high-value payouts are unusually common, leading players to believe that a jackpot is just around the corner. Many payouts are less than the player's initial wager, creating the impression that the player has won even though he has merely lost a smaller amount. Payouts can be made to vary from machine to machine, creating the appearance of "hot" and "cold" machines. Meaningless choices are presented as though they matter—for example, players are asked to pick a random reward during a bonus round. None of these choices affect the odds of

3. "There is considerable evidence that gamblers hold a range of mistaken beliefs about their chosen form of gambling. Perhaps the most important of these is a form of the gambler's fallacy: that the worse the run of luck, the more certain you can be that a change in luck is near." Zangeneh, Blaszczynski, and Turner, *In the Pursuit of Winning: Problem Gambling Theory, Research and Treatment,* 31.

4. "Some lottery players say that, despite the fact that they know they will lose, they so enjoy the fantasy of winning, and dreaming of what they will do with their winnings, that it is well worth the price of the lottery ticket. One such gambler said that he had gotten more imaginative satisfaction out of his lottery tickets over the years than out of anything else in his life. Though he still hasn't ever had a winning ticket, he doesn't care." Sutton-Smith, *The Ambiguity of Play,* 70.

winning in the slightest, but they contribute to the imaginary causal chains that make the overall experience more enjoyable.[5]

The power of imagined anticipatory chains is also harnessed in non-casino games. For example, online role-playing games such as *World of Warcraft* are usually designed to provide players with the opportunity to "grind" for rare "drops" (random in-game rewards). Grinding involves completing the same encounter over and over again, hoping that eventually the random reward will be something unusual and valuable. Grinding is, by definition, boring. If you are enjoying an encounter for its own sake, then you aren't grinding. You aren't grinding until the immediate play of the scenario has been exhausted. You know all the moves the monsters are going to make, and you have played through the encounter so many times you know exactly what you need to do to beat it. You're enjoying the encounter only for the opportunity it provides to weave an imaginary web of expectation. Chris Bateman refers to this phenomenon as "grip":

When a particular game gets the player into a state of wanting "just one more go," it is because of grip; the feeling that one might succeed (or do better) on another attempt fosters the desire to persevere. Slot machines depend upon this for their appeal (if you didn't win with that coin, surely you will have a better chance of winning next time!)[6]

The construction of satisfying grinding experiences is closely related to the construction of satisfying gambling experiences. A good grind consists of many small moments of reinforcement, a collection of near misses and false wins that suggest that the big drop lies just around the corner. There are many minor decisions to be made that, though meaningless, hint at being strategically advantageous. There are suggestions of "hot" and "cold" grinding opportunities—locations or times in the game at which big payouts are more likely to occur. A good grinding experience transforms a stochastic process into an anticipatory romp in the mind of the player.

Resolving Anticipation

No matter how long we spin out anticipatory play, eventually we have to make a move that will actualize our predictions. Sometimes a decision is forced upon us by the unstable state of the game. Other times we choose

5. Harrigan and Dixon, "PAR Sheets, probabilities, and slot machine play: Implications for problem and non-problem gambling."

6. Bateman, *Imaginary Games*, 34.

to act when we reach a point at which there is no more meaningful anticipatory play to be had within the current horizon. We have explored our options and chosen the best move, and any further loops through the cycle of play feel pointless and tedious.

This is where our predictions will be either confirmed or falsified—where our anticipatory play is resolved. We imagined that a certain set of choices within a certain set of constraints would lead to a certain range of outcomes. If our predictions are confirmed, we feel a rush of satisfaction. In part this satisfaction is a result of getting what we want, but in part it's a result of predicting correctly. The thrill of success in a game with anticipatory gameplay is twofold—the enjoyment of achieving a desired outcome is mingled with the enjoyment of having correctly predicted it.

In fact, "correctly predicting the outcome" is a meta-goal that cuts across all games. Players usually want to win. But even when they don't, they take consolation in anticipating the nature of a loss. A win is more satisfying than a loss, but an anticipated loss is more satisfying than an unanticipated loss. Depending on the game and the players, an anticipated loss may sometimes be *more* satisfying than an unanticipated win—the player may feel that it's better to fail honestly than to triumph through a fluke. An accurate prediction, no matter what the outcome, is itself a form of victory.

When something happens "the way it should," we feel a rush of satisfaction, as though something meaningful has "clicked into place." The satisfaction of achieving an anticipated outcome is so strong that it can make even a very tight set of constraints fun to play with.

There are many videogames that use a "Simon says" model of play. Players are presented with a sequence of control inputs that they are required to mimic within a fixed time window. The first videogame example of such play was the 1983 arcade hit *Dragon's Lair*, but since then it has appeared in many different incarnations. Music games such as *Guitar Hero, Rock Band, and Dance Dance Revolution* are built around this simple play model. In these games, players are presented with a continuously scrolling series of control inputs that they must perform in time with the beat. Endless runner games such as *Canabalt* and offer a similar mechanic—players must time their jumps to avoid the continuous stream of obstacles toward which they are running.

At first glance, "Simon says" mechanics hardly seems like play at all (as we have defined it). There is very little freedom in these sorts of games. Players are told exactly which buttons to press, and in what order. The only decision open to them is *when* to press the button—and even that is barely a decision, since there is only one correct choice: one must hit the button on the right beat, or before time runs out.

But what these games lack in freedom, they make up in satisfaction. There is only one correct move in each horizon of action, but the results of making that move are so rewarding that players are willing to overlook the tightness of the constraints. Hitting the right button at the right time in a "Simon says" game gives an immediate double dose of satisfaction: "I did the right thing, and I *knew* it was the right thing to do."

The fixed time window is a crucial part of the design of "Simon says" mechanics. Our anticipatory play when we play *Guitar Hero* isn't directed toward the ramifications of our possible choices, but toward exactly matching the timing of each incoming beat. It's similar to the satisfaction we feel during a game of catch. When you throw a baseball to me, my horizon of intent is very narrow. There is only one "right move": to position my glove so that the ball lands in it. However, the satisfaction involved in quickly moving my glove to the correctly anticipated position is so strong that it overcomes the narrowness of the horizon. The tight time window is essential—without that hard constraint on my possible moves, my horizon of intent would be so open-ended that it wouldn't support interesting anticipatory play. Expert players sometimes encounter exactly this sort of tightly focused anticipation even in games with broad horizons of action. In a first-person shooter there might be many things I could theoretically do at a certain moment, but if I know the game well my internal constraints may collapse that broad horizon of action into a very narrow horizon of intent. My enemy comes around the corner, my crosshairs are on his helmet, and BANG! There were many things I could have done, but there was only one *right thing* to do. Knowing the right thing to do and then doing it is profoundly satisfying.

As we get better at games, we find that our choices grow fewer but our opportunities for satisfaction increase. "Simon says" games provide a short-cut from inexperience to mastery. Instead of asking us to figure out the right course of action from horizon to horizon, they make the correct choice obvious: "Here is a thing to do. Do this thing and you will have the satisfaction of having done the right thing."

Achieving Closure

No game goes on forever. At some point, someone wins, or time runs out, or play is interrupted by external circumstances, or the players simply give up out of fatigue, annoyance, or boredom. Often we can see the end coming, and can account for it in our anticipatory play. We are aware that the timer is ticking down, that we're down to our last life, or that we're almost across the finish line, and our expectations contract accordingly.

But sometimes the end comes unexpectedly. As an extreme example, imagine you are in the middle of an exciting boss battle and the electrical power in your neighborhood goes out. Your mind is still racing ahead to plan your next attack combo, but the screen is dark and there is nothing more you can do. Such a moment is intensely frustrating. All your carefully constructed expectations come crashing down around you as the play space collapses abruptly.

Similar frustration occurs whenever the end of anticipatory play fails to correspond to the end of immediate play. The rules (or external circumstances) dictate that the game must end, but our minds still busy sifting through contingencies that will never play out. This happens frequently in race-style board games in which the object is to be the first player to arrive at the finish line. (*Candy Land* and *Snakes and Ladders* are examples.) Even though the game is officially over when the first player reaches the goal, it is common for one of the remaining players to say "Let's keep going to see who comes in second!" Regardless of what the rules say, the game will not feel as if it is over until the players have exhausted their opportunities for anticipatory play. This is *closure*. Closure is achieved when anticipatory play ends. It is brought about by giving the player cues that the game is almost over, or by gradually shutting off avenues for anticipatory play. One reason that boss battles are effective as conclusions is that they tend to discourage players from thinking any farther into the future: Don't worry about conserving ammo, or whether you followed the right path, or what is going to happen next—just focus all your effort and attention on defeating this giant squid *right now*.

Game designers often intuitively build cues to facilitate closure into their designs. Games are full of progress bars, counters, and timers, all intended to give the player feedback on how close he is to success or failure. If your goal is to kill twenty goblins, it is very satisfying to have a counter that tracks your kills, even though it doesn't have any effect on your immediate tactics. The counter isn't there to help you kill goblins; it's there to help you stop thinking about killing goblins when the quest ends. Without some kind of progress indicator, you will still be deep in anticipatory play when the final kill comes. Your thoughts will still be racing along various lines of potential action. An unexpected announcement of victory is an unpleasant surprise that yanks you abruptly out of anticipatory play. However, if the game tracks your progress, you can adjust your expectations in advance, shutting down anticipatory play as the final kill draws near. Consequentially, when you do finish off the twentieth goblin you experience an immediate feeling of satisfying completeness. Not only is the quest over because the rules say so; the quest also *feels* as though it is over, because you are no longer planning for it. Closure has been achieved.

Movement toward closure can be triggered in a number of ways:

Progress displays   These often take the form of explicit meters and counters, but information about progress can also be presented less directly. For example, in *Diablo III* the map shows areas you have already visited. By glancing at the map, you can easily see how much of the current level remains unexplored. When you finish a level, you know there is nothing left to do, because the map is entirely filled in.

Strategic resolves   In games with strategic play, players are working toward various long-term goals. Decisions are made not just for their immediate benefit, but because they move the player closer to a distant destination in the play space. As closure approaches, these long-term anticipatory chains have to be resolved. For example, in the Japanese role-playing game *Skies of Arcadia* you spend a large part of the middle of the game recruiting new crewmembers for your flying battleship. Completing your "crewmember collection"—finding someone to fill every position—is one of the ways the game winds down your anticipatory experience.

Advancement plateaus   While a game is gradually shutting down existing anticipatory chains, it also should avoid initiating new ones. As the end approaches, there are fewer and fewer opportunities to make new long-term plans. For example, *Sorcery*, an action-adventure game I helped design, has an alchemy system. Players use ingredients they discover in the world to unlock character upgrades. Although you can brew upgrade potions right up to the final boss battle, you discover your last new ingredient about an hour earlier. As the end approaches, the upgrade system still exists as a tool, but it is no longer a source of significant anticipatory play.

Immediate challenges   As has already been mentioned, the demands of fast-paced immediate gameplay can crowd out anticipatory play. If you are concentrating desperately on staying alive right now, you don't have enough mental bandwidth to consider what you are going to do in the future. For example, the ending of *Ocarina of Time* includes a frantic dash out of a collapsing tower after the final boss has been defeated. There is no time to plan your escape (or anything else)—the time pressure is so strong, and the threats come so quickly, that all you have time to do is react to them.

Barren horizons   A good indication that the end is approaching is that the play space simply offers you fewer and fewer new things to do. In the game *Civilization V*, for example, you have the option to keep playing after the game has been won or lost. You can continue to tinker with your civilization and wrap up any long-term projects you started, but there is no opportunity to score more points or defeat your enemies. This little bit of "dead space" at the end of the full game gives you the opportunity to wind down any anticipatory play that might still be in progress at the moment of victory.

The existence of closure elements such as health bars and progress meters is sometimes criticized as "gamey" and "unrealistic." After all, tasks in the real world usually don't come with such clear indications of our progress toward success or failure. This is true, but immaterial. Tasks in the real world are structured by random and arbitrary constraints, and as a result they are often boring, confusing or frustrating. The real world isn't designed to provide us with either satisfaction or closure. A game, on the other hand, is a system of constraints designed to encourage the consistent production of satisfying horizons of intent. Closure is important not because it mimics how the real world operates, but because it provides the sort of clarity the real world lacks. A well-designed play space not only provides us with opportunities for anticipatory play but also brings anticipatory play to a close at the proper moment.

Playing with Others

When we play a game against other human beings, our horizons are determined not only by the rules of the game and our interpretations of those rules but also by the moment-to-moment actions of our opponents. And, of course, the relationship is reciprocal. My actions become constraints for you, just as your actions become constraints for me.

Successful multi-player games are structured so as to channel actions performed out of self-interest into interesting choices for the other players. When I hit a pop fly in baseball, the arc of the ball through the air creates a cascade of entertaining opportunities for action by the members of the opposing team. I didn't hit the ball to make things fun for my opponents, but the rules of baseball are structured so that my playful actions naturally lead to interesting horizons for others.

This feature of multi-player games is so fundamental that it's almost invisible. Taking a trick in bridge, performing a head shot in a first-person shooter, driving downfield in soccer—virtually every action we take in a well-designed multi-player game serves a dual purpose. It is fun in and of itself for the player performing it, but it also triggers interesting evolutions of the state for the other players. This creates an interesting challenge for the designer. In a single-player game, every action can be judged by a single criterion: Is it interesting to do? But in a multi-player game, we also must take into account whether the action is interesting to have done to you. Sitting in a turret and mowing down wave after wave of enemies can be really fun in a single-player game. But repeatedly charging an impregnable base in a multi-player game isn't. It isn't enough for a multi-player game to create interesting opportunities for action for an individual. The results of those actions must also translate into meaningful constraints for the other players of the game.

Furthermore, if you are shaping my experience, my experience will differ from yours, and vice versa. Each of us will chart his or her own unique trajectory through the game's phase space. If the game is competitive, your experience of winning will necessarily be balanced by my experience of losing. As your horizons consistently provide opportunities for satisfaction, my horizons will lead only to repeated frustration. No matter how fairly a competitive multi-player game is designed, there is an inherent asymmetry to multi-player play: In order for one player to succeed, another player must fail. This asymmetry exists even in cooperative play. Even if the entire team is working toward a common goal, the actions of each individual player will preclude similar opportunities for future action by his teammates. Because I intercepted the pass and took the shot on goal, my teammate next to me didn't. Because I was first through the doorway and was attacked by the monsters, my teammate was able to sneak in and grab the treasure. My moment-to-moment choices within a multi-player game will alter its evolving state so that the other participants will not have the same choices that I had.

When we understand a game, it is because we have internalized enough of its constraints to engage in anticipatory play. When some constraints are provided by other human players, all sorts of interesting possibilities appear. Human beings are far more complicated than any videogame, and so anticipating their future actions is a far greater challenge than anticipating the future actions of an AI. As a result, it is common for players to spend much longer playing the multi-player version of a game than they spend playing the single-player version. The complexity and variety of the external constraints generated by other human beings offers a far wider range of potential horizons, and it takes much longer (sometimes longer than a single human lifetime) for such a game to be played out.

When you first encounter a new opponent, you respond only to his actions. His moves change the state of the game and reconfigure the external constraints that define your current horizon of action. But as you play against him longer and longer, you do what people do with all external constraints: construct a corresponding set of internal constraints that you can use to anticipate future evolutions of the state before they occur. The longer you play against an opponent, the more you come to understand him, and the better you can predict his future behavior in the game.

Furthermore, while you are furiously working to assemble a set of internal constraints that will allow you to predict your opponent's actions, he is doing the same with regard to you. That means that if you really want to understand your opponent, you must self-referentially include his understanding of you in whatever internal framework you construct to model his behavior. The result is a regressing chain of abstraction: I have internal constraints to simulate your internal constraints to simulate my internal constraints to simulate your internal constraints … and on and on.

The simplest example of this sort of self-referential anticipatory play is the feint—a tactic that crops up in a variety of multi-player games, including fencing, basketball, and first-person shooters. A feint is a gameplay action whose entire purpose is to trigger the construction of a particular set of constraints in the mind of an opponent. You move the blade of your foil in a particular downward arc that suggests that you are attempting to slip under my guard. I counter with the standard parry for that attack, but your blade has abruptly changed direction and is now circling *over* my guard instead. I quickly return my foil to its original position to counter, only to discover that your second move also was a feint; you really did intend to attack low all along. Now I am too confused to respond, and you slip under my defenses and score an easy touch. In an actual fencing bout, this entire chain of action and reaction would take place in a fraction of a second. In order to pull it off, you not only have to understand how I will respond to a particular threat; you also have to understand how I understand *you*. In fact, in the seconds leading up the attack, you may even have been purposely performing a sequence of actions intended to make me *misunderstand* you. For example, to encourage me to expect something different, you may have launched a couple of low attacks that were intended to fail. I'm watching for the first feint, and you know I'm watching for it, and you use that knowledge to defeat me. Effective team play requires the same sort of intuitive understanding. Every move performed by a quarterback depends on the other members of his squad executing a precise set of actions in a particular order. His moment-to-moment horizons of action are shaped not just by what the other members of his team do, but also by what he *expects* them to do in the future. Their actions place strong constraints on him, but stronger still are the internal constraints he has constructed to model their behavior. He fades back and throws the ball, confident in his knowledge that the receiver in the distance will not suddenly stop running and sit down for a rest in the grass.

The internal constraints we use to model other players loom large in our experience of playing a multi-player game. In day-to-day life, it is often difficult to predict what other people will do. Their motivations may be obscure or unknown, and our interactions are often fleeting and contradictory. But within the framework of play, the rules impose a structure that puts tight limits on our potential interpretations of the actions we witness. If, while playing in a football game, we see a player running across the field while carrying the ball, we can be reasonably certain that he is attempting to score a touchdown. He isn't fleeing from the police, or trying to catch a bus, or jogging for exercise, or any of the many other reasons why someone might be running across a field in real life. The result is a peculiar transformation of our relationship with the other players in the game, particularly members of our own team. Their actions are comprehensible and their motivations are clear in a way that is rare in day-to-day life. As we grow accustomed to playing with them, we become better and better at anticipating how they will respond in any particular situation. Often we find ourselves imagining a particular sequence of events playing out, and then, almost as if by magic, what we imagined actually happens. The receiver cuts across the field just in time to catch our pass, the priest heals us just at the moment when our health is about to give out, the sniper picks off the grunt as he charges our base.

In the heat of the moment, our anticipation of the actions of our teammates can easily be misinterpreted as agency. It is as though, by simply thinking about someone doing something, we are able to cause them to do it. We become, for a time, more than a mere individual: we expand to encompass a team. We collectively act with a unity of vision and purpose that transcends our normal, solitary existence.

The transcendence of team play is not telepathy. There is no interconnected "team mind," only a collection of individuals each imagining the thought processes of the others. But that doesn't mean that it isn't a powerful thing to experience. When we play with others we aren't alone, and not merely because of the social interactions that naturally occur during most games. The act of play itself creates a sense of oneness with the other players in the game.

There is also a downside to playing with others: the possibility of cheating. When you play by yourself, the universe of the game is yours and yours alone. Your moves are bounded by a single set of internal constraints that you have constructed inside your head. Every move you make necessarily

falls within the range of acceptable actions defined by those internal constraints—even moves that may violate the official external rules of the game.

Consider solitaire as an example. Many versions of solitaire feature face-
down cards that the player isn't supposed to peek at. However, since the
player himself is responsible for enforcing this constraint on his actions, he
may choose to ignore it. The official rule may be "Don't peek at face-down
cards," but the game the player is actually playing may have the rule "Peek
at face-down cards if you want to" or even "Peek at face-down cards only
if you're really stuck." The player may refer to this activity as cheating, but
it's a different sort of transgression than the type of cheating that occurs in
multi-player games. The rules exist to provide an entertaining experience
for the player, and if your solo experience is enhanced by rewriting the rules
you play by, then those rewritten rules become the true active constraints
of the game.

But in a multi-player game the ramifications of cheating are quite different. Each player is operating under his own set of internal constraints,
so actions that are legal under one set of constraints may be illegal under
another. When I'm playing solitaire, I can unilaterally decide to amend the
rules to allow peeking. But when I'm playing poker, I can't make the same
sort of unilateral choice; every action I take must be legal not only to me
but also to the other players in the game.

This prohibition against amending the rules even extends to single
player games if they are being played within the context of a broader community. I can play solitaire any way I want if it's solely for my own enjoyment. But if I want to compare my score with others, or brag about my skill,
or debate strategies, I must follow the same rules as other players.[7]

As a result, most multi-player games have fixed sets of official rules to
which all players consent in advance. The price of admission for play is

7. For a deeper discussion of the ethics of single-player cheating within a community of players, see Sicart, *The Ethics of Computer Games*, 119–120. Sicart goes further
to argue that cheating in a single player game is a moral transgression even in the
absence of other players: "These phenomena are not limited to playing with other
players. Playing a single-player game is also an act of moral relevance. A player introducing cheat codes, for instance, affects the game balance and the carefully crafted
game experience, thus shattering the game experience as it was intended and opti-
mized." Sicart, *The Ethics of Computer Games*, 91. Equating moral play with obeying
designer intent is problematic for multiple reasons: Often we don't have any way of
knowing what the designer's intent was. Games often admit interesting ways to play
that the designer didn't foresee. Some designs may not mesh well with the abilities
of some players. And the ability of designers to deliver optimum experiences often
falls short of ideal.

agreeing to submit to the authority of the communal rule set. These official rules—for example, the text in the official rulebook of baseball, or the binary code written on the disk of a PlayStation game—are external to all players. Sometimes their authority will be upheld by the players themselves; sometimes they will be enforced by a human referee or by the game software. But no matter how they are enforced, play can't happen unless the players are all in agreement as to which actions are permitted and which actions aren't.

What happens when one player performs an action that violates another player's internal constraints? Successful play depends on our ability to construct internal constraints that allow us to anticipate what may happen next. But when another player performs an action that we consider illegal, we can no longer be sure of what the future holds. Once one rule is broken, *all* the rules become suspect. As a result, we lose the capacity to construct meaningful horizons and play collapses. Huizinga puts it this way:

All play has its rules. They determine what "holds" in the temporary world circumscribed by play. The rules of a game are absolutely binding and allow no doubt. Paul Valéry once in passing gave expression to a very cogent thought when he said: "No skepticism is possible when the rules of a game are concerned, for the principle underlying them is an unshakable truth … ." Indeed, as soon as the rules are transgressed the whole play-world collapses. The game is over. The umpire's whistle breaks the spell and sets "real" life going again.[8]

In his discussion of cheating, Huizinga makes a distinction between two types of transgressors: the cheat and the spoilsport. The cheat acknowledges the authority of the communal rule set, even while he violates it. But the spoilsport refuses to submit to the authority of the rules at all. Of the two, the spoilsport's crime is greater. It is still possible to play with a cheat; we can shame him into following the rules, or even reconfigure our own internal constraints to redefine his illegal behavior as legal.[9] But with

8. Huizinga, *Homo Ludens*, 11.
9. My grandparents were avid *Scrabble* players. Several times a week they would set up the board and play against each other. As my grandfather aged, his mental capacities began to fail, and he began to cheat. Instead of drawing his tiles randomly from the box, he would peek to make sure he got the letters he wanted. My grandfather wasn't particularly subtle about it, and my grandmother quickly caught on to what he was doing. But she didn't stop him. Her mind was still sharp, and without my grandfather's little cheat she could have beaten him easily. But with him picking the letters he wanted and her picking randomly, they could still have a challenging game. She reconfigured her internal constraints to make his cheating legal. And as a result, the two of them were able to keep playing together for several years longer than if she had insisted on faithfully following the official rules.

a spoilsport, no such accommodation is possible. The spoilsport denies the validity of the game itself, and that makes it impossible for play to even begin. Huizinga writes:

It is curious to note how much more lenient society is to the cheat than the spoil-sport. This is because the spoil-sport shatters the play-world itself. By withdrawing from the game he reveals the relativity and fragility of the play-world in which he temporarily shut himself in with others. He robs play of its *illusion*—a pregnant word which means literally "in play" (from *inlusio*, *illudere*, or *inludere*). Therefore he must be cast out, for he threatens the existence of the play-community.[10]

Cheating isn't a transgression against the game itself or the intent of the designer. It is a transgression against the other players. It's an act that has meaning only within a social context. When I play a game all by myself, I'm free to construct whatever internal constraints I want in my quest for an interesting play experience. But when I play with others, my internal constraints must be functionally equivalent to theirs.

10. Huizinga, *Homo Ludens*, 11.

6 Mastery

When we looked at frustration and satisfaction in chapter 4, we focused mostly on what happens when a player is incapable of performing an action. But frustration can also arise from lack of understanding. If we believe that a troll is vulnerable to sword hits, but it turns out it can only be killed by fireballs, it doesn't matter if we execute every joystick twitch and button press impeccably. We will still die, and we will still feel frustrated.

It is useful to make a distinction between these two different types of frustration:

Skill-based Our understanding of the game's constraints is sufficiently accurate for us to correctly anticipate future outcomes. However, we aren't able to perform the appropriate actions.

Knowledge-based We have the necessary skills, but our understanding of the game's constraints is incorrect or incomplete.

The two different types of frustration are often intertwined. For example, we may have a solid understanding of a game's rules but fail to make accurate predictions under time pressure. Or our lack of skill at imagining long causal chains may interfere with our anticipation of future events.

Still, the distinction between these two types of frustration is useful. For one thing, they happen at different times. Skill-based frustration occurs during immediate play, whereas knowledge-based frustration occurs during anticipatory play. And we experience each type of frustration differently. Our response to a moment of skill-based frustration is "I can't do this!" Our response to a moment of knowledge-based frustration is "I don't know what to do!"

One important difference between the two types of frustration is how much time it takes to resolve them. Overcoming skill-based frustration involves practice and training. If I consistently miss an important jump in a platforming game, I have to practice over and over until the correct timing is ingrained in my muscle memory. If I am consistently outrun by my opponents while playing soccer, my only recourse is train harder so as to increase my speed and endurance. Resolving skill-based frustration takes effort over time. But knowledge-based frustration can be resolved almost instantaneously. The mismatch between recent events and the expectations created by our internal constraints can trigger an abrupt snap to a new set of internal constraints that resolve the inconsistency—often with an accompanying "aha" moment. Out of the blue, we suddenly discover the winning move, the gap in our opponent's armor, or the solution to the puzzle. No training or practice is involved. It's simply a matter of reconfiguring the internal constraints that we are using to make predictions about the future behavior of the game.

The new constraints that resolve a moment of knowledge-based frustration can even come from an outside source. Instead of learning how to play a game through trial and error, I can watch a walkthrough on the Internet, or read a strategy guide. It is instructive to note what walkthroughs and strategy guides can do for a player and what they can't. They can teach us the sequence of button presses that trigger a powerful combo, and under what circumstances that combo will be most effective, but in order to successfully execute the move in game, we have to practice it. Strategy guides and walkthroughs can resolve our knowledge-based frustration over about *what to do*, but actually *learning to do it* still requires time-consuming training to improve our play skills.

The difference between these two types of frustration has important ramifications for game design. Over the course of a game, our skills tend to grow gradually. As we practice familiar moves over and over, we slowly become more proficient with them. The timing of our jumps improves, our shots become more accurate, our dodges get more fluid. As a result, most games are designed with the expectation that the skill-based challenges will get *gradually* more difficult as the game progresses to match the slow improvement in our ability to execute the appropriate moves. Knowledge-based challenges, on the other hand, can fluctuate between easy and difficult throughout the game. They are not nearly so dependent on the gradual accumulation of expertise.

An example of this is the design of the classic boss battle. In a boss battle, we are expected to use skills that we have practiced over the preceding hour or two of play, but we are asked to use them in unfamiliar ways. We typically have (or are on the verge of having) all the tools we need to accomplish the task, but the task itself is unfamiliar. Discovering what to do is part of the challenge. The boss may attack using strange patterns of movement, or present unexpected windows of vulnerability that must be exploited. Our ability to anticipate the outcomes of our actions collapses, and we must observe and interact with the altered system to gradually build up a new, more useful set of internal constraints.

Good boss battles are built around moments of both skill-based and knowledge-based frustration.[1] The actions we are asked to perform usually lie right at the edge of the level of mastery we are expected to have achieved by this point in the game. And the boss supplies a fresh set of external constraints that beg to be internalized. We are asked to stretch ourselves both by slightly increasing our skills and by making huge leaps in our understanding.

My wife and I sometimes play videogames together, and we have discovered that it's particularly fun, even in a single-player game, to collaborate on boss battles. I manipulate the controls to direct the action while my wife watches the patterns of the boss and calls out moves and strategies. Basically, I assume responsibility for the skill-based frustration and she assumes responsibility for the knowledge-based frustration. And since knowledge-based frustration is easily resolved through a reconfiguration of internal constraints, the necessary information is easily shouted across the living room—for example, "Hit him on the tail! That's his weak spot!" More significant, even though only one of us is holding the controls, both of us are *playing*. The uncertain nature of the unfamiliar constraints creates numerous opportunities for wide-ranging and open-ended anticipatory play. Figuring out the boss's weaknesses and developing a plan of attack is fun in and of itself, even if you aren't the person who actually executes the necessary moves to carry the plan out.[2] Sadly, this sense of collaborative play typically evaporates after the boss battle is over. The average single-player videogame doesn't provide enough anticipatory challenges in the non-boss-battle sections to sustain the interest of a "player" who isn't actively controlling a character.

1. "Often, the intensity [of a game] is increased at the end of a level by a 'boss monster' who can only be defeated through a mix of puzzle solving ('Oh! I have to jump on his tail, and that makes him drop his shield for a second!') and dexterity ('I only have a second to shoot an arrow into that narrow gap!')." Schell, *The Art of Game Design*, 184.
2. "A number of players I have worked with love the idea of the *Legend of Zelda* series but get frustrated as their attempts lead to a few minutes of joystick mashing and then death. So they play together. Furthermore, adopting a 'co-pilot' role allows one to notice aspects of the game that are missed in the role of primary player." Newman, "The Myth of the Ergodic Videogame."

Cruxes

Predicting future outcomes is a large part of gameplay. But sometimes our predictions are wrong. Our internal model of the system is deficient, our estimation of our abilities is incorrect, or we are thwarted by sheer randomness. I call such a moment a *crux*.[3] A crux is a rupture between the internal and external parts of gameplay. It's an indication that our predictive capacities are deficient— that our understanding of the system has diverged from its reality.

A crux is a moment of knowledge-based frustration, but it is also a moment of opportunity. A rupture between internal representation and external reality, when it occurs, is an invitation to learn. Learning about a system as you play—internalizing its constraints on the fly—requires the repeated construction and resolution of cruxes. Frustration, rather than something to be avoided, becomes an important component of the play experience.

When a crux is resolved, we feel a rush a pleasure. The incongruity in our frame has been resolved, our predictive capabilities have been restored, and everything is right with the world. Frustration isn't fun, in and of itself, but frustration creates the possibility of resolution—the thrill we feel when the unknown becomes known, when the broken pieces are reintegrated into the seamless whole. As Dorothy and Jerome Singer write in *The House of Make-Believe*:

The "fun" of children's play … may be a consequence of the gradual reduction of a high level of ambiguity or extreme novelty in a stimulus complex to a manageable cognitive structure the child can manipulate and over which, in contrast with the "real" adult world, he or she can experience some power.[4]

As we trace our trajectory through a play space, our experience tends to oscillate between satisfaction and frustration. Intervals of satisfactory outcomes are periodically punctuated by cruxes that spur us toward a deeper understanding of the system of constraints.

The ratio of satisfaction to frustration depends on the type of the game and on the intended audience. Games intended for dedicated gamers tend

---

3. 'Crux' is a term I have borrowed from paleography. In that field, a crux is a point in a historical text that resists translation or interpretation because of a misprint, or a loss of cultural context. The large interpretive challenges posed by historical texts seemed to be a useful metaphor for the smaller interpretive challenges posed by other experiences.

4. Singer and Singer, *The House of Make-Believe*, 203.

to have a greater frequency of cruxes, forcing a player to repeatedly respond to a variety of challenges that lie at the edge of his abilities in order to progress. Casual games targeted at the mass market tend to devote themselves to delivering long stretches of relatively crux-free gameplay. The goal is not to give a player a set of challenges to overcome, but rather to present a player with a series of interesting choices within a familiar and stable configuration of constraints.

Flow

Mihaly Csikszentmihalyi is a Hungarian psychologist whose work over the last four decades has focused on the origins of happiness. How do human beings achieve contentment? What sorts of physical and mental activities result in feelings of satisfaction and enjoyment? And, conversely, what are the sources of dissatisfaction and frustration?

Csikszentmihalyi's central idea is the concept of *flow*. Flow is the condition of "optimal experience." It's the state of mind that we achieve when we completely lose ourselves in an activity. When we experience flow we not only lose our awareness of the outside world and the passage of time, we also lose our awareness of ourselves as distinct individuals who exist separately from the world around us. Csikszentmihalyi writes:

It is what the sailor holding a tight course feels when the wind whips through her hair, when the boat lunges through the waves like a colt—sails, hull, wind, and sea humming a harmony that vibrates in the sailor's veins. It is what a painter feels when the colors on a canvas begin to set up a magnet tension with each other, and a new *thing*, a living form, takes shape in front of the astonished creator. Or it is the feeling a father has when his child for the first time responds to his smile. Such events do not occur only when the external conditions are favorable, however: people who have survived concentration camps or who have lived through near-fatal physical dangers often recall that in the midst of their ordeal they experienced extraordinarily rich epiphanies in response to simple events as hearing the song of a bird in the forest, completing a hard task, or sharing a crust of bread with a friend.[5]

Most of us who are gamers can probably remember experiencing flow. It's that magical moment when our actions in the game become transparently effortless. We aren't just responding mindlessly or reflexively. Rather, we are concentrating so intently that the game expands to become, for a limited time, our entire universe of being. We are faced with challenges, but the challenges are so closely matched to our skills and knowledge that they

5. Csikszentmihalyi, *Flow*, 3.

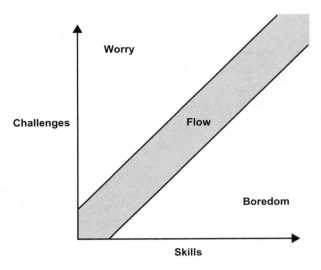

Figure 6.1
The flow channel.

seem to melt away before us. The result is a sense of total dominance. The game is our universe and we are its master.

Csikszentmihalyi identifies flow as occurring in moments when "people perceive opportunities for action as evenly matching to their capabilities."[6] In his 1975 book *Beyond Boredom and Anxiety* he provides a graphic illustration of the flow state. When a person believes that the challenges he faces are too great for his skills, he will experience worry and anxiety. On the other hand, if the challenges that he faces are too easy, he will experience boredom (figure 6.1). Flow arises when skills and challenges are closely matched. And for flow to be sustainable, skills and challenges must increase in parallel.

Csikszentmihalyi has identified eight major components of flow[7]:

Goals are achievable.
Concentration is possible.
Goals are unambiguous.
Feedback is immediate.
"Normal" life is temporarily forgotten.
Outcomes are controllable.

6. Csikszentmihalyi, *Beyond Boredom and Anxiety*, 50.
7. Csikszentmihalyi, *Flow*, 49.

Self-awareness is suspended.

Time sense is disrupted.

In a variety of different studies, people who have experienced flow have described the experience as consisting of at least one, and often all, of these components.

The list above contains a mix of causes and effects. Some of the entries are criteria that must be met for flow to occur; others describe quality of the experience after it is actually achieved. For present purposes, we will concentrate on the conditions for flow and examine how they relate to the framework for play that we have constructed.

Flow occurs only when you are *doing* something. It's a by-product of a particular type of activity, not a general emotional state such as happiness or sadness. It emerges as part of a process, and then melts away when that process comes to an end.

Activities that are likely to produce flow have the following four characteristics:

Distractions are minimized.

Goals are unambiguous and achievable.

Actions determine outcomes.

Outcomes have an immediate causal link to actions.

There is a lot of overlap between these properties and the heuristics that we developed in chapter 4 to describe successful play spaces. There is nothing particularly surprising in this. Csikszentmihalyi himself devotes an entire chapter of *Beyond Boredom and Anxiety* to analyzing how chess players experience flow, and numerous game scholars have cited his research.

Because there is such a strong overlap between play and flow, it is very tempting to equate the two. But play can be fun and satisfying even if it doesn't rise to the level of Csikszentmihalyi's transformative "optimal experience." Flow requires a precise balance between our skills and the challenges we are facing. According to Csikszentmihalyi,

One might visualize it as a strip of movie film. Each synchronic slice of the action ... is like a frame of the film. When the action is too easy or too difficult, the film stutters and the actor is very aware of the black borders of each frame, the negotiation of the ego construct. But when the difficulty is just right, action follows action in a fluid series, and the actor has no need to adopt an outside perspective from which to consciously intervene. Awareness of the individual frames disappears in the unbroken flow of the whole.[8]

8. Csikszentmihalyi, *Beyond Boredom and Anxiety*, 85–86.

Flow is certainly a desirable element of good play, but it isn't an essential one. When flow occurs, we relish it as a special, magical experience; however, we can have satisfactory play experiences without flow. We can enjoy a game even if there is a significant mismatch between our skills and the challenges we face.

Playing Outside the Flow Channel

In his 2004 book *A Theory of Fun for Game Design*, Raph Koster makes the case that games are fundamentally systems for learning. Rule-based play provides a safe environment for practicing and mastering a variety of skills that then can be applied outside the game in various real-world situations. Games are fun because they teach us things, and clarifying what lessons the game is intended to teach should be an integral part of the design process.[9]

I disagree with Koster's definition of fun. There is certainly a strong element of learning in many games, but there are just as many games in which the opportunities to gain new knowledge are minimal. Learning is an element of fun, not its totality.

The most obvious example of simple, mindless fun is probably familiar to anyone who owns a computer running Windows. *FreeCell* is a solitaire program that has been supplied as part of the Windows operating system since 1995. I probably have played several thousand games of *FreeCell*. It's a classic time waster, a little diversion that is ideal for killing a few extra minutes between bigger tasks. It's difficult enough to present a challenge, but easy enough that you don't really have to concentrate.

I suppose there was a time, long ago, when playing *FreeCell* taught me something new, but that time has long since passed. Now, when I play it, it's because I enjoy the familiarity of it. The arrangement of the cards is always different, but the strategies I use to help me solve the puzzles are always the same. I know which techniques work and which ones don't, and it's fun to simply click on the cards and cruise serenely through the horizons of action as they unfold.

It isn't hard to find other play experiences that resemble *FreeCell*—a little bit of learning right at the beginning, followed by a long stretch of mostly mindless fun. If you are playing a game of *Monopoly* with your children, or a game of Frisbee golf with your buddies, or a game of *Super Smash Bros.* with your sister, or a game of *Candy Crush Saga* on your phone, you probably

---

9. "Fun, as I define it, is the feedback the brain gives us when we are absorbing patterns for learning purposes." Koster, *A Theory of Fun*, 96.

aren't increasing your mastery; you're probably just enjoying the casual challenge of responding to each new horizon of action. Occasionally something unexpected may happen, and you may learn some new technique, strategy, or trick. But most of the time, while you are playing, you will be having fun without learning anything new at all. Cruxes are few and far between.

Koster has noticed this flaw in his thesis, and his response, amazingly, is to state that if you're having fun without learning anything you should stop:

[T]he point at which a player chooses to repeatedly play a game they have already mastered completely, just because they like to feel powerful, is the point at which the game is betraying its own purpose. Games need to encourage you to *move on*. They are not there to fulfill power fantasies.[10]

This is an unsatisfactory argument in a book that sets out to explain the nature of fun. When confronted with evidence that the way many people play contradicts his central thesis, Koster's response is to reply, in essence, that if people are having fun playing that way, they shouldn't be. They're doing it wrong.

Maybe it's a waste of time for people to play games that don't teach them anything new. But that doesn't mean that they aren't having fun while they are doing it. It's akin to arguing that because Big Macs are junk food they don't really taste good, and that people who enjoy the taste of Big Macs are deluding themselves. But Big Macs *do* taste good, and *FreeCell is* fun to play, even if it's better to enjoy both in moderation. And any theory that attempts to explain the nature of fun should take this fact into account.

Resolving cruxes is certainly *part* of the fun of playing a game. It is deeply satisfying to come up with a new strategy or a new understanding. Applying a fresh set of interpretive constraints to a familiar game can open up enticing new horizons of intent. But it's also fun to operate within a fixed and familiar framework. As long as the game itself continually presents us with new and unfamiliar configurations of the state, we still have fresh horizons to explore. And the pleasure of exerting mastery can be just as compelling as the pleasure of attaining it.[11]

The pleasure of exerting mastery creates another problem for equating flow with play. David Myers has observed that it is also quite possible to

10. Koster, *A Theory of Fun*, 134.
11. Jesse Schell defines fun as "pleasure with surprises" (*The Art of Game Design*, 26). This formulation very succinctly captures the tension between satisfaction and frustration that I have been describing.

have fun by completing challenges that are nowhere near the limits of our skills:

> This latter definition of flow, as a proper ratio of challenge to skill, is close to what I found elicits a positive computer gaming experience. However, I have not found that boredom "always happens" when challenges surpass skills [sic]. In a significant amount of computer game play, players enjoy returning to previously mastered sequences of play and replaying these in a meditative, trance-like state quite different from boredom, a state which in fact combats boredom in many instances. Higher levels of complexity, that is, that is, increasingly greater challenges, may be required to remain in flow, as Csikszentmihalyi defines it, but these are not necessarily required to remain in computer game play.[12]

Flow occurs when there is a careful balance between skills and challenges. But there are broad bands of playful activity on both sides of the narrow flow channel. On the high end we find the learning-dominated play that Koster has identified in *A Theory of Fun*: Challenges are difficult, the potential for frustration is high, cruxes occur often, and the player is continually updating his internal constraints to adapt to new situations. On the low end, we find the doing-dominated experience identified by Myers: Challenges are easy, the potential for satisfaction is high, cruxes are rare, and the player's internal constraints remain mostly stable (figure 6.2).

All of the experiences across this continuum are acceptable forms of play. Sometimes all we want out of a game is a few minutes of mindless button-mashing. We don't want to be challenged to reconfigure our internal constraints; we just want to perform a familiar action in a familiar context that promises a strong possibility of a desirable outcome. And the reverse is also true. Sometimes the familiar and comfortable are boring. We want to be stretched and frustrated. We want to be prodded to learn new things about the game and about ourselves.

Nicole Lazzaro has explored the idea of play outside the flow channel with her model of the four types of fun. Lazzaro categorizes play experiences by the sorts of emotions they evoke in players[13]:

Hard fun Triumph / Frustration / Boredom
Easy fun Curiosity / Surprise / Wonder
Serious fun Excitement / Relaxation
People fun Envy / Love / Gratitude / Generosity

12. Myers, "Time, Symbol Transformations, and Computer Games," 441–457. The phrase "challenges surpass skills" is almost certainly a typographical error. From the sense of the rest of the passage, it is clear that Myers intends to say that boredom isn't automatic when *skills surpass challenges* and not the other way around.
13. See Lazzaro, "Understand Emotions," in *Beyond Game Design*, ed. Bateman.

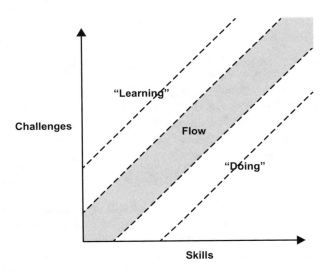

Figure 6.2
Play outside the flow channel.

Hard fun explicitly involves wandering back and forth across the flow channel. The other types of fun have a more complicated relationship with the balance between skills and challenges. Easy fun is the fun of exploration and invention, which means (paradoxically, in view of its name) that it exists almost exclusively within the high-crux band of learning-dominated play. However, the frustration that frequent cruxes can cause is mitigated by a play space in which winning is de-emphasized. Easy fun is the fun of just fooling around, of figuring out a new play space (or a new way to play in an old play space). It's easy not because we aren't playing hard, but because we aren't pushing ourselves to achieve a particular victory condition. Instead, we are seeking out new unexplored vistas within the game.

Serious fun, in contrast, tends to be the product of doing-dominated play. It's the fun we experience when we "zone out" while relaxing with a familiar favorite. It's also the fun we have when we feel that the act of playing is improving us in some way—it's training our minds, making us physically stronger, making us better at something that is worth being better at. Serious fun has few cruxes. If we're just playing to relax, we don't want to be frustrated or seriously challenged. And if we're playing to sharpen our skills, we want our play to be focused and repetitive. *Practicing* is serious fun. When we practice, we don't push ourselves to the limits of our abilities. Instead, we perform familiar moves over and over again, so that when we do push ourselves later we are able to reach farther.

Lazzaro's "people fun" is the type of fun most removed from the flow model. In people fun, the game exists to create a framework for social interaction. When we play a casual parlor game, such as *Monopoly*, the social interactions we have with the other players around the table form a large part of the experience. Losing ourselves in the mechanics of the game works against this sort of fun—if we are completely absorbed in navigating the immediate challenges before us, the social aspect of the experience can recede into near invisibility. As a result, games that focus on social fun tend to have simple rules, large amounts of randomness (to discourage extended anticipatory play), and extended downtime between decision points.

With many games, our play experience drifts back and forth across the flow channel. When we begin to play, the challenges we face are often beyond our capabilities. Our experience is dominated by failures and cruxes as we build up a reliable internal model of how the game functions. As the game becomes more familiar to us, we move out of learning-dominated play and into the flow channel. At this point Csikszentmihalyi's "optimal experience" opens up for us. We are still learning new things, but our increasing control over the challenges we face gives us a sense of moving effortlessly past obstacles as they appear before us.

Eventually, if we keep playing at the same level, we move out of the flow channel and into doing-dominated play. Now our control over the game has increased to the point where the challenges exert only minimal pressure on us. Instead, the pleasure of playing comes mostly from the continual reward of correctly anticipating the game's evolving state. This phase of play can be called *mastery*. The game has very little left to teach us, but the pleasures of "going through the motions" remain (figure 6.3).

Eventually, mastery segues into staleness. The horizons that we encounter are so familiar and "played out" that even the satisfaction of perpetual victory isn't enough to stave off boredom. At that point the only options open to us are either to quit playing or to move on to a higher level of challenge. This may entail progressing to the next level, or finding more skilled opponents to play against, or even introducing new internal constraints of our own ("Hmmm; can I clear level 2 in less than 3 minutes?"). Increasing the challenge moves us back into the flow band, or even all the way into the learning band, and the process begins anew (figure 6.4).

Regardless of what other rewards the game may offer, the achievement of mastery is a powerful reward in and of itself. In an effort to keep players from getting bored, some videogames are designed as uninterrupted series

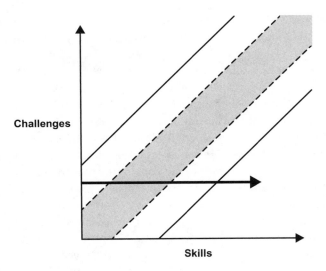

Figure 6.3
The evolution of player engagement.

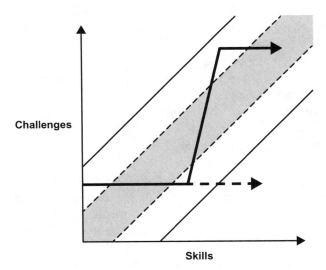

Figure 6.4
Oscillating across the flow channel.

of challenges. As sooner as a player has mastered one skill, he is thrust into a fresh situation that challenges him in new and different ways. This approach to game design can certainly satisfy our desire to learn, and may even allow us to achieve flow, but it will almost certainly deny us the feeling of deep confidence and control that comes from the successful exercise of familiar mechanics. Often a better approach is to allow the player to oscillate back and forth between frustration and satisfaction. Each major crux is followed by an interval of relative stability that allows the player to put his newly acquired skills to use. The achievement of mastery provides a strong piece of feedback that the new internal constraints that the player has constructed are working effectively and that the recent crux has been successfully resolved.

Before the invention of videogames, most games revolved around human-versus-human competition. There were some exceptions, of course (card-based solitaire games, pinball machines). But generally, if you wanted to play a game before the 1970s, your first step would be to round up one or more other people who wanted to play with you. This is significant because human-versus-human gameplay has significant limitations in the sort of experiences it can deliver. Specifically, it isn't very good at providing a sustained sense of mastery. When you are playing against a human opponent, mastery is a zero-sum game—the more that one player experiences mastery, the less that the other player does. As one side's satisfaction increases, the opposing side's satisfaction decreases in proportion. And if one side's experience is composed almost exclusively of frustration, their interest in continuing to play will dwindle away until they eventually quit.

Multi-player games incorporate a number of internal and external mechanisms to prevent matches from becoming too uneven. Casual board games include a high degree of randomness, lessening the chance that any one player will dominate.[14] In games in which skill is significant, ranking systems make it easier to match up players with other players who have similar skills. Handicapping systems allow players of different ability levels to play against each other fairly. Even the notion of "fairness" itself is a part of this equalizing framework. A fair game isn't necessarily one in which both sides are subject to exactly the same constraints; it's one in which each

---

14. "*Alea* does not have the function of causing the more successful to win money, but tends rather to abolish natural or acquired individual differences, so that all can be placed on an absolutely equal footing to await the blind verdict of chance." Caillois, *Man, Play and Games*, 18.

side has a decent shot at victory. A baseball game that pitted the New York Yankees against a Little League team might be equitable, but it wouldn't be fair.

In human-versus-human games, mastery is expected to occur intermittently, not continually. Certainly there will sometimes be situations in which one team is completely overmatched by their opponents, or a player will be so "on" that he completely obliterates his competition. But if the imbalance persists, the players will try to fix the inequality by adding new constraints to make the competition "fair" again, or by simply ending the game.

All of this changes when the other player is a computer. When we play a single-player videogame, we don't have to worry that our opponent will become frustrated and quit. Even after being stomped into the dust a hundred times, the computer is still ready for another match. Good sportsmanship ceases to be an issue when your opposition is incapable of emotion, thought, or awareness. As a result, it is possible for videogames to deliver an experience of sustained mastery. We can create situations in which the player moves relatively effortlessly through minimal challenges and still has a good time. To those of us who grew up playing board games and sports, this may seem wrong or broken. We have so internalized the idea that challenge is essential to play that we find it difficult to shift frames and think about designing for doing instead of for learning. Sometimes it is hard to think of a game as an experience to have and not an obstacle to be overcome.

The Experience of Play

The game designer Marc LeBlanc has created a taxonomy of game pleasures, a collection of the different ways that a game can provide enjoyment to the player[15]:

Sensation The fleeting sensory pleasures that a game provides. This could be the heft of a beautifully carved chess piece in your hand, or the satisfying "thunk" that your battleaxe makes when it connects with the head of an orc.

Fantasy The element of make-believe. Who does the game allow me to pretend to be? A lot of the fun of *Guitar Hero* comes not from its "Simon says" gameplay but from the way it lets me pretend to be a rock star.

15. Hunicke, LeBlanc, and Zubek, "MDA: A Formal Approach to Game Design and Game Research."

Narrative The sense of drama and rising expectation. Regardless of whether or not a game explicitly tells a particular story, it will usually have an implicit arc of progress and accomplishment.

Challenge The thrill of overcoming obstacles. As we achieve goals within a game we feel a strong sense of accomplishment. The more challenging the game, the stronger the sense of satisfaction when we finally beat it.

Fellowship The pleasure of playing with others. This encompasses both the rewards of teamwork, the dark pleasures of dominating an opponent, and the various types of camaraderie that accompany any shared human activity.

Discovery The enjoyment of learning new things about the game, the real world, our opponents, or ourselves.

Expression The construction of identity. How we play is an expression of who we are, and the choices we make in a game can be a means of defining ourselves as individuals.

Submission The pleasure of submitting to authority. Whatever the challenges we overcome during a game, the initial act of deciding to play is an act of surrender.

LeBlanc acknowledges that this list isn't exhaustive, and Jesse Schell has pointed out other pleasures that could be added to it: schadenfreude, generosity, humor, pride.[16]

The items in LeBlanc's list are undeniably parts of the experience of play. It is true that games are abstract systems of rules, but our encounters with them are inevitably embedded within a social and personal context. If I sit down on my couch to play *Flower* or *God of War* or *Fat Princess*, I'm not merely a theoretical abstraction of a player; I'm an actual human being with my own needs, desires, and agendas. My engagement with the game isn't solely a matter of navigating constraints—the manner of my playing sets up opportunities for these other sorts of pleasures to emerge. Maybe, as a professional game designer, I'm appreciating the artistry of the game's execution. Maybe I'm enjoying a moment of camaraderie with my teenage son. Maybe I'm feeling wistful about a similar game I played 20 years ago. Maybe I'm relishing an opportunity to feel powerful after a long and stressful day.

The point is that there is more to playing than just play. Play is a particular process, a particular way of thinking and doing within the context a particular structure of constraints. It is an end unto itself, but it is also a means toward other ends. These other ends depend on the existence of play for

16. Schell, *The Art of Game Design*, 111.

their existence—without the system of constraints called *Settlers of Catan*, my family wouldn't have spent last Saturday evening sitting around the kitchen table laughing and talking. The rules constructed a nexus of playful activity that providing the basis for an extended social encounter. The game was fun not only because the play space was interesting to navigate on an abstract level, but also because the act of playing provided a common meeting ground for human interaction.

The pleasures in LeBlanc's taxonomy are inexorably intertwined with our real-world experiences of play. We can't strip away the camaraderie of playing on a baseball team from of the experience of playing baseball. We can't replace the lush, detailed world of *Uncharted* with a stick figure moving through a world of gray boxes without changing how the game plays. A gray box may provide the same constraint on movement as a beautifully modeled jungle hut, but it doesn't support the same fantasy. Over the past six chapters, we have looked very closely at the structure of play. But it is important to keep in mind that this structure isn't a totalizing framework. It isn't a description of the entirety of what play *is*; it is a description of how play *works*. While playing a game, we are freely navigating a systems of constraints, but freely navigating a system of constraints isn't the only thing we are doing. This observation will become increasingly important later in this book as we turn our attention to other sorts of experiences and the pleasures they provide. In the chapters to come, we will look for play in some unexpected places. But the identification of play elements in non-game experiences shouldn't be taken to imply that somehow, fundamentally, everything is play. It simply means that play is one of a variety of elements contained within many experiences. Play is central to *Tetris*, but play is also a non-trivial element of *Moby-Dick*. *Moby-Dick* doesn't demand that we play the way that *Tetris* does, but it does provide an opportunity for play that is difficult to avoid. Teasing out how play operates in the context of literature, or theater, or music requires us to acknowledge that play can be an element of an experience without constituting its totality.

The previous chapters have laid out a framework for understanding the experience of play. In short, we experience play as an unfolding sequence of interesting choices.[17] Sometimes these choices represent physical

---

17. "What makes a *thing* into a *game* is the need to make decisions. Consider Chess: It has few of the aspects that make games appealing—no simulation elements, no roleplaying, and damn little color. What it's got is the need to make decisions. The rules are tightly constrained, the objectives clear, and victory requires you to think several moves ahead. Excellence in decision making is what brings success." Costikyan, "I Have No Words & I Must Design."

moves—the sort of immediate play we encounter when we aim at a target in a first-person shooter and pull the trigger, or kick a soccer ball and send it sailing down the field. But more often, these choices reside within a chain of anticipatory play—our moves exist entirely within our minds. Imagining a course of action, working through its ramifications, and exploring long chains of cause and effect all are play just as much as mashing the "jump" button.

The heuristics of play describe what sorts of moves are interesting to make. A good play space offers us several options at any moment. Because these options vary over time, the choices we are asked to make are always shifting. Our decisions have consequences—the course of action we pick now determines what choices we will be offered in the future. And these consequences are predictable—we can plan out chains of future moves and use these chains to navigate toward privileged positions within the play space.

However, our ability to predict the future is limited. Good play spaces offer unexpected twists and turns that thwart our ability to perfectly anticipate what lies ahead. This uncertainty prevents us from quickly exhausting the entire play space in one quick run of anticipatory play. Instead, we find ourselves constantly confronted by new and unexpected lines of investigation. Our exploration of the play space is a ramified and iterative process in which our imagination continually flickers out along shifting, branching structures of potentiality, probing different lines of action to determine which is most likely to lead us to our goals.

In a good play space, our goals are always achievable, although sometimes to the path we have to take to reach them is obscure or hidden. The result is an ongoing oscillation between satisfaction and frustration, between choices that carry us toward our destination and choices that carry us away. Each moment of frustration forms a crux, a fleeting rupture in the system of internal constraints that forms the basis of our anticipatory play. Frustration triggers a reconfiguration of these internal constraints to bring them more in accord with the external structure of the playfield. The longer we play within the play space, the better we understand it, and our increased understanding opens up new avenues for play. But play is more than just internalizing a complicated system. There is also deep satisfaction to be had from knowing what to do and then doing it, and from predicting the future and then having that prediction proved correct. This process is possible because of the constrained nature of a well-designed play space. Day-to-day life also presents an unfolding sequence of choices, but these choices aren't shaped by a coherent system of rules. In day-to-day life, our choices are often too many, or too few. We are faced with the same choices over and over again, or our decisions have no effect on the overall trajectory of our lives. Sometimes it is obvious how matters will work out; at other times we are surprised by events that change our circumstances without warning. Frustration may not lead to understanding, and satisfaction is far from assured.

Well-designed constraints are necessary for play not just because we enjoy being constrained, but because they provide the structure to channel us into situations in which we repeatedly have interesting choices to make. A rule set is, fundamentally, not a mechanism for challenging or limiting the player (although it will certainly provide challenges and limits). Rather, it is a mechanism for structuring an experience to provide a series of interesting choices—choices that will lead, ultimately, to frustration and satisfaction, to the particular pleasures of learning and doing.

The Discourse of Play

The heuristics of play are themselves a set of rules designed to structure a play space. They are intended both as a description of how play spaces operate, and, simultaneously, as constraints on a field of discourse about play.

In chapter 1, I discussed the problems we face when we define terms. There is a tendency to think of definitions as either correct or incorrect. Correct definitions successfully encapsulate the essence of the thing that they refer to; incorrect definitions don't. By advancing a definition of play and creating a set of heuristics that describes how it works, it may seem as though I'm saying that *this is what play is.*

I'm not.

My words for describing play do not encapsulate the essence of play. Rather, they are bounds on a discursive field that contains play as its subject. They are a means of demarcating a particular phenomenon within the totality of experience. (And I say this with the caveat that even referring to the subject of the demarcation as a "phenomenon" incorrectly implies that the subject precedes the definition. In fact, the phenomenon becomes identifiable as a phenomenon only as a result of the demarcation.)

Different choices of bounds would result in different discursive fields. The question is not "Which is the correct definition?" The question is "Does this definition structure an interesting or useful discursive field?" There many different ways to define play other than the way that I have chosen. There are different ways to describe the experience of play other that the heuristics I have laid out. I have chosen these rules not because they are the only rules possible, but because the discursive field they structure makes it easier to make interesting moves and say interesting things. Just as choosing polar coordinates instead of Cartesian coordinates can make some calculations easier to perform, this particular formulation of an aesthetic of play is designed to make some critical moves easier to make.

Of course, in addition to making some critical moves easier, this particular aesthetic also makes some critical moves harder. In many ways, this aesthetic cuts against the grain of the main body of existing videogame scholarship. Certain elements of play that are usually taken to be central (interactivity, competition, learning) have been shifted to the periphery while other elements (choice, anticipation, doing) have been moved closer to the center.

In part, this reflects my own taste in games and my ideas as to the direction in which they should be moving as an artistic enterprise. I think there is a lot of interesting play to be had from spaces that emphasize stillness over action, contemplation over interactivity, and layered meaning over explicit challenges. I think that previous critical approaches to videogame design have borrowed too heavily from traditional games—zero-sum play spaces in which extended stretches of individual mastery are discouraged in order to keep all the participants, winners and losers alike, interested.

But I have also chosen this particular frame because I think it allows us to say interesting things about cultural enterprises other than games. There is an element of play in visual art, in music, in literature, but it's difficult to perceive it when play is viewed largely through a lens of competition and conflict and interaction. You can't win a symphony. The words in a novel don't rearrange themselves in response to our actions. You don't have to struggle with a piece of sculpture to view it from different angles. And so games feel like a radically different form of expression, a radically new way to structure experience.

But if we choose different constraints to structure our discursive field, a completely different set of critical moves becomes available—moves that are much more applicable to other media of expression. Instead of treating conflict and interaction as essential to play, we can treat them merely as medium-specific techniques for generating interesting horizons of intent. This means that we can use the heuristics of play as a critical tool for understanding how art in general goes about structuring experience.

Seen from this perspective, it isn't that games are themselves a radically different medium. Rather, it is that analysis of games can provide us with a radically different perspective on how we navigate *all media*. An aesthetic of play gives us a new way to talk about what literary theorists call "presence"—the quality of "being-inside" that necessarily accompanies any interval of aesthetic engagement.[18] This aesthetic isn't a new way to interpret art (although it has a lot to say about the mechanics of interpretation). Rather, it is a new way to talk about the process of reception—a new way to analyze how letters, pigments, tones, bodies, or even ideas can function as constraints on a trajectory through a constructed play space.

More important, an aesthetic of play gives us a language for talking self-referentially about the experience of critical analysis itself. It is a frame for understanding the feeling of "being-inside" that occurs during the process of critical thought. When we analyze a work critically, we typically think of ourselves as standing outside of our immediate experience of it—we situate ourselves apart from the work in order to study at how it shapes the reader/viewer/player/listener's experience within it. But critical analysis is itself a mode of engagement. In constructing a critical space that allows us to stand outside our immediate experience and observe and comment on it, we are merely replacing one play space with another. Critical thought is itself a form of play, and the success or failure of different schools of critical thought hinges largely on what sorts of moves they allow within their relative fields of discourse.

We will explore these issues in much greater detail later in book. However, before we can do so, we need some more critical machinery. In part II, we will take a step back from games and turn our attention to questions of understanding and meaning: What are we talking about when we say that we understand how to play a game? What are we claiming when we say that a work of art means something? What is the relationship between particular objects in the world (games, artworks, texts) and our mental representations of those objects?

This may seem an odd philosophical turn in a book that has (up to this point) focused on the practicalities of constructing interesting play spaces. But it is a necessary one. In order to understand games (and other works of art) as meaning-making experiences, we need a better grip on *meaning* itself. With that goal in mind, in the next few chapters we will construct a set of constraints that define a new discursive field around the idea of meaning. As with our definition of play, this discursive field will not be an ontological claim about what meaning is; rather, it will be a functional model for describing how meaning-making unfolds.

In constructing this model of meaning-making, we will begin by looking at the relationship that exists between external and internal constraints in a play space. We will then take this basic model and extend it by connecting

18. Gumbrecht, *Production of Presence*.

it to a specific philosophy of knowledge. Using pragmatic epistemology, we will examine how the relationship between external and internal constraints can be understood as a special case of the more general relationship between things in the world and our ideas about those things. From philosophy, we will move on to neuroscience. We will explore how the brain stores information at the neural level, and use this information to further refine our epistemological model. We will look at a how constraint-based meaning-making can be embodied in a physical brain, and how the low-level properties of brains affect moment-to-moment experience. Finally, we will turn our attention to semiotics. By tweaking the classical definition of the relationship between words and objects, we will develop a modified semiotics that better coheres with both pragmatism and neuroscience. This ludic semiotics will be specifically directed toward analyzing the transmission of meaning through play spaces. It will give us a framework for talking about how systems of constraints can structure situations in which meaning is produced.

The result will be a new theoretical discourse for analyzing games (and other play spaces) as meaning-making activities. We will then put this discourse to the test in part III, where we look at how literary texts can also be analyzed as systems of constraints, and how the meaning-making process of textual interpretation also obeys the heuristics of play.

II Minds

7 Understanding

Up to this point, we have incorporated learning into our model by describing it as "internalizing external constraints." The idea is that as we learn to play a game we take rules that are part of the external constraint set and construct internal analogues of them. In some cases, the self-enforcement of these internal rules is an essential part of playing the game. However, even in situations in which the rules are externally enforced, the construction of internal analogues is necessary for anticipatory play. If we want to think our way through chains of possible future actions, we need to have a set of internal constraints to explore.

But what does it mean for an external constraint to be "internalized"? In the case of the rules of a game such as chess the answer is pretty straightforward. It means that a player has stored, somewhere in his brain, a set of constraints that are equivalent to the official written rules of chess. If a bishop can only move and capture diagonally, that particular chunk of information must be encoded by some pattern of neural activity. The constraint has an internal, mental representation. And if that internal representation corresponds with the external rules, we can say the constraints have been correctly internalized. The player knows the rules and understands the game.

But if we attempt to apply this interpretation to videogames, it falls apart. In the first place, the external constraints of a videogame are typically not exposed to the player. The "rules" of the game are coded into the game's software, not written down in a rulebook to be read. When we play a videogame we encounter an evolving state that *implies* the underlying nature of the rules, but the rules themselves remain hidden.[1]

---

1. "In a boardgame the structure is mostly contained in the literal rules, although aspects may be contained in the topology of the board, information printed on pieces or cards or other components, etc. The structure is therefore directly perceivable by

Furthermore, even if the rules were exposed, they likely wouldn't be of any use to us. The simplest videogame is far more complicated than the most detailed board game, requiring hundreds of lines of software to produce even the most basic gameplay effects. Even if we could memorize all the specific programming instructions that make up a game's rule set, we still would lack the cognitive skills to apply those hundreds (or thousands) of constraints during anticipatory play. The system is just too complicated to understand the way we can understand a board or a card game.

Then what is going on when we learn how to play a videogame? If we aren't constructing internal analogues for the external rule set, what does it mean when we say that the constraints have been internalized? How can we possibly understand something so complex?

The key is to realize that very different sets of constraints can yield very similar horizons. In order to correctly anticipate future outcomes in a videogame, we don't need to precisely replicate the external constraints inside our heads. Instead, it is sufficient to construct an alternate set of internal constraints that mimics the behavior of the actual constraints coded into the game. These internal constraints aren't merely crude versions of the true constraints. Rather, they are a completely different rule set that produce similar outcomes.

For example, a videogame may perform a series of line-of-sight checks that compare a line between an enemy and the player with the polygons that make up the world geometry. The results of these line-of-sight checks are then fed into a state machine that triggers different enemy behaviors on the basis of a hierarchy of threats. One high-priority behavior may be to pass a message to other enemies to trigger a standard search-and-destroy combat behavior. It is a complicated rule system requiring hundred of lines of software to implement. But as players, we can understand all it as "If that sentry sees me, he'll call for help."

the player, although understanding it requires effort on his part—he or she must learn and master the rules. Electronic games work differently; much of their structure is invisible to the user. It's contained in compiled software code. In a boardgame, players are responsible for operating the game as well as playing it, it you will; when a calculation must be made or an algorithm applied, the must do so, referring to the rules if necessary. In an electronic game, the 'rules' are incorporated in the software; a player gains understanding of them through experience, by playing the game, and may well remain in ignorance of their specific details, instead gaining a 'gut,' intuitive understanding of their operation." Costikyan, "I Have No Words & I Must Design."

Note that our internal constraints aren't merely a scaled-down version of the external system that they are intended to model. We aren't performing fewer line-of-sight checks, or fudging the behavior hierarchy. Instead, we are attributing the sentry's behavior to an entirely different mechanism. However, despite their differences, the horizons generated by both sets of constraints are very similar. We step around the corner and the sentry lets out a shout and the other nearby soldiers turn and charge toward us.

Now, if we nitpick, we can identify particular circumstances where the mismatch between these external and internal constraints produces anomalous results. For example, since the sentry doesn't actually "see" us, it might be possible to poke an elbow or knee into view without being detected. As long as the mathematical line-of-sight checks fail, whether we actually are in view doesn't matter. Similarly, since the other soldiers can't really "hear" the warning, it can't be drowned out by a loud noise, as it could in real life.

Experienced players may discover these discrepancies and develop more sophisticated internal constraints to exploit them. For most players, however, the constraint "If the sentry sees me, he'll call for help" is sufficient. A player who internalizes this particular constraint can reasonably be said to "understand" that aspect of the game, even though the constraint he has constructed doesn't actually replicate the corresponding external rules. What is important is not that the external constraints themselves are replicated, but that their effects are.

Thus, when we say that we "understand" a game, that doesn't mean that we have memorized its rules. It means that we have constructed a set of internal constraints that are sufficient for us to play it. Specifically it means that we have constructed a set of internal constraints that correctly predict future evolutions of the game's state, and thus that we can make meaningful decisions in our navigation of the play space. These functional internal constraints may include memorized versions of the rules, but they can also include alternative rules that produce the same effect and simple strategic constraints such as the "Open in a corner" rule taught to beginning *go* players.

Furthermore, once we arrive at this definition of what it means to understand a game, it resolves a subtle epistemological question: How can we claim that any pattern of mental activity "represents" some aspect of the external world? The rule "Roll two dice and move that number of spaces forward" can be encoded by a string of symbols printed on paper. But when we read that rule and internalize it—when we convert it into a pattern of mental activity in our brains—how can we say that it is the same rule? We can't compare our neurons to the words one by one to see if they correspond—memories aren't inscribed on our brains the way words are inscribed on a page. The only meaningful comparison we can make is a functional one. We can say the mental representation is correct because it leads us to do what the written representation says we should do: roll two dice and move that number of spaces forward. The correctness of the mental representation isn't due to correlation with its written counterpart; it is due to functional equivalence.

Thus, even when we consider something as simple as memorizing a written rule for a board game, we are still forced into a position of accepting a functional definition of understanding. Understanding a game isn't about learning rules; it is about constructing internal constraints that accurately predict future outcomes. And *any* internal constraint that allows a player to correctly anticipate the future evolution of a game's state can be a useful means of understanding that game, whether or not it corresponds to any particular aspect of the game's external system.

Interpretation

If a game has any appreciable degree of complexity, it is likely that different players will understand it in different ways. If the game has explicit rules, the players will mostly agree on those, but still there is room for divergence.[2] For example, it is possible for two players to successfully play a game of chess even if they have different understandings of how *en passant* captures work. And if the game requires strategic thought, each player will almost certainly have his own set of higher-level internal constraints. Each player's understanding of the game will be determined by his previous cruxes, and since each player's history is unique, it isn't likely that they will arrive at exactly the same knowledge of how to play.

In fact, a major element of competitive play is the clash between players' differing systems of internal constraints. If I am playing tennis against an opponent, some of my success (or failure) is due to my physical prowess:

2. "[The rules of a game] are expressed in words every time someone describes a game or explains how to play it. Not everyone will have exactly the same understanding of grasp of the game, so they aren't likely to transmit their knowledge in exactly the same form of words. These rules are, therefore, not a known quantity, but an average of all the understandings of all the players. As such they may contain inconsistencies. The totality of rules of all but the simplest games are not exactly a cloud of unknowing, but could be described as a cloud of fuzzy knowing." Parlett, "Rules OK or Hoyle on Troubled Waters."

How fast can I run? How accurate is my backhand? How fast is my serve? But a bigger factor is how I understand the tactical elements of the game: Where do I position myself to respond to my opponent's next shot? Where do I aim my shots to pull my opponent out of position? What does my opponent expect from me, and how can I thwart those expectations? A player can be physically inferior to his opponent, but still win because he has a superior understanding of the game.

We can think of these different understandings as *interpretations*. An interpretation is any internal constraint that doesn't correspond to an external rule in a play space, but which, nevertheless, has predictive value. The construction of a new interpretation is inherently a creative act on the part of the player. An interpretation isn't some hidden, pre-existing part of the game waiting to be uncovered; it is a brand-new thing, independent of the game's original structure.

Once we adopt this frame for talking about interpretations, we can make an interesting observation: There may be some useful interpretations that the game's creators didn't intend. In other words, players may develop ways of understanding a game that weren't anticipated by the game's designers.

For example, consider the evolution of the game of chess. Chess originated on the Indian subcontinent sometime in the seventh century. From the beginning, it was a war game played with pieces representing different types of units on an 8-by-8 game board. In the centuries since, it has spread around the world, evolving into dozens of different regional variants.[3]

The modern European version of chess settled into its now-familiar form in the seventeenth century. Though there have been some minor changes since (how pawn promotion is handled, for example), the rules have remained largely the same for several hundred years. But how chess is *played* has changed considerably during that time. Despite the stability of the rules, expert players have developed new ways of understanding the game that have altered the experience profoundly. Probably the most striking of these was the invention of positional play in the middle of the nineteenth century. Before then, the Romantic style had dominated high-level competition. The Romantic style emphasized tactical brilliance—overwhelming one's opponent with clever attacks and dazzling sacrifices. Little attention was paid to defense or to long-term strategy. Positional play, pioneered by the great theoretician Wilhelm Steinitz, changed all that. Steinitz advocated a wide range of new techniques that emphasized controlling the

---

3. Parlett, *The Oxford History of Board Games*, 278–279.

board over capturing pieces. The goal was no longer to slash your enemy to ribbons; now it was to maneuver him into a position where his opportunities to attack withered away into nothing.

Not all of Steinitz's opponents appreciated his innovations. In contrast to the old freewheeling style of play, Steinitz's approach was meticulous and grinding. When Adolf Anderssen, the previous world champion, was asked to assess Steinitz as a player, he replied bitterly: "Steinitz is a pickpocket, he steals a pawn and wins a game with it."[4] Despite the disdain of the existing chess establishment, positional principles came to dominate high-level chess within a generation. Steinitz's new understanding of chess was more effective than the old Romantic style and quickly drove it into extinction.

Positional play wasn't designed into chess. Chess existed in various forms for more than 1,000 years before Steinitz invented his new interpretation. At each stage in its development, players tweaked the game by trial and error, keeping the variants that were fun to play and discarding the boring ones. But at no point did any of chess's "designers" anticipate Steinitz's way of playing.

Another example is the invention of strafe-jumping in *Quake*. Strafe-jumping is a technique for boosting forward movement speed by exploiting a loophole in how the game handles diagonal movement. During normal play, you control your forward movement with a keyboard key, typically "w." When you hold down "w," your character accelerates forward until you reach a speed limit set by the game. You also have two strafe buttons (typically "a" and "d") that allow you to slip from side to side. If you press the key that controls forward movement and one of the strafe buttons at the same time, you move diagonally.

Now, diagonal movement is subject to the same speed limit as forward movement. However, some players noticed that if you quickly jump as you switch from moving straight to moving diagonally, your diagonal velocity is briefly less than the maximum allowed, and the game accelerates you. But because of the angles involved, some of that acceleration is also applied to your forward movement, briefly boosting your forward speed past the limit.

Now, if you keep running diagonally your direction of travel will change and the speed limit on diagonal movement will reduce your speed. But if you quickly jump again as you switch from strafing left to strafing right, you can get another boost in speed before you hit the diagonal speed limit.

4. *New York Times*, January 23, 1887.

Quickly toggling between left and right strafes while jumping can increase your forward speed by more than 20 percent—a big advantage in many situations.

This technique wasn't intended by the designers of *Quake*. In fact, the cap on diagonal movement was itself intended to thwart strafe-running, a similar exploit in *Quake's* predecessor *Doom*. The invention of strafe-jumping was first documented in an editorial by Antony Bailey posted on the Planet Quake website on October 12, 1997:

What we've discovered is indeed a way to increase the speed at which you run without cheating. The speed-up isn't as good as that provided by strafe-running in DooM [*sic*]; at best, one can manage about a 22% speed increase, which is approximately only half that which strafe-running gave (that is, if you were doing it right.) And, like strafe-running, it is awkward to use and takes a bit of practice. But we think this is all to the good—the more skillful you are and the more you practise [*sic*] this technique, the faster you will be. This is a brand new technique.[5]

Strafe-jumping proved so useful that it quickly became one of the skills that an experienced *Quake* player was expected to master. Even though it wasn't originally intended to be part of the game, newer first-person shooters such as *Jedi Knight II* and *Call of Duty* have preserved it.

Sometimes a designer may intentionally design a hidden way to play into a game. And if, as a player, you discover that hidden way to play, you can use that knowledge to play more effectively. But the fact that you discover a new way to play doesn't prove that it was waiting there, hidden, all along. Like Steinitz or the *Quake* strafe-jumpers, you may have invented an entirely new interpretation that meshes nicely with the game's existing rules. You have learned something new, but it isn't a lesson that the designer intended to teach.[6]

Portability

Suppose for a moment that understanding a game were merely a matter of memorizing its rules—that is, that every internal constraint had an external analogue. Your knowledge of chess would consist entirely of facts such as

5. Bailey, "Zigzagging through a Strange Universe."
6. "Even non-computerized games have interactions the designers did not intend. ... The player cannot be bothered to interpret the will of the game designer as far as which moves are 'fair' and which moves are not, or which moves are intended and which moves weren't. It's irrelevant anyway. The player knows only moves that lead to winning and moves that don't." Sirlin, *Playing to Win*, 24.

"A bishop can move any number of vacant squares in a diagonal direction" and "The king cannot engage in castling if it has already moved." None of your internal constraints would be interpretive. If knowledge of that sort were the only knowledge you possessed, you still could play a passable game of chess if you spent enough time thinking about your actions. All computer chess programs depend to some extent on this "brute-force" approach, mindlessly sifting through millions of possible future positions to find the optimal move.[7] It isn't an efficient or an elegant way of predicting future outcomes, but it can be effective. However, such an understanding of chess would be useful only for playing chess. A constraint such as "A queen can move any number of spaces in any direction" makes sense only within the context of chess. It doesn't tell you anything you anything useful about backgammon, or *go*, or hockey. And it certainly doesn't tell you anything useful about real-world queens.

Contrast that with the sort of understanding that is developed when we learn interpretive constraints. One of the most basic elements of positional play in chess is "Control the center." It is one of the first strategic principles that beginning players typically learn. But unlike "A queen can move any number of spaces in any direction," "Control the center" can apply to a wide number of different domains. You can apply it to a soccer game, to a real-time strategy game, to tic-tac-toe, or even to a presidential election. Such a constraint is *portable*. It is valid in many different contexts. Once you have learned that "Control the center" is a useful interpretive constraint in chess, it becomes a multi-purpose tool that you carry around with you and try in other circumstances.

Now, that doesn't mean the tool will work every time you try it. One of the counterintuitive aspects of learning to play *go* is that controlling the center early in that game is a bad idea. You build a strong position in *go* by dominating the corners early, then moving to control of the sides of the board, then extending your reach into the center in the middle of the game. A chess player who is learning to play *go* may try to apply "Control the center" and fail badly.

Thus, an interpretation doesn't represent some sort of deep universal principle. All such knowledge is provisional. Sometimes it will be useful; sometimes it will not. But the fact that it is useful at all outside its original context is significant. Sometimes games teach us facts, but more often they teach us tools. These tools then become part of our conceptual

7. For more on this brute-force approach to playing chess, see Shannon, "Programming a Computer for Playing Chess."

background—a collection of ready-made interpretations for other situations we may face in this game, in other games, or in life.

That games work this way is interesting from a practical design perspective, but it also means that games aren't limited to being trivial, self-contained pastimes. Depending on the portability of the internal constraints they encourage us to construct, they may have expressive power that extends far beyond the play experience.

For example, consider the videogame *Journey*. In *Journey* you play an anonymous traveler in the desert. You are on a pilgrimage to a distant mountain, and the gameplay consists of a series of platforming and enemy-avoidance challenges as you navigate an increasingly treacherous series of ruins. There are a number of things to learn as you play the game, including how to time your jumps and where to find hidden scraps of cloth that work as power-ups, but most of these interpretive constraints make sense only within the context of *Journey*. They form a frame of limitations and affordances to navigate as one plays, but they don't have any utility afterward. However, *Journey* includes an interesting twist. If you play it online, you will be randomly matched with another player on the same pilgrimage. You and the other player can't talk to each other, and the game doesn't force you to cooperate, but you are subtly rewarded if you work together. Staying close to each other recharges the meters that determine how high you both can jump. As result, "Stick together" is an interpretive constraint that most players quickly internalize.

Without being ordered to, most players find themselves slipping into a supportive, cooperative relationship with a random, anonymous stranger. Experienced players help inexperienced players who get lost. If one falls behind, the other waits for him to catch up. Players carry on "conversations" using the wordless chime that the pilgrims have in place of a voice. The constraint "Stick together" is, at first, a practical interpretation. It is a convenient way to understand the rules encoded in the game's software for character proximity and jump duration. However, over time this practical constraint bleeds out into a variety of other behaviors in the game. What was born of utility quickly becomes habit. Near the end of the game you reach a stretch where you cross a snowfield high in the mountains. By that point, your ability to jump has been rendered useless. It is severely limited by the cold, and, in any case, there nothing to jump to in the endless field of white. However, every time I have played *Journey*, and every time I have watched it being played, both players have continued to stick together through the snowfield, trudging slowly forward, shoulder to shoulder, into the storm. And when the game is over, the constraint lingers. Not overtly, though—*Journey* doesn't offer that sort of neatly packaged lesson. Rather, what remains is an impulse toward a way of being, a habituated trace of the mechanics of "sticking together-ness." This trace is much more than just the easy moralizing of "We should all stick together"; it bounds a wide range of different stances regarding responsibility and duty and selfish advantage and safety and risk and fellowship. The portable constraint "Stick together" isn't a thing with a single meaning. It is a tool for the production of multiple meanings—or, rather, it *can be* such a tool. The construction of interpretations is an inherently idiosyncratic process—a function of a player's specific encounters within the play space and the background he brings to the experience. Interpretations are always solutions to practical problems of engagement: How do I, as a player, go about building a frame for anticipatory play within the system I currently find myself? *Journey* is *about* "sticking together" not because some essence of "sticking together" resides within it, but because the system it provides functions nicely as a play space when some form of "sticking together" is added to it as a constraint.

This way of thinking and talking about meaning has broader philosophical implications. If we accept that play is a human universal then, the structure of play—the rules for rules—must be grounded in basic features of human cognition. We play the way we play because play is a by-product of how our minds exist within the world. Because of this, our frame for understanding games can be used as a starting point for understanding the relationship between thoughts and things—for understanding *understanding*.

8 Epistemology

As we move through a level in a first-person shooter, the walls around us form a system of constraints. They define the boundary between where we can go and where we can't. The game enforces these constraints—if we try to make our character walk through a wall, the game prevents it. However, as players we quickly learn to avoid these collisions before they occur. We know that we can't walk through walls, so we don't try to. The external constraints have become internalized. And so, as we explore the level, our movement is constrained less by the actual restrictions that the software imposes upon us, and more by our understanding of those restrictions.

However, our understanding is an interpretation. We don't understand a wall the way the game does. The game understands a wall as a set of triangles, and a collision with that wall is the result a numerical calculation to determine if our character's bounding cylinder intersects any of those triangles. But we don't make our way through the level thinking about triangles and bounding cylinders. We understand the walls *functionally*— a wall is something that blocks movement. And, in fact, the underlying implementation of the wall is immaterial for the purposes of the game. We could replace the existing wall code with an entirely different algorithm, and as long as the two implementations were functionally equivalent—that is, as long as the new code prevents us from walking through walls, as the old one did—our understanding of walls would still be valid.

Understanding is about knowing what things *do*, not what things *are*. This is true in the real world just as much as in games. We encounter walls all the time in the real world, and they block our movements just as the walls in games do. And we understand them the same way: through their function. Walls in the real world aren't blocking our movement because our bounding cylinder has intersected one of their triangles, they are blocking our movement because the electrons orbiting their atoms repel the electrons orbiting our atoms. But as we walk through a real-world building, we don't think about electrons and electrostatics. We avoid walking into walls because we understand walls functionally, whatever the underlying mechanism.

If we cared only about where we could walk, a wall made out of polygons and a wall made out of atoms would be equivalent. However, real walls do other things besides block movement—for example, they attenuate sound, they catch fire, they crumble when damaged, and they can be painted. If our understanding of walls were limited to "walls block movement," we wouldn't be able to anticipate what might happen in other circumstances.

In practice, most people have a complicated "theory of walls" that encompasses a number of related constraints regarding how real-world walls behave in a variety of circumstances. If I ask you to imagine a wall being hit by a sledgehammer, you are capable of forming an expectation in your mind of what will happen. This is true even if you have never actually seen a wall being hit by a sledgehammer, or even previously thought about a wall being hit by a sledgehammer. Your understanding of walls consists of a collection of constraints that describe how walls behave. And the functional nature of this understanding means that you can anticipate how previously unobserved or unimagined scenarios involving walls will play out.

This notion of functional understanding is central to the aesthetic of play. It gives us a way to talk about how games (and other forms of play) can function as knowledge-generating activities. Thus, in the rest of this chapter we are going to delve more deeply into the ramifications of this particular approach to knowledge. What does it mean to have a functional understanding of the world? What mechanisms underlie this model of knowledge production? How can we use those mechanisms to improve our understanding of the experience of play?

Positivism

It is tempting to think that science has allowed us to replace our old fragmentary functional understanding of what walls *do* with a more rigorous unified understanding of what walls *are*. Saying that a wall is a collection of atoms seems to be a description of fundamental nature of the wall, not just a description of its properties. But if we examine the notion of an atom more closely, we discover that this isn't so. Atoms are made up of more fundamental objects—electrons, protons and neutrons—and it turns out that we don't have a particularly good grasp of what electrons, protons and neutrons actually are either. Sometimes they act like particles and sometime they act like waves. Sometimes the waves don't even act like waves; they act like the probability distributions of waves. Thus, if we closely examine the understanding that physics provides, all we see are more functional descriptions. These descriptions may be more accurate and generalized than our intuitive everyday understanding of how walls work, but they still tell us only what walls do, not what they are.[1]

We could take the position that as we learn more and more about how the universe works, and as our understanding of physics gets better and better, eventually we will reach the point where our functional description of the world will converge on a single undeniable truth. We will not just be saying "Here is a set of rules that predict how this system behaves." We will be able to say "Here is what this system is." This was the position of logical positivism, the dominant philosophy of science for the first half of the twentieth century. The idea was that science, through a series of increasingly careful and subtle experiments, would be able to prove that one particular description of the universe was the correct description—that science could arrive at one ultimate understanding, which would be congruent with the nature of the reality itself.

However, there are several flaws in this approach. The first has to do with the problem of induction. In order to make a claim about the nature of reality, we must proceed from specific observations to general principles. But we can never be entirely certain that we haven't overlooked something in our observations. For example, if I observe a flock of swans on a lake, and notice that they are white, I can hypothesize that all swans are white. If I want to be more confident about my assertion that all swans are white, I can travel from lake to lake and make many observations of many different swans. But no matter how many lakes I visit, I can never be entirely sure that I haven't overlooked one somewhere that contains a black swan. And one black swan suffices to invalidate my hypothesis.[2]

---

1. "But what of the terms of our theories? To what do they refer? This question has proven troublesome to empiricists. For in speaking of fields, waves and sub-atomic particles, we are not referring to anything that is directly observable. Of course we observe the effects of these things; this is precisely what the theory *says*. But we do not observe the *things themselves*. Sometimes theoretical entities seem inherently paradoxical, like the entities studied in quantum mechanics, which are both waves and particles, and concerning which there may be no categorical truths, only probabilities." Scruton, *Modern Philosophy*, 190.

2. "Now it is far from obvious, from a logical point of view, that we are justified in inferring universal statements from singular ones, no matter how numerous; for any conclusion drawn in this way may always turn out to be false: no matter how many instances of white swans we may have observed, this does not justify the conclusion that *all* swans are white." Popper, *The Logic of Scientific Discovery*, 4.

Thus, even if science leads us to draw particular conclusions about the nature of the universe, we can never be entirely sure that there isn't a black swan lurking somewhere in the shadows. In physics in the late nineteenth century, the laws of Newtonian mechanics seemed good candidates for a fundamental explanation of the nature of reality. Newton's simple laws of motion and force seemed adequate to explain every facet of the material world, from the trajectories of artillery shells to the motions of the planets. But then series of experiments by Albert Michelson and Edward Morley at Case Western Reserve University in 1887 proved to be the unexpected black swan that invalidated any claims that Newtonian mechanics was congruent with the true nature of reality. At the time, light was understood to be a wave, and the luminiferous aether was thought to be the medium through which light waves propagated, just as air was the medium through which sound waves propagated. The aether was thought to fill all space. The Michelson-Morley experiment was designed to detect it by taking two measurements of the speed of light several months apart. Since the earth's orbital speed is about 30 kilometers per second, and since the earth moves in opposite directions at opposite extremes of its orbit, the earth's velocity *relative to the stationary aether* should fluctuate by about 60 kilometers per second over the course of a year. Light itself travels at about 300,000 kilometers per second, so measurements of the speed of light taken six months apart should vary by about 0.02 percent—a tiny amount, but well within the accuracy of Michelson's interferometer. However, Michelson and Morley's experiments showed no variation in the speed of light over the course of several months of observation. This unexpected result led to the collapse of the theory of the luminiferous aether, and to Einstein's subsequent formulation of special and general relativity and the rise of a new physics. Newtonian mechanics had appeared to be a complete description of how the universe worked only because certain observations hadn't yet been made. No matter how all-encompassing our theories may seem to be, we can never be certain that an unexpected result from a future experiment will not overturn them.

For this reason, the epistemology of science since middle of the twentieth century has focused not on *verification*, but on *falsification*. The point of science is not to formulate theories that are true—i.e., that correctly describe the nature of the universe—but to formulate theories that makes testable predictions. We can treat these theories as provisionally true—they are the best descriptions we have at the moment to explain the evidence at hand, but they aren't true in the sense that they are congruent with what reality is. The "truths" of science are simply functional descriptions—systems of constraints that allow us to accurately anticipate the unfolding of the world around us. They don't make any claims as to what that world actually is.

Even if we allow that at some point in the distant future humans may converge on one manifestly superior way of understanding everything, it is clear that we haven't done so yet. Our present techniques for making our way through the world are based not on knowledge of how the world actually is but on knowledge of how it behaves. Even if we suppose that humans may eventually be able understand the world as it truly is, that way of understanding would be completely different from the current way. Thus, if we are trying to understand what it means to understand things, it does us no good to construct an idealized version of understanding that bears no relation to how we go about understanding things on a daily basis. I know how to drive to a car, and I know what John Keats did, and I know where Australia is, and I'm able to know all these things without having anything other than a provisional, functional understanding of how cars, Keats, and Australia exist within the world.

Pragmatism

The way of thinking about knowledge I described in the preceding paragraph is called pragmatism. It was first articulated by the American philosopher Charles Sanders Peirce in the 1870s, then picked up and amplified by William James, John Dewey, and others. The central idea of pragmatism is that truth is always provisional and contingent. When we say that something is true, we might seem to be saying "This is how things are" but in fact we are really saying "This way of thinking yields useful results in my current circumstances." And in this context "useful results" means "accurate predictions about the unfolding of the world around me."[3]

Pragmatism represents a radical break in the history of Western philosophy. Since the time of Plato, one of the fundamental questions posed by philosophers has been "What is the true nature of existence?" This yearning for metaphysical clarity is certainly understandable. Our lives are awash in errors, ranging from tiny misunderstandings to life-threatening delusions. Living in such a broken world, it is comforting to think that if we dig deeply enough beneath the illusions that surround us, we will eventually reach

---

3. "Consider what effects might conceivably have practical bearings you conceive the object of your conception to have. Then your conception of those effects is the WHOLE of your description of the object." Peirce, "Issues of Pragmatism," *The Essential Peirce*, volume 2, 346.

bedrock—that if we look and think hard enough we will eventually arrive at an understanding of the world not merely as it seems to be, but as it truly is.

However, pragmatism rejects the entirety of this endeavor.[4] What pragmatism says is that discovering the true nature of things is logically contradictory. "Getting at the true nature of things" is not what understanding is. (A more correct way to put this is that "getting at the true nature of things" isn't what understanding *does*, since even understanding itself doesn't have a true essence. Our understanding of understanding is itself necessarily functional. We can describe how understanding works, but we can't say what it is.)

The pragmatic position is that the whole of ontology and metaphysics— that is, a large chunk of what has historically constituted philosophy—is predicated on an error. The error is thinking that there is some particular relation that must exist between ideas and objects, a relation that must be analyzed and explained. The error lies in thinking that ideas exist as one sort of thing and objects exist as other sorts of things, and that if we want to separate true ideas from false ones we must find a way to reconcile the essential nature of our ideas with the essential nature of the objects our ideas are about.[5]

In contrast, what pragmatism says is that understanding is a matter of being able to predict what will come next. There is no "deeper understanding" or "more fundamental truth" that lies beyond being able to predict what will come next. Some ways of understanding may be more general than others—for example, understanding a wall as a collection of atoms may allow you to make predictions that you can't if you understand a wall as a barrier to movement—but they aren't more "true."[6] And, in fact,

4. "[Pragmatism] will serve to show that almost every proposition of ontological metaphysics is either meaningless gibberish ... or downright absurd." Peirce, "What Pragmatism Is," *The Essential Peirce*, volume 2, 338.

5. "If philosophy comes to an end, it will be because this picture is as remote from us as the picture of man as a child of God. If that day comes, it will seem as quaint to treat man's knowledge as a special relation between his mind and its object as it now does to treat his goodness as a special relation between his soul and God." Rorty, *The Consequences of Pragmatism*, 33.

6. "The intuitive realist thinks that there is such a thing as Philosophical truth because he thinks that, deep down beneath all the texts, there is something which is not just one more text but that to which various texts are trying to be 'adequate.' The pragmatist does not think anything like that. He does not even think there is anything as isolable as 'the purposes which we construct vocabularies and cultures to fulfill' against which to test vocabularies and cultures." Rorty, *The Consequences of Pragmatism*, xxxvii.

understanding a wall simply as a barrier to movement is often a more useful way of thinking in many real-world situations. It's a better way to understand walls if you are running through the house to answer the doorbell, for example.

Thinking and arguing from a pragmatic perspective is often difficult because ontological assumptions are woven into the very fabric of our language. For example, if I say something like "Play is free movement within a system of constraints," it sounds as though I'm claiming that reality contains a thing called "play" and that I have identified the true properties of that thing. But that isn't what I'm claiming at all. What I'm really claiming that it is easier to see how certain situations will unfold if we consider those situations as systems of constraints. Unfortunately, it is hard to say that clearly in English. 'Is' is such a powerful and useful word that to write without using it is difficult, even though every sentence is a whispered affirmation of a questionable metaphysical stance.

Pragmatic epistemology maps directly on to our constraint-based model of interpretation. Here is how William James describes the process of encountering and resolving a crux:

> The observable process ... is the familiar one by which any individual settles into new opinions. The process here is always the same. The individual has a stock of old opinions already, but he meets a new experience that puts them to a strain. Somebody contradicts them; or in a reflexive moment he discovers that they contradict each other; or he hears of facts with which they are incompatible; or desires arise in him which they cease to satisfy. The result is an inward trouble to which his mind till then had been a stranger, and from which he seeks to escape by modifying his previous means of opinions. He saves as much of it as he can, for in this matter of belief we are all extreme conservatives. So he tries to change first this opinion, and then that opinion, and then that (for they resist change very variously), until as last some new idea comes up which he can graft upon the ancient stock with a minimum of disturbance to the latter, some idea that mediates between the stock and the new experience and runs them into one another most felicitously and expediently.[7]

James is talking about how we form new beliefs in general, not only when we are playing a game. Each of us possesses a body of constraints that structure his or her anticipation of future events. As we pass from moment to moment, our minds continually probe ahead along the lines of affordance that these constraints offer. Mostly these expectations are confirmed—the chair that we sit on solidly supports our weight, we hear a familiar step in the hallway and a friend appears at the door, the sun goes down and

7. James, "What Pragmatism Means," *Pragmatism and Other Writings*, 24.

the sky grows dark. This continual process of anticipation isn't a conscious one—we aren't deliberately working to think about what will happen next. Rather, anticipation is the carrier wave of thought, the medium in which thinking takes place.

We exist within a ceaseless epistemological cycle, continually anticipating the unfolding of the world around us and then adjusting our internal constraints to accommodate any failures of anticipation. And if we think in functional terms, we can construct a model of how this epistemological cycle operates. This model isn't a description of what understanding is. It is a description of what understanding does. It's a system of constraints that make predictions about how our knowledge of the world evolves from moment to moment in response to the sensations we experience.

Modeling the Epistemological Cycle

Peirce associates this cycle of anticipation and crux with three different types of reasoning: inductive, deductive, and abductive.[8] Each of these different types of reasoning plays a role in process of knowledge formation.

Inductive reasoning is the process of arriving at general premises from specific facts:

All the swans I've seen are white.
Therefore, all swans are white.

Deductive reasoning, on the other hand, is the process of arriving at specific facts from general premises:

Kirby is a dog.
All dogs have fleas.
Therefore, Kirby has fleas.

Abductive reasoning (the least well known of the three) is the process of forming a new premise in the light of new, contradictory facts. Specifically, it is the process of forming a *reasonable* new premise—one that does the least damage to all the other premises that make up our understanding of the world.

For example, suppose that after years of seeing nothing but white swans I suddenly see a black one. This is a crux—a moment when my expectations have been thwarted. In order to accommodate this new information I need to modify my internal constraints. But how should I modify them? I have a variety of new constraints I can adopt:

8. Peirce, "Three Normative Sciences," *The Essential Peirce*, volume 2, 205.

A trick of the light has caused a white swan to look black.
Some swans are black.
That's not a swan, it's a crow.
Someone dyed that swan black.
All swans are black. The animals I previously saw were doves.
My eyes now see white objects as black.
I'm dreaming.
I'm hallucinating.

If we encounter a fact that runs counter to our expectations, there are always a large number of different explanations that will resolve the crux. Abductive reasoning is the process of adopting, provisionally, whichever explanation causes the least disruption to our current system of interpretive constraints. If, after a lifetime of seeing white swans, I suddenly see a black one, my most reasonable response is "The light must be playing a trick on me" followed closely afterward by "I suppose some swans are black." Either explanation has a relatively small ripple effect on my overall understanding of the world around me. However, if I insist on preserving my belief that all swans are white no matter what, then I'm forced to resolve the crux with more complicated explanations with more significant consequences. "I'm hallucinating" has a much more dramatic effect on my anticipation of future events than "Some swans are black."

Now, this doesn't mean that the simplest resolution for any crux is always the best one. Abductive reasoning provides a reasonable first guess that must then be tested deductively. If our reasonable first guess fails this test, the process repeats as we attempt to resolve the crux through increasingly more extreme modifications to our system of internal constraints. Eventually we may arrive at "I'm hallucinating" as the only constraint that can explain a sequence of events that we have observed, but such an extreme disruption of our explanatory framework is always a last resort when other explanations that aren't as sweeping fail. Abductive reasoning is thus an essential step in an iterative epistemological process that is able to correct both small and large flaws in how we understand the world.

Iterative abductive reasoning can be nicely illustrated by a bit of dialogue from the opening of the old TV series *Superman*:

"Look! Up in the sky! It's a bird."
"It's a plane."
"It's Superman!"

Whenever you see a flicker of movement up among the clouds, it *may* be a flying space alien with superhuman powers. But deciding that Superman

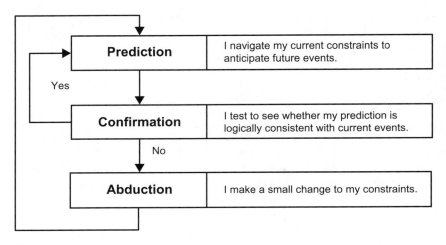

Figure 8.1
The pragmatic epistemological cycle.

is real has far-reaching consequences. Thus, you are better off starting with less disruptive explanations—a bird, or a plane—and moving on to Superman only when your earlier abductions fail their deductive tests.

We live our lives within this epistemological cycle (figure 8.1). We use induction to predict how the world will unfold, and then deductively confirm if our expectations agree with what we observe. If our expectations are incorrect, we make minor abductive tweaks to our constraints until we find a new set that resolves the rupture. The tweaks to our constraints start small, becoming larger only if more minor adjustments fail to repair the breach in our understanding. Eventually we reach to a state of predictive equilibrium where the unfolding of the world again matches our expectations of it. And the cycle begins anew.

It may seem odd at first to think of knowledge in terms of being able to predict what will happen in the future, because so much of what we know right now concerns what has already happened in the past. For example, I know that George Washington was the first president of the United States. This is knowledge of something that happened in the past. I don't know that at some point in the future George Washington *will be* president of the United States. I know that during the years 1789–1797 George Washington *was* the president of the United States. So how can knowledge of something that happened more than 200 years ago be said to structure anticipation of how the world will unfold in the future?

The key is realizing that knowledge is something that is bound to individual human brains. Past and future are defined in relation to the temporally bound viewpoint of the person doing the knowing. When I anticipate the unfolding of the world around me, I'm not anticipating the unfolding of the world in general; I'm anticipating the unfolding of the world as it is experienced by *me*, a particular human being situated in a particular time and place.

"George Washington was the first president of the United States" is an interpretation I have adopted to explain a variety of experiences I have had. I've read books that claim that George Washington was the first president of the United States. I've been told the same thing by my elementary school teachers. I've been to Mount Vernon and seen the Washington Monument. I've seen George Washington's face on the dollar bill. My past is filled with a variety of experiences that can all be explained by adopting "George Washington was the first president of the United States" as one of my internal constraints.

The expectation formed by this constraint isn't that George Washington will be president in the future. The expectation is that in the future I will continue to have experiences that are in agreement with the statement "George Washington was the first president of the United States." If I see a list of presidents, I expect his name to be at the top. If I read a history of eighteenth-century politics, I expect to find him mentioned. If "George Washington was the first president of the United States" is a useful constraint, then I should continue to stumble across evidence that this constraint predicts and explains. And if, suddenly, these predictions fail, I will experience a massive crux. If I read a book that claims that the first president of the United States was a man named Adam Weishaupt, then I need to find a way to resolve this rupture in my understanding. If the crux is an isolated event, I probably can explain it away as an error or a joke.[9] However, if more and more evidence contradicting my understanding that George Washington was the first president of the United States piles up, eventually I will have to make a more radical re-adjustment of my internal constraints. If Adam Weishaupt's face is on every dollar bill, and his name is in every history book, and if my every attempt to find evidentiary traces of George Washington ends in failure, I will gradually and grudgingly be forced to admit that my original belief about George Washington had been a delusion.

This is as true for my knowledge of the immediate world around me as it is for my knowledge of events that happened in the past. For example, I know that I am sitting at a table in a coffee shop in Los Angeles as I type these words. But when I say that I know that there is a table here in front

9. Shea and Wilson, *The Illuminatus Trilogy.*

of me, what I mean is that my memories of recent patterns of light on my retina and recent patterns of pressure on my fingertips can be conveniently explained through a "theory of table," and that this "theory of table" makes consistent predictions about other patterns of light and pressure that I will experience as the world unfolds around me.

The philosopher Edmund Husserl uses the terms *retention* and *protention* to describe how our understanding of the unfolding of the world is anchored in time. When we observe an object, such as a table, the encounter isn't a single, isolated event. It is always an ongoing process in which our sense of the object's existence is an amalgam of our current sensory traces, interpretations of past sensory traces (retentions), and expectations of future sensory traces (protentions). We never experience anything as pure, unadulterated sensation. Our engagement with the world is always mediated by interpretive constraints and predictions within the epistemological cycle.

The clearest illustration of this principle is how we experience music. Consider the simple tune "Three Blind Mice." It's just a sequence of pitches: E, D, C, E, D, C, and so on. When we here it performed, we hear one pitch at a time. First one tone sounds, then a different tone, then another, until all the tones have been played and the tune is finished. At any moment, we are hearing either a single tone or the silence between them. However, we don't experience "Three Blind Mice" as a sequence of isolated tones separated by silence. We experience "Three Blind Mice" as a *melody*. A melody feels like a *thing*. It is an evolving structure that moves and curves and swells and retreats. But it's a purely mental thing. It has no existence apart from the way that our brains organize sequential tones into a structure with temporal extent.[10]

The day-to-day world that we inhabit—the world of tables and melodies and George Washington and coffee shops—is filled with mental things of exactly this kind. When we encounter a table in our everyday world, we

10. "Let us take a particular melody or cohesive part of a melody as an example. The matter seems very simple at first; we hear a melody, i.e., we perceive it, for hearing is indeed perception. While the first tone is sounding, the second comes, then the third, and so on. Must we not say that when the second tone sounds I hear *it*, but I no longer hear the first, and so on? In truth, therefore, I do not hear the melody, but only the particular tone which is actually present. That the expired part of the melody is objective to me is due—one is inclined to say—to memory, and it is due to the expectation which looks ahead that, on encountering the tone actually sounding, I do not assume that that is all." Husserl, *The Phenomenology of Internal Time-Consciousness*, 43.

aren't encountering the thing in itself. We are encountering a cognitively convenient strategy for engaging with a particular interval of sensory experience. Our understanding of the table says nothing about what the table truly is. It is a system of constraints that explains past sensory events and makes predictions about future ones.

This way of thinking about the world may seem strange at first. Reality, as we experience it, feels ... well ... *so real*. If I'm not paying attention to where I'm going and I walk into a wall, the wall doesn't feel like a convenient fiction arranged by my brain to explain a collection of sensory inputs. It feels like a solid, impenetrable wall. Not until we begin to dig deeper into the behavior of the world around us does the constructed nature of the reality we seem to inhabit begin to make itself apparent. When we try to find "where the melody is," we discover only individual pitches. If we go looking for the "wallness" of a wall or the "tableness" of a table, all we find are atoms and forces and probabilities, which are themselves just labels for other functional descriptions of the world's unfolding.

Epistemological Parsimonies

An interesting aspect of this way of thinking about knowledge is the emphasis it places on algorithmic efficiency. The epistemological cycle isn't a mechanism for finding truth. Rather, it is a mechanism for finding workable explanations with the smallest expenditure of mental resources. It is computationally parsimonious at each stage of its execution, always striving to minimize effort, time, and memory.

For example, our minds do not continually reconsider the validity of our entire understanding of the world. At any moment, we take most of what we know as given. We pause to consider that there may be a flaw in our understanding only when we encounter a crux—when something happens that we hadn't expected to happen. It is easy to see why this parsimonious strategy is useful. If we spent all our time sifting through possible explanations, we would never have time to actually engage with the world.

Furthermore, when we do experience a crux, our impulse is to resolve it with the smallest possible adjustment to our constraints. Resolving a crux with an abductive leap takes a non-zero amount of time. The larger the disruption to our system of constraints, the longer the validation step will take. By considering smaller adjustments before larger ones, we perform the quickest tests first.

However, the short-term efficiency that comes from minimizing disruption to our existing constraints must be balanced against the long-term efficiency of minimizing the total number of our constraints. It is possible to resolve any crux trivially by constructing a one-off explanation. For example, if I crash into the wall in a racing game, I can always minimize the disruption to my existing understanding by blaming the crash on a momentary glitch in the game's logic. This approach will certainly resolve the crux without disturbing my previous internal constraints, but such extreme short-term parsimony will generate large numbers of special-case constraints with little predictive value. The principle that we should avoid unnecessary *ad hoc* explanations is usually called Occam's Razor: We prefer simpler explanations over more complicated ones, even if those simpler explanations require us to abandon some elements of our previous understanding.

We also prefer constraints that can be navigated quickly and easily. Although we want our predictions to be as accurate as is possible, a prediction is worthless if the future arrives before we finish predicting it. So we strive to keep our system of constraints simple enough that it can generate useful predictions in a timely fashion. For example, if I knew the precise physical characteristics of every car around me on the highway—the mass of their chassis, the coefficient of friction of their tires, the tensile strength of each rod in their suspensions—I could theoretically calculate their future trajectories with a great deal of accuracy. But such a computation would take a long time, and I have to decide whether to brake or turn *right now*. Thus, rather than working from an extremely precise understanding of each car *in particular*, I'm better off working from a fuzzier understanding of how cars behave *in general*. The answers that this understanding gives me will be less accurate, but they will be answers that I can use in a fraction of a second when the car ahead of me begins to skid.

And we prefer constraints that are as concise as they can be. Gregory Chaitin, one of the founders of algorithmic information theory, has gone so far as to define understanding as form of data compression—that is, to suggest that to understand a thing is to possess a mental representation that is simpler than the thing itself but is still capable of describing the thing's behavior:

For any finite set of scientific or mathematical facts, there is always a theory that is exactly as complicated, exactly the same size in bits, as the facts themselves. (It just directly outputs them "as is," without doing any computation.) But that doesn't count, that doesn't enable us to distinguish between what can be comprehended and what cannot, because there is always a theory exactly as complicated as what it explains. A theory, an explanation, is only successful to the extent to which it compresses the number of bits in the facts into a much smaller number of bits of theory.

Understanding is compression, comprehension is compression! That's how we can tell the difference between real theories and *ad hoc* theories.[11]

I think that Chaitin goes too far in associating understanding *entirely* with data compression, simply because such a stance doesn't take into account the need for understanding to operate within the time frame of lived experience. As anyone who has opened a compressed document knows, there is a tradeoff between compression and speed of access, and sometimes the most concise description of a thing isn't the most convenient. $E = mc^2$ is a very concise expression of the relationship between energy and mass, but we can't re-derive the entirety of physics and chemistry from a small number of such concise expressions every time we want to make a cup of coffee.

Our understanding of the world is situational and heterogeneous. Our knowledge is tailored to the uses that we intend to put it to, and we often possess multiple useful ways of knowing about the same thing. I can understand a car as a collection of atoms, or as a looming threat, or a means of transportation, or as a status marker, or as an investment, and each of these ways of knowing is a computationally convenient way to arrive at different sorts of predictions about the unfolding of the universe. Furthermore, I arrived each of these different ways of understanding *independently*. It isn't as though I started with one fundamental way of understanding cars and then derived all the other ways of understanding cars from it. Rather, each of these ways of understanding cars is the product of separate lived experiences—watching cars, driving cars, buying cars, owning cars. While these different ways of understanding cars are all lumped together under the common signifier 'car'" they aren't organized into any sort of hierarchy. We generally try to maintain some degree of coherence between our different ways of understanding—outright contradictions will trigger a crux—but for the most part each way of understanding functions as an independent predictive system.

This way of thinking about knowledge is what the literary theorists Gilles Deleuze and Félix Guattari would describe as "rhizomatic."[12] A rhizome is an intermeshed root system, with multiple points of connection

---

11. Chaitin, "Epistemology as Information Theory: From Leibniz to Ω."
12. "A rhizome ceaselessly establishes connections between semiotic chains, organizations of power, and circumstances relative to the arts, sciences, and social struggles. A semiotic chain is like a tuber agglomerating very diverse acts, not only linguistic, but also perceptive, mimetic, gestural, and cognitive: there is no language in itself, nor are there any linguistic universals, only a throng of dialects, patois, slangs, and specialized languages." Deleuze and Guattari, *A Thousand Plateaus*, 7.

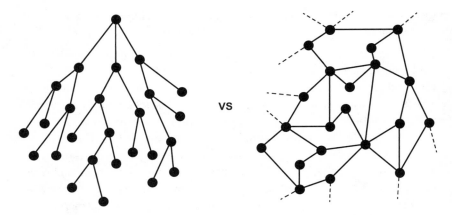

Figure 8.2
Root vs. rhizome.

linking multiple individual plants. Deleuze and Guattari use the rhizome as a metaphor for non-hierarchical interconnectedness. They present it as an antidote to the more traditional way of thinking about knowledge as a ramified root system branching out from a single point of origin (figure 8.2).

In a hierarchical epistemology, everything we know about the world links back to a single central truth, some fundamental way of understanding that justifies everything else that we know. But in a rhizomatic epistemology there is no such center. In a rhizomatic epistemology, all we have are a collection of different interpretive constraints, each invented on the fly in response to the exigencies of a particular situation as our brains attempt to parsimoniously resolve a crux. Some of these interpretive constraints may be long-lived and portable, others fleeting and narrow, but all are provisional and pragmatically justified. The fact that sometimes some of these contingent, provisional truths may appear to be the root of a fundamental way of understanding is merely an accident of perspective—the result of finding ourselves temporarily suspended within a bubble of epistemological stability.

Knowledge and Play

From the perspective of game design, one practical consequence of understanding the parsimonious nature of the epistemological cycle is that it gives us a way to anticipate the abductive leaps that players will tend to make within a play space. A significant element of structuring any play experience is guiding the player toward the construction of a successful set of internal constraints—a particular way of understanding the game. Often these internal constraints are interpretive—the result of the player's attempts to resolve cruxes early in the play experience. If we have a sense of the player's conceptual background we can anticipate the sorts of cruxes he is likely to encounter and the sorts of interpretations that he is likely to choose to parsimoniously resolve them.

However, this way of thinking about epistemology also illuminates something much more fundamental about the relationship between knowledge and play. Our brains are engines of anticipation. What we call knowledge is simply a collection of constraints that have demonstrated the ability to generate correct predictions about the unfolding of the world around us. The structure of this knowledge, the way that we understand things, has no relationship to the world around us other than a functional one: We don't know what things are, merely how they behave. We construct fragmentary, provisional systems to model this behavior—a heterogeneous collection of strategies of engagement, each the result of a particular sequence of cruxes within our lived experience. The distinction between good and bad strategies is determined by various parsimonies. What is the most concise explanation that yields accurate predictions? Which way of understanding gives us answers in the timeliest fashion? What interpretation minimizes the disruption of our existing constraints?

Play is the idealized distillation of our preferred epistemological stance. It is a system of external constraints that has been organized so as to allow us to slip comfortably through repeated iterations of the epistemological cycle, where it is easy to predict what will come next, and where our predictions mostly come true. Play is a place where the cruxes we experience can be quickly resolved through parsimonious abductive leaps, and where the correctness of our abductions can be easily established through quick bursts of deductive reasoning. It is a place where our interpretive choices form the basis for new, more subtle types of prediction—where there is always something exciting and new to discover, but we are never more than a few steps away from the safe and the familiar.

The heuristics of play are guidelines for building an ideal situation for the mind. They work to facilitate the smooth functioning of the epistemological cycle. And, in fact, the existence of play as a human (and animal) activity justifies pragmatic epistemology as a useful discourse. If we define knowledge simply as a connection between objects of the mind and objects of the world, play makes no sense. Why should we enjoy an activity that provides no material benefit, no reproductive edge, no useful information?

But if we define knowledge as a system of constraints that generates accurate predictions, the picture changes. In that case, we should expect animals like us (animals who depend on knowledge of the world to survive) to seek out situations in which highly predictive and variable constraints can be found in abundance.[13] We don't play *in order* to learn things; we play as an inescapable consequence of being *able* to learn things.

13. "It is therefore the fact that games have this fundamental quality of multilayered contingency that allows them both to mimic and constitute everyday experience, and this is what makes well designed games compelling. If we, as humans, are pattern-noticing machines (so to speak), then the unfolding of contingent outcomes in a semibounded domain such as a game is inherently compelling, presenting as it does just the right mix of the expected and the unexpected (provided it is well designed, whether by a game designer or by the practices of tradition)." Malaby, "Beyond Play: A New Approach to Games."

9 Neurons

In the previous chapter, we looked at how knowledge can be understood as a system of predictive constraints. In this chapter, we will examine how this pragmatic model of knowledge intersects with our current understanding the physical brain.[1]

The epistemological cycle is a functional description of the process of knowledge production. It is a simple way to conceptualize how observations are transformed into understanding. But this simplicity necessarily obscures certain practical nuances. Physical brains do not proceed from prediction to confirmation to abduction in the tidy, linear way that the model implies. And the information contained in a physical brain isn't stored as a set of discrete, well-defined constraints. In contrast to what the model suggests, physical brains are tightly interconnected networks where multiple cascades of competing activity unfold simultaneously, and where the constraints governing these cascades are distributed across hundreds or thousands of different locations.

The epistemological cycle is a useful *interpretation* of this physical process, but it isn't *analogous* to it. The operation of the physical brain deviates

---

1. The brief description of the brain in this chapter necessarily omits a great deal of nuance. For example, there is no mention of the structural divisions of the brain, or of the subtle differences between different types of neurons, or of the role that glial cells play in providing a metabolic substrate for the brain's computations, or of the distinctions between short- and long-term memory. Contrary to the abbreviated picture I present, the brain isn't simply an undifferentiated mass of identical neurons. However, treating the brain as an undifferentiated mass of identical neurons does make it easier to explain certain basic principles of its operation that would otherwise be obscured beneath a welter of anatomical and biochemical details. Readers who are interested in learning more about the structure and function of the brain are directed toward the encyclopedic *Principles of Neural Science*, which is the source of much of the information contained in this chapter.

from this model in small but significant ways, much as the algorithmic line-of-sight checks in a videogame will deviate from a player's understanding of "what the sentry sees." Our goal in this chapter is to lay out a more nuanced explanation of the neural processes that underlie what the epistemological cycle describes. This neural model is more unwieldy than the epistemological cycle, and more difficult to work with as a critical tool, but understanding its details (and how it deviates from the predictions of the epistemological cycle) will prove useful when we examine how physical brains share information in the next chapter.

Neurons and Constraints

The human brain consists of about 85 million neurons. A typical neuron has a large central cell body (the soma) and a number of smaller filaments that branch out to connect to other neurons (the axons and the dendrites) (figure 9.1). The axon is a thick root-like structure that carries outgoing signals; the smaller and more numerous dendrites receive incoming signals from the axons of other neurons. This web of axon-dendrite connections is very dense—on average, each neuron in the human brain connects to about 7,000 of its neighbors.

Each of these connections is a small gap called a synapse. Messages are transmitted across this gap by little squirts of chemicals called neurotransmitters. When a neuron fires, it sends a wave of electricity rippling down its axon. This electrical impulse stimulates the release of neurotransmitters across thousands of synapses. These neurotransmitters are then absorbed by the corresponding dendrites.

There are a large number of different neurotransmitters, but the two most common are glutamate and GABA (gamma-aminobutyric acid). When these chemicals are absorbed by a dendrite, they stimulate the opening of

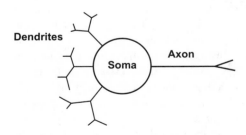

Figure 9.1
Schematic of a neuron.

ion channels, allowing charged ions to flow into or out of the neuron. These ion flows alter the neuron's internal voltage. A squirt of glutamate raises the voltage of the neuron, whereas GABA lowers it. So when a neuron sends an electrical pulse down its axon, the proximate result is an increase or decrease in the voltages of thousands of neighboring neurons.

If the voltage of one of these neighboring neurons is high enough, that neuron will itself fire and send an electrical pulse down its own axon, and the process will start all over again. In this way, a single neuron can trigger a chain of events that can ripple across the entire brain. One neuron fires, which excites its neighboring neurons, triggering some of them to fire, which excites *their* neighbors, triggering some of *them* to fire, and so on in an outward-spreading cascade.

Not all synapses are excitatory; some are inhibitory. If two neurons are connected by an inhibitory synapse, then when the first neuron fires the second neuron will have its internal voltage reduced. This reduction offsets the excitatory signals the neuron may be receiving from its other neighbors. These inhibitory impulses are an essential part of the functioning of the brain. Without them, any excitatory impulse would rapidly spread through the entire brain, creating a chaos of competing signals: a seizure. And, indeed, the cause of many seizure disorders can be traced back to a malfunction of the inhibitory synapses.

From a functional perspective, we can think of a neuron as working like a digital counter. It is connected to thousands of inputs that are constantly nudging its internal count up and down by small increments. If the count gets high enough to cross some threshold, then the neuron fires, incrementing or decrementing the counts of its neighbors. After it fires, its own count drops to zero and the process starts all over again (figure 9.2).

When we examine the brain at the cellular level, *all* of our mental activity is the result of millions of these tiny counters quickly counting and firing, sending waves of excitation rippling back and forth within our skulls. Every thought, every memory, every sensation that we experience is the product of cascades of excitation within the web of neurons that make up our brains. Every move that we make within a game, and every chain of anticipation that we pursue is the result of this distributed counting process. Even consciousness—our sense of being a self-aware observer embedded within the physical world—is an emergent property of this rapidly incrementing and decrementing network. How this effect is produced is uncertain. We don't yet understand how a collection of interconnected counters can generate the experience of self. But we are driven to the conclusion that somehow it must, because when we look

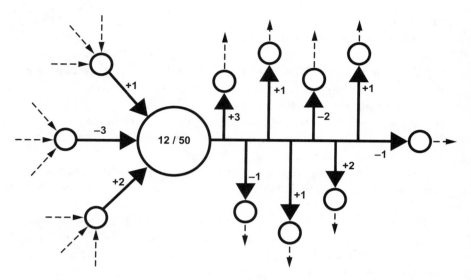

Figure 9.2
Neuron as counter.

closely at the brain, a collection of interconnected counters is all that we find.

How is knowledge of the world stored in the brain? It seems to be encoded in the strength of individual synapses.[2] If we think of a ripple of excitation passing through the brain, the path that it follows will tend to run along a chain of synapses with high excitation strength. The ripple will also spread across synapses with low excitation strength, but these routes are more likely to be damped by competing inhibitory inputs. Considered collectively, arrangements of synapses with high excitation or high inhibition strength act as negative or positive constraints on the path of the ripple through the web of neurons.

The spread of a ripple of excitation through the brain resembles a forking lightning bolt. It rapidly branches out along thousands of different paths, but most of these quickly peter out as inhibitory synapses counteract the effects of the excitatory synapses. The paths that survive are those where excitation is high and inhibition is low. Which neurons wind up being

2. With short-term knowledge, each synapse merely increases or decreases how much neurotransmitter it releases. With long-term knowledge, the actual number of synapses can also increase or decrease, baking the size of the response into the structure of the brain itself. Whichever mechanism is used, the result is the same—greater or lesser excitation of neighboring neurons.

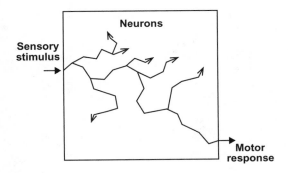

Figure 9.3
Excitation across a network of neurons.

activated at the end of the chain is determined by the specific strengths of the synapses along the chain's entire length (figure 9.3).

The particular swath that a ripple of excitation follows is determined by thousands of tiny synaptic events along the way. Slightly increase the response of a few excitatory synapses here, slightly decrease the response of a few inhibitory synapses there, and the ripple will be nudged toward a different swath. Changing one synapse will not cause a significant shift in the pattern of excitation—there is too much redundancy and parallelism along the way—but changing hundreds of synapses can.

When we know something—the rules of a game, a fact about the world—that knowledge is stored in the collective strengthening or weakening of hundreds or thousands of synapses. That pattern of strengthening or weakening will change the swath that a ripple of excitation will take through the brain, and, as a result, the course of our thoughts.

For example, imagine a very simple electronic game: A box with a light on the top, and two buttons, a red one and a green one. Periodically, the light will come on and the player can turn it off by pressing either button. Pressing the green button when the light is on scores a point, and pressing the red button deducts a point.

There is a simple, obvious winning strategy to this game: "When the light comes on, press the green button." A player who knows that strategy will press the green button whenever the light comes on. Knowing this strategy is a matter of having certain synapses strengthened and others weakened. When the light comes on, the visual stimulus triggers a cascade of synaptic events. A ripple of excitation passes through the brain. The knowledge of the winning strategy introduces a bias in the course that the ripple takes. Eventually the ripple terminates in neurons whose axons

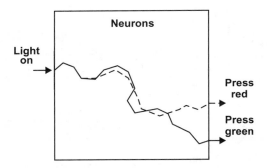

Figure 9.4
Knowledge differential produces path differential.

connect through the nervous system to the muscles, and those motor neurons transmit impulses that move the player's hand so that it presses the green button (figure 9.4).

If we change the game so that the red button wins instead of the green, all we need to do is tell the player: "Now when the light comes on, press the red button." This new knowledge is encoded as a subtle shift in the strength of a number of synapses. The next time the light comes on, the ripple of excitation will follow a slightly different course, and a slightly different set of output signals will be sent to the player's muscles. Now, instead of pressing the green button, the player's finger presses the red one.

The constraints that make us this knowledge are encoded as a pattern of differential excitation across a large number of synapses, not just one. The new path to "Press Red" isn't created by a single definitive forking, but by a large number of tiny branching events that gradually accumulate into a different outcome. In fact, not only is a single piece of knowledge not encoded by a single synapse, a single synapse may take part in encoding multiple pieces of knowledge. For example, a synapse that takes part in encoding "When the light comes on, press the red button" may also take part in encoding "George Washington was the first president of the United States." The brain has no way to "assign" a synapse to a particular fact. If a synapse takes part in a neural event associated with one piece of knowledge, it will be strengthened or weakened accordingly, even if that strengthening or weakening degrades its effectiveness in neural events associated with other pieces of knowledge.

At the cellular level, *this is what it means to know something*. A fact is a set of synaptic potentials that can alter the course of a ripple of excitation.

Knowing to press the green button results in a different set of motor signals than knowing to press the red button. Knowing that George Washington was the first president of the United States results in a different set of
motor signals than knowing that Simon Weishaupt was. Suppose you ask
me "Was George Washington the first president of the United States?" The
motor impulses that cause me to nod or shake my head are the result of a
long cascade of neural events. And the particular neural events that make
up this cascade are determined by the excitatory or inhibitory strength of
thousands of synapses.

The idea that knowledge consists of functional constraints maps very
nicely onto what we know about the low-level operation of the brain.
When we get down to the synaptic level we don't observe a mechanism for
storing data the way a book or a computer does. We simply observe a distributed mechanism for biasing neural events toward or away from certain
motor outcomes. We observe a system of constraints.

Dopamine and Learning

The adjustment of synaptic weights within the brain is controlled through
the release of a third neurotransmitter called dopamine.[3] It is a general rule
within neuroscience that "neurons that fire together, wire together."[4] However, recent research suggests that this wiring only takes place when the
firing occurs in the presence of dopamine. A neuron can fire repeatedly
during the course of normal brain activity and the strength of its synapses
will remain relatively stable. But if a separate neural event simultaneously triggers other nearby neurons to release dopamine, then the neuron
will respond by increasing the strength of its connections when it fires.
Basically, the dopamine system is the brain's way of encoding significance.

3. The bulk of information in this section on recent research on dopamine is drawn
from the 2010 survey article "Dopamine in Motivational Control: Rewarding, Aversive, and Alerting" by Bromberg-Martin, Matsumoto, and Hikosaka. The description
of the role of dopamine here refers primarily to the functioning of the mesolimbic
and mesocortical dopamine pathways.

4. This principle is known as Hebb's Rule: "Let us assume that the persistence or
repetition of a reverberatory activity (or 'trace') tends to induce lasting cellular
changes that add to its stability. ... When an axon of cell A is near enough to excite
a cell B and repeatedly or persistently takes part in firing it, some growth process or
metabolic change takes place in one or both cells such that A's efficiency, as one of
the cells firing B, is increased." Hebb, *The Organization of Behavior*, 49–50.

The presence of dopamine tells a neuron: "This pattern of firing that you are taking part in right now is important. Do it more strongly in the future."[5]

There are several circumstances that can trigger a release of dopamine. The first and most powerful is receiving a reward. Animals that are given food or water experience an immediate dopamine spike. The spike has the effect of reinforcing whatever pattern of neural firing is in progress when the reward is offered. This response is how the brain associates actions with outcomes, and is the mechanism underlying classical Pavlovian conditioning. If you ring a bell when you offer food to a dog, the resulting dopamine spike will strengthen the connections between the neurons that are responding to the bell and the neurons that are responding to the food. Do this repeatedly and the connections become strong enough that the dog will salivate in response to a bell even if food isn't present. At its most fundamental level, this value response makes sure that behaviors that are associated with positive outcomes are encouraged, and behaviors that are associated with negative outcomes are discouraged.

However, our dopamine reward system also contains an additional, subtle twist. Dopamine only spikes when we receive an *unexpected* reward. If we predict a positive outcome before it arrives, then our response to it vanishes. Instead, the dopamine spike comes at the moment when we first predict the outcome. The value response is displaced from the reward itself onto the cue that foreshadows it. The displacement of the value response from outcome to anticipation allows us to link behaviors into causal chains. The dopamine spike originally associated with eating a piece of bacon can be displaced onto the act of picking it up off the plate, or the act of cooking it, or the act of buying it at the store, or the act of driving to the store, or the act of finding our missing car keys. Situations or actions that we recognize as steps toward goals become intermediate goals themselves.

This displacement of the value response results in a second dopamine trigger: salience. Salience is the property of a sensory event that causes it to stand out from the background. For example, a charging lion is a salient stimulus, whereas a pile of rocks is not. Salience coding is how our brains

5. Like all the neuroscience in this chapter, this is somewhat of a simplification. Research with rats that lack the capability to produce dopamine demonstrates that other neurotransmitters can fill in for dopamine in a pinch. Learning can occur without dopamine, but the alternate mechanisms are much weaker. Dopamine is still the primary neurotransmitter responsible for the adjustment of synaptic weights. For more information, see Cannon and Palmiter, "Reward without Dopamine."

distinguish important stimuli from unimportant ones. Ultimately, what determines the salience of an event is the weight assigned to it by the value response—an important stimulus is one that tells us something good or bad may be happening soon. However, the salience response differs from the value response in that it isn't just triggered by rewards, *but also by penalties*.

Whereas the value response biases our actions toward positive outcomes, the salience response biases our attention toward meaningful patterns. We are constantly bombarded by a stream of diverse sensations, and we need to be able to quickly extract patterns from the stream that imply positive or negative outcomes.

The third circumstance that triggers a dopamine response is when something unexpected happens. The unexpected event need not be important; it need only be unforeseen. For example, suppose you walk into the kitchen and notice your coffee mug sitting on the counter, even though you don't remember getting it out of the cupboard. The location of the mug isn't particularly significant in and of itself. What makes it significant is that its location not something you expected. Having your expectations thwarted is enough by itself to trigger a spike in dopamine.

This is called the alerting response, and it ties into both the salience and the value responses. In general, we direct our attention toward things that our salience response has taught us are important—unless we are surprised by something that is out of the ordinary. And in general, we pursue courses of action that our value response has taught us are beneficial—unless our actions produce a result we weren't expecting. The alerting response acts as an error-correction mechanism on the other two responses. It weeds out synaptic connections that may have been formed by coincidence. For example, suppose that the first time I meet a dog, he snarls at me. My value and salience responses will lay down a pattern of synaptic firing that will make me warier the next time I encounter him. However, if he surprises me by not snarling the next time I meet him, my alerting response will trigger in response to my thwarted expectations and moderate my wariness.

We can summarize the relationships between the three different dopamine responses with a diagram (figure 9.5). Value neurons release dopamine when we receive a reward, or when we receive evidence that a reward is forthcoming. This reinforces broader patterns of neural firing, encouraging us to repeat thoughts and behaviors that correlate with rewards (even if the correlation is mere coincidence). The displaced triggering of the value neurons sets the criteria for what we consider important. The salience

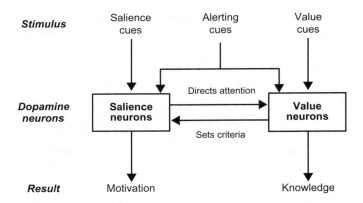

Figure 9.5
The three dopamine pathways.

neurons use these criteria to direct our attention toward certain stimuli and away from others, sharpening the response of the value neurons. Both of these systems can be overridden by the alerting response. When something unexpected happens, our attention is drawn to it, even if it isn't something we would ordinarily consider important. And if our thoughts and behaviors don't yield the outcomes we expect, the alerting response prompts the value neurons to nudge us toward a new set of synaptic weights that are more accurate.

These three pathways are the dominant mechanism by which *all* new information is encoded in the brain. Our understanding of the world consists of a collection of synaptic constraints, and these constraints change when one of these pathways—value, salience, alerting—triggers a spike of dopamine. This is why our thoughts and actions are so easily hijacked by food, sex, status, or money. And why it is easier to learn new information about topics we care a lot about. And why we remember unique occurrences more easily than everyday ones.

These three dopamine pathways have a significant effect on the structure of play spaces. The value pathway biases our behavior toward the pursuit of goals, whereas the displacement of the value response allows us to construct intermediate goals that are steps toward accomplishing other goals. The salience pathway directs our attention to features of the play space that the value pathway has identified as important. And the alerting pathway overrules the others when a crux occurs. What this means is that we learn things more readily in situations in which the knowledge is clearly applicable to accomplishing something that we want to accomplish, and where the knowledge represents a surprising insight—the resolution of an unexpected crux.

The way that these dopamine pathways structure our mental lives also reveals something fundamental about how our brains work: Before an alerting cue can warn us that our expectations have been thwarted, our brains first need to *have* expectations. And since we can never know where a surprise will come from next (otherwise it wouldn't be a surprise) we need to have expectations about *everything*. The existence of the alerting cue implies that, rather than simply responding to the unfolding world around us, our brains actively anticipate it, and that much of what we experience from moment to moment is the product of this active anticipation.

Motor Control and Anticipation

All creatures with brains have one thing have in common: They move around. Not everything that moves around has a brain, but, without exception, everything that has a brain moves around (or will move around in the near future). In fact, creatures that stop moving around as part of their life cycle quickly shed their brains as unnecessary extravagances. A prime example of this is the sea squirt. In its larval form, it resembles a tadpole. It has one eye, and a simple brain, and it survives by swimming around to avoid predators while seeking out a suitable rock to make its permanent home. When it finds such a rock, it attaches itself and, as a first step toward adulthood, digests its own brain. Once a sea squirt stops moving around, its brain no longer serves any useful purpose.[6]

It is easy to see why brains are linked to moving around. Any sort of organized movement requires an assortment of muscles to contract in a specific sequence. This is true whether we are talking about a human's walking gait or about the full-body undulation of a swimming flatworm. In order to the muscles of a moving creature to twitch in the appropriate pattern, there has to be a nervous system that controls the timing of each muscle contraction.

Furthermore, movement is always more useful if it is directed toward a goal. Moving around at random may accidentally carry a creature toward food or away from a predator, but a more successful strategy is to sense

6. This anecdote comes from Wolpert's talk "The Real Reason for Brains."

a reward or danger and adjust your movement accordingly. For example, flatworms have tiny eyespots they use to detect light. These eyespots don't form images—flatworms don't see the way we think of seeing—but they do generate neural signals that bias the flatworm's undulations toward the direction where the light is fainter. The flatworm's tiny brain transforms information about photon intensity into a coordinated swimming behavior that allows the worm to avoid bright light.

Simple brains such as the flatworm's respond to the state of the world as it is right now. But more complicated brains are capable of making predictions about how the world is likely to be in the future. If a creature is capable of directed movement, the usefulness of making accurate predictions is obvious. If I'm a frog trying to catch a fly with my tongue, I want to aim for where the fly will be a few milliseconds in the future, not where it is right now. If I'm a gazelle running for my life from a ravenous lion, I want to zig in a direction opposite to the direction the lion is going to zag. While simple brains take sensory stimulus and translate it directly into motor response, more complicated brains use the stimulus to generate a prediction of how the world will unfold in the future, and then derive a motor response from that prediction.

A complicated moving creature, such as a human being, has to make a lot of little predictions just to navigate the world. While it might be theoretically possible to calculate each prediction directly from sensory evidence, it is much more efficient to maintain a single general predictive model that is continually tweaked and corrected by input from the senses. This single general model can drive a large number of different actions without having to start from scratch each time. And neuroscientists have found evidence for just such a model by studying the role that anticipation plays in motor control.

For example, suppose you are holding a ketchup bottle upside down and shaking it to get the ketchup to come out. In order to keep the bottle from slipping, you need to tighten your grip at the bottom of each shake. If you equip the bottle with a force sensor, you can measure how much your grip changes and when. When test subjects perform this task, their grip tightens in synch with the increasing load. If they were tightening their grip in response to *feeling* the bottle slipping, there would be a little lag. Instead, experiments show that the test subjects know exactly how much to increase their grip *before* they receive any sensory input.

Furthermore, this effect can be disrupted simply by having someone else tap the bottle. If the increased load comes from an external source, the test subjects still tighten their grips, but their response lags behind the tap, and is stronger than necessary to stop the bottle from slipping.[7] What this means is that our brains are constantly anticipating intended movements. When we shake a ketchup bottle, the force of our grip is in synch with the varying load because the motor signals sent to our hand are the output of a chain of neural events that models the action before it occurs.

Even more interesting is the fact that although our grip alternates between being stronger and weaker as we shake the bottle, *it feels as though our grip remains constant.* Not only are we anticipating how much force we need to exert to keep the bottle from slipping; we are also anticipating how much pressure our fingertips should feel as a result of this force. And if the expected pressure matches the actual pressure, then we experience the sensation of maintaining a steady grip, even though our grip isn't steady at all.

This seemingly mundane experimental observation has profound episte-mological implications. We have an intuitive sense that our senses operate like a window on the world. We experience things, and it seems very much like what we are experiencing is a direct product of the world around us: I see a tree in front of me because there is a tree there in front of me for me to see. But what the ketchup bottle experiment demonstrates is that our naive sense of how our senses function is incorrect. We don't experience the world as it is; we experience it as a computationally convenient neural construct.

Our brains (and the brains of other complicated animals) support a con-stant cyclical cascade of neural events. Ripples of excitation flow through the densely interconnected web of neurons. The paths they take are gov-erned by the excitatory or inhibitory potential of trillions of synapses. These free-running cognitive loops generate motor signals to control our muscles, but they also spit out a collection of sensory predictions. These predictions are an abstraction of the sensory traces we can expect to encounter in the near future if the understanding of the world encoded in our synapses is correct (figure 9.6).

7. "When dealing with such unpredictable objects, our grip force is modified reac-tively in response to sensory feedback from the fingertips, with the consequence that the grip tends to lag behind. However, when we direct behavior toward objects in the environment that exhibit stable properties, predictive control mechanisms can be effectively exploited. For example, when the load is increased by a self-generated action, such as moving the arm, the grip forces increases in parallel with the load force with no delay. Sensory detection of the load is too slow to account for this increased grip force which relies on predictive processes." Wolpert and Flana-gan, "Motor Prediction."

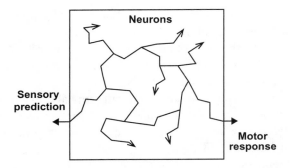

Figure 9.6
Free-running loops generate actions and predictions.

Thus, when I "see" a tree in front of me, there isn't a simple cause-and-effect chain tying the photons emitted by the tree to the image of the tree in my mind. The image of the tree in my mind is a neural construct.[8] It is a prediction based on the knowledge of the world that is encoded in my synapses. I don't see a tree because there is a tree in front of me to see. I see a tree because seeing a tree is the expected consequence of my current understanding of the world.

Of course, seeing things that aren't there isn't of much use. If I think I see a tree in front of me, then it should be because there really is the functional equivalent of a tree in front of me. And so our brains continually test our sensory predictions against the incoming signals from our sensory receptors. The results of those tests are then used to tweak the behavior of our free-running neural loops by slightly adjusting the strength of the relevant synapses (figure 9.7). This tweaking is done through the alerting response of the dopamine system. When our senses disagree with what our brains predict, it triggers a spike of dopamine that drives the active synapses to adjust their weights until the disagreement is eliminated. The intruder in the hallway suddenly resolves into a shadow on the wall; the fleeing stray cat becomes a plastic bag tumbling in the wind.

This is the neural counterpart to the epistemological cycle. Free-running patterns of neural excitation driven by our synaptic constraints generate

8. "The disposition of matter and energy in the world is accessible to the brain exclusively through the mediation of its sensory apparatus (which includes the five external senses and the various interceptive channels). No matter how veridical some of the information provided by these senses is, the representations they feed into are necessarily VIRTUAL computational constructs." Edelman, *Computing the Mind*, 419.

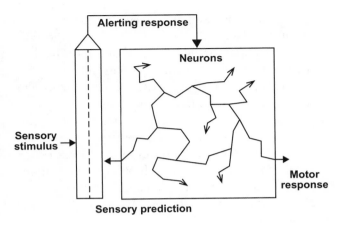

Figure 9.7
Using sensation to tweak the free-running loops.

predictions of future sensory experience. Mismatches between these predictions and our actual sensations are cruxes. These mismatches trigger a release of dopamine that perturbs the patterns of excitation until they generate matching predictions that resolve the crux. Once the crux has been resolved the process continues with new synaptic weights (our new constraint-based understanding) governing the future course of our thoughts.

Knowledge construction isn't something that we do only through deliberate effort; it's the natural, automatic way that our brains function from moment to moment. And the anticipation of future events isn't merely a state of mind that we adopt from time to time; it is woven into the most fundamental fabric of our mental experience. Our brains are engines for predicting the future, and the experiential world we inhabit is the product of those predictions.

The predictive model that is formed through this process is situational and heterogeneous. Our understanding of any aspect of the world—a tree, a teapot, a taxicab—is the product of a lifetime of encounters with trees, teapots and taxicabs. Each new encounter creates opportunities for new cruxes and the possibility of forming new constraints. These new constraints are shaped by the circumstances of their formation, and so our understanding of the world is inevitably an assemblage of disjointed solutions to a multiplicity of situational challenges. Concise, general constraints that repeatedly demonstrate predictive value across a broad range of circumstances tend to get more reinforcement, and so tend to dominate over the long run, but they co-exist with narrow, idiosyncratic interpretations that linger on long after the wayward dopamine spikes that accidentally inscribed them on our synapses. For the most part our thoughts flow safely along the broad courses defined by our dominant constraints, but they also leak out along narrower lines of affordance, leading us sometimes to odd and unexpected states of mind, strange eddies of neural activity, unexpected insights, random associations, and curious discontinuities and ruptures.

This neural model offers an explanation for how we go about constructing knowledge at both the small and the large scales. It gives us a way to understand how we assemble sensory traces into coherent experiences, and how we distill these experiences into broader interpretations. It describes how we take the accidental, unmediated flux of the unfolding world and organize it into a set of functional constraints that will allow us to navigate life from moment to moment (or from year to year).

However, not all of the sensory traces we experience are accidental. Many of them arise from objects or situations that are intended to have a specific effect on us. Videogames, short stories, traffic signs, symphonies, billboards, conversations, police uniforms, history books, action movies, theme parks, instruction manuals, oil paintings, courtrooms, basketball courts, war memorials, pop songs, gold coins, skyscrapers, science museums, candy wrappers—all of these things exist in order to drive our epistemological cycles toward particular ways of understanding the world. And analyzing these sorts of intentional knowledge-generating experiences is the topic of the next chapter.

Semiotics is the study of mediated meaning-making.[1] It examines how certain objects and situations can be imbued with symbolic weight that transcends their physical form. As a result, it offers a framework for understanding how arbitrary sensory patterns can trigger the construction of particular mental states. For example, semiotics addresses the question of how reading a sentence such as "The cat is on the mat" can lead to knowing that the cat is, in fact, on the mat, or how seeing a red traffic light can lead to knowing that it would be dangerous to enter the intersection.

It is important to accommodate semiotics within our play-based critical framework because so much of play involves the exchange of symbols between players. If I'm playing a game of basketball and I call out that I am open, that is a meaningful move within the play space. I'm attempting to change the unfolding of the game by constructing a particular internal constraint in the mind of my teammate. Some games are only interesting when you take into account the welter of tiny communicative acts that pass back and forth between players while they are being played. Poker, for example, become a fairly dull game of odds if you strip away the multiple layers of feint and indirection as players bluff to gain advantage.

1. Like neuroscience, semiotics is a vast and ramified field, and a brief introduction can't do justice to the many different schools of thought that it contains. Rather than attempting to engage with the full breadth of semiotic scholarship, I am instead borrowing certain core concepts that relate directly to the understanding of play and modifying them to operate within a ludic framework. Besides drawing on the foundational work of Saussure and Peirce, this chapter touches on the work of Roland Barthes, Umberto Eco, Jacques Derrida, Daniel Dennett, and John Searle. For a good general overview of semiotics, I recommend Chandler's *Semiotics: The Basics*, particularly the opening chapters on signs. A more detailed exploration of the foundational issues in this chapter can be found in Barthes' *Elements of Semiology* and Eco's *Theory of Semiotics*.

Semiotic play is important even in single-player games. There the communication is not from player to player, but from designer to player. If
I'm designing a game and I want it to communicate a particular mood or
idea to the player, it is useful to have a model for how this communication
can occur. If players are allowed to choose their own trajectories through a
play space, how can a designer hope to create a game that is intentionally
meaningful—a game that says what the designer intended for it to say?
Thus, in this chapter we are going to take a look at how communicative
acts can be modeled, and at how this model can be incorporated into our
discourse of play.

The core concept of semiotics is the sign. Roughly speaking, a sign is
when one thing stands for another thing. For example, if I write the word
'dog', that pattern of marks on the page stands in for a dog. When you read
the word you think about dogs, even if there are no dogs nearby.

A sign is a relationship. It is the linking of two different things so that
one can stand for the other. The most common formulation of the sign
relationship was developed by the Swiss linguist Ferdinand de Saussure near
the end of the nineteenth century. Saussure's signs consist of two elements,
a signified and a signifier (figure 10.1).[2] The signified is a thing—an object,
a concept, an emotion—and the signifier is an arbitrary symbol that has
been chosen to stand for that thing. The two arrows represent the reciprocal nature of the relationship between the signifier and the signified—the
signifier can trigger thoughts of the signified and the signified can trigger
thoughts of the signifier. Reading the word 'dog' can make you think of
dogs, and seeing a dog can make you think of the word that refers to it.

A central element of the concept of the sign is the arbitrary nature of the
signifier. The linkage of signifier to signified is a matter of convention, not
necessity. For example, the word 'dog' bears no resemblance to a real dog. I
could have typed 'chien' or 'perro' or 'inu' instead. Words are tags that we
attach to things so we can talk and think about them, but the sounds and

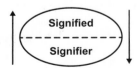

Figure 10.1
The Saussurean sign.

2. Saussure, *Course in General Linguistics*, 65–70.

the marks that we choose as tags have no inherent meaning. They mean what they mean because we have assigned those meanings to them.

Strictly speaking, Saussurean signs are entirely mental constructs. The linkage between signifier and signified occurs in our heads, so the signifier actually refers to our mental image of a symbol, and not to the symbol out in the world. Similarly, the signified refers to our understanding of a thing, and not to that thing out in the world. A sign is the linkage between our *perception* of the word 'dog' and our *conception* of dogs, not between the word 'dog' and actual dogs—although this distinction is often overlooked. Printed or spoken words are often referred to as *signifiers*, and the objects they stand in for as *signifieds*.

The distinction between things in the world and our internal mental representations of those things is made explicit by the alternate formulation of the sign put forward by Charles Sanders Peirce. Peirce developed his semiotics independently of Saussure's; he arrived at his notion of the sign not through linguistics, but through his exploration of pragmatic epistemology. And whereas Saussure was primarily interested in the two-way relationship between words and ideas, Peirce used signs as a way to formalize the three-way relationship between words, ideas, and the things that those words and ideas are directed toward.

As a result, whereas Saussurean signs are dyads, Peircean signs are triads.[3] They contain three elements instead of two (figure 10.2). The *representamen* corresponds to Saussure's signifier; the *interpretant* corresponds to Saussure's signified. Both are internal mental constructs. But also contained within

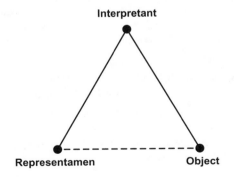

Figure 10.2
The Peircean sign.

3. Peirce, "Sundry Logical Conceptions," *The Essential Peirce*, volume 2, 272–273.

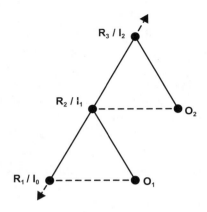

Figure 10.3
The Peircean semiotic chain figure.

the Peircean sign is the *object*, the external thing to which the sign refers. For example, in Peirce's system our perception of the word 'dog' is a representamen, our understanding of dogs is the corresponding interpretant, and the physical existence of dogs in the world is an object.

Peirce's triadic signs can be linked together to form *semiotic chains* (figure 10.3). A mental state that serves as the interpretant in one sign may serve as the representamen of a different sign. So, for example, our knowledge that we have read the word 'dog' acts as the interpretant in a sign that has the word on the page as the object. But it also acts as the representamen in a sign that has our understanding of dogs as the interpretant and real-world dogs as the object. And our understanding of dogs can then act as the representamen in a third sign that has our understanding of loyalty as the interpretant, and so on. Reading the word 'dog' will not necessarily result in us just thinking about dogs; it can trigger a long sequence of associations as our thoughts hop from sign to sign along the semiotic chain. Eventually we might wind up at a sign whose object is quite remote from the original triggering stimulus—Alaskan sled races, ritual uncleanness, Egyptian gods, duck hunting, and so on. The Peircean sign isn't merely a description of the relationship between a symbol and an idea. It is a modular building block for conceptualizing the iterative process of translating a symbol into an idea about something in the world.

While both Saussurean and Peircean signs have been widely used over the last hundred years, both formulations have some deficiencies if we want to incorporate them into a play-based critical framework. The first is the problem of "floating," "sliding," or "empty" signifiers. Both definitions of the sign contain the implicit assumption of a stable one-to-one correspondence between symbols and ideas—that we can neatly pair up signifiers with matching signifieds. This assumption works well enough for many practical forms of discourse; if I say "Please hand me the screwdriver," it is likely that you and I will both connect the signifier 'screwdriver' to similar ideas of what constitutes a screwdriver, i.e., similar signifieds, and the resulting shared sign will be relatively stable. But the stability of signs begins to break down when we consider their application to more nuanced and ambiguous forms of communication.

As an extreme example, consider the lyrics of songs such as "I Am the Walrus" and "Lucy in the Sky with Diamonds." The lyrics of these songs are meaningful, but it isn't possible to arrive at that meaning simply by considering them as a sequence of fixed signs. Even the Peircean notion of semiotic chains is inadequate to describe the "piling up" of meaning that accrues as these songs unfold, the way that each sign caroms off the signs that preceded it, sending our interpretations skittering off in unexpected directions. The interpretation that each individual listener arrives at is likely to be highly idiosyncratic, and may even be different from one hearing of the song to another.

The literary scholar Jacques Derrida raises this point explicitly in his essay "Structure, Sign and Play in the Discourse of the Human Sciences," in which he points out that the multiplicity of moves within a discourse cannot be reduced to the meaning of the concepts used to structure the discourse:

> The movement of signification adds something, which results in the fact that there is always more, but this addition is a floating one because it comes to perform a vicarious function, to supplement a lack on the part of the signified.[4]

In other words, the play within a system of signs can produce meanings not found within the signs themselves. The multiplicity of signifieds that emerge in the process of play will inevitably float free of the finite pool of signifiers.

The second issue with accommodating signs within a play-based critical framework is the problem of *ineffable signifieds*. When we play a game, there are many things we understand that aren't paired with signifiers. For example, in a racing game, we can *feel* what we need to do in order to weave

---

4. Derrida, "Structure, Sign and Play in the Discourse of the Human Sciences," in *Writing and Difference*, 292.

in and out through a tight pack of cars, but it is difficult to articulate the nuances of this feeling or reduce it to a clear-cut set of rules. There isn't a signifier that stands for our understanding of how to weave through packs of cars the way that 'dog' stands for our understanding of dogs. Much of the understanding that we gain when we play games is simply expressed through the act of playing them. We know what we should do and we proceed to do it, even if there isn't a name or symbol that can be used to stand for that knowledge.

Of course, it is possible to construct a signifier that stands for anything *after the fact*. We could decide that from now on we are going to refer to a particular sort of racing-game understanding as "pack-weaving technique," and we could then use that signifier as a shortcut for discussing how players weave through packs. But such a step, though possible and perhaps desirable, is *not necessary in order to play the game*. We can execute our pack-weaving technique just fine without ever having a signifier attached to it.

These two problems—floating signifiers and ineffable signifieds—are a large part of the reason why it is difficult to use semiotics to talk about games. Many of the strategies that emerge as we play have no corresponding signifiers, and the signifiers that we do encounter are often ambiguous and prone to floating free from any sort of fixed meaning.

Nevertheless, a sign-like theoretical construct can be still a useful tool for understanding how certain sensory traces can be used by one actor to intentionally drive the epistemological cycles of other actors toward particular states. Stated more simply, signs are still a good way to talk about how people communicate. For that reason, I am going to propose an alternate definition of the sign—one that shares many of the properties of both Saussurean and Peircean signs, but that fits more neatly within a play-based discourse.

The Ludic Sign

Our understanding of the world is encoded in the weights of our synapses. These synaptic weights act as constraints on looping cascades of excitation within our brains. These cascades generate a set of predictions about the unfolding of the world, and those predictions are continually tested against the evidence of our senses. Mismatches between prediction and sensation trigger minor adjustments to our synaptic weights until the crux is resolved.

As an abstraction of this process, we can think of a pattern of stimulus as causally linked to a corresponding set of constraints. For example, if I see a bear, my neural loops rapidly converge to include a set of constraints

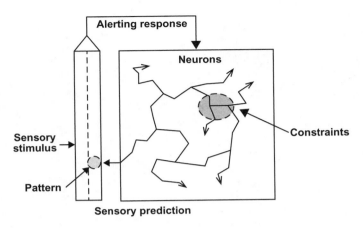

Figure 10.4
The functional relationship between pattern and constraint.

that mirror the "bearish" sensations I'm receiving. Those "bearish" constraints become part of my neural cascade because they provide the best predictive match for my sensory flow. This relationship between pattern and constraint is bidirectional. A pattern of stimulus triggers the activation of particular constraints because those constraints are capable of generating a matching pattern (figure 10.4).

However, my understanding of bears consists of much more than just knowing what they look like. I also know that bears are strong, and can run fast, and are capable of killing humans, and the synapses that encode all that information (and much more) are also linked to the synapses that encode what bears look like. Furthermore, the excitation of one neural pathway related to bears is very likely to trigger the excitation of the others. So when I see a bear and my cognitive loops lock onto the constraints that generate a "bearish" pattern, a large number of other constraints are brought into play as well, altering the overall direction of my thoughts. Eventually these new cascades of excitation may ground out in "bearish" motor responses—I might freeze in place, or run away, or raise a rifle, or exclaim "That's a bear," or merely reach out and touch the glass of the zoo enclosure to reassure myself. And all of these responses will be the result of "bearish" constraints becoming active in order to account for "bearish" sensations.

I call the encapsulation of this causal relationship *the ludic sign*. The ludic sign is a dyad that links a pattern to a set of constraints. The relationship is bi-directional. The constraints generate the pattern, and the presence of the

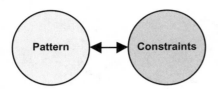

Figure 10.5
The ludic sign.

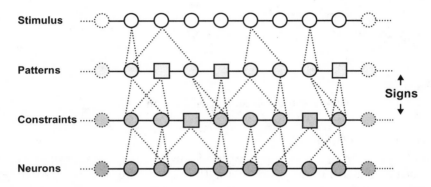

Figure 10.6
A hierarchy of "leaky" mappings.

pattern triggers the activation of the constraints (figure 10.5). In traditional semiotic terms, the pattern corresponds to the Saussurean signifier (or the Peircean representamen) and the constraints correspond to the Saussurean signified (or the Peircean interpretant).

However, it is important to note that this relationship between pattern and constraint depends on the overall activity of our brains. The constraints don't generate the pattern in a vacuum—rather, they do so only within the context of an ongoing cascade of other neural events. Given a pattern, the cascade will not necessarily converge on one default set of constraints. Rather, it will lock onto whichever constraints are first to generate a match. The ludic sign is not a representation of some fundamental relation between signifier and signified; it's merely shorthand for a transient neural event.

We can conceptualize this entire system as a hierarchy of mappings (figure 10.6). At the lowest level are the individual synapses—the actual working circuitry of the brain. At the second level are the constraints that structure our thoughts; each constraints is encoded by hundreds or thousands of synapses, and one synapse may take part in encoding multiple constraints. At the third level are sensory patterns that are tied to constraints through the epistemological cycle; one pattern can link to multiple constraints, and one constraint can link to multiple patterns. And at the top level are the sensory traces arriving from the external world. Semiosis flows from the top to the bottom of this hierarchy. Features within our sensory stream are as assembled into a pattern. This pattern is the result our neural loops converging on constraints that generate a match. And these constraints are physically realized by a cascade of excitation through our synapses.

However, there is slippage and leakage at each level. The patterns we perceive aren't absolute; they are merely the best match our neural loops can achieve at the moment. The particular constraints that happen to generate that match aren't inevitable; they can vary depending on our overall neural cascade. And the particular neurons that participate in the match aren't dedicated solely to that single pattern; they may also generate tangential patterns of excitation unrelated to the initiating stimulus.

Defining the sign in this way has several significant consequences. The first is that *all* signifiers are inherently floating. Which constraints generate a match in response to a particular pattern is dependent on our overall neural cascade. The stable relationship between signifier and signified implied by traditional semiotics is abandoned. Signifiers have no fixed signifieds, only *likely* signifieds given certain normative assumptions. A request such as "Please hand me the screwdriver" seems simple because I can be relatively certain that your current state of mind will probably cause the signifier 'screwdriver' to trigger the activation of a very particular set of matching constraints. However, this easy certainty vanishes in many other situations. I can't be nearly so certain about which constraints will become active when you hear the phrase "sitting in the blue corner of the unbidden." The resulting neural cascade is too idiosyncratic.

The second consequence is the recognition that not all constraints have corresponding patterns—in other words, that it is possible to know things without having a word or symbol that refers to that knowledge. We experience these ineffable constraints all the time when we play games or music; we can *feel* what we should do next, even though we find it difficult to articulate that feeling, or even think about it symbolically. Signs can be used to bring constraints into play, but a system of existing constraints can function as a play space even without any signifying acts.

Similarly, the pattern associated with a sign need not correspond to any real-world object; it's simply an arbitrary trigger for the activation of a particular set of constraints. For example, when I read the word 'unicorn' I think about unicorns, even though that particular set of constraints isn't tied any real-world entity. I can know lots of things about unicorns without ever seeing a real unicorn because knowing about unicorns is merely a matter of particular constraints' being linked to the pattern "unicorn." Or consider the word 'duty'. I know what duty is, even though I can't see duty the way I can see a bear. Knowing the word 'duty' gives me a way to tie together a wide variety of constraints that can't easily be triggered by an object or event in the real world.

Viewed from this perspective, *signs are a technology for the manipulation of internal constraints*. Words and symbols give us a way to bring particular constraints into play, even if the real-world objects that those constraints are directed toward are absent. By saying "bear" I can get you to think bearish thoughts without showing you a bear. Furthermore, signs allow us to construct collections of constraints that don't correlate with *any* real-world patterns; I can write a sentence such as "Captain America always does his duty" and it will make sense even though Captain America is a fictional character and "always" and "duty" are abstract concepts.

However, there is a catch. Although hearing the word 'bear' can stand in for seeing a bear, the substitution isn't exact. When I hear you say "bear," the constraints on which I converge will be directed not only toward the possible existence of a nearby bear, but also toward your beliefs and intentions. Are you telling the truth? Are you reliable? Do you intend for the word 'bear' to mean something other than the animal? The spoken word 'bear' doesn't just signify the animal, it also signifies a number of things about the speaker. And so, in order to understand how the ludic sign works to structure communication between human beings, we need to take a brief detour to explore how intentional actors are represented within a play-based epistemology.

The Intentional Stance

The philosopher Daniel Dennett has identified three broad conceptual frameworks that humans use to navigate reality: the *physical stance*, the *design stance*, and the *intentional stance*. These stances represent three different ways to use constraints to make predictions about the unfolding of the world around us.

The physical stance is how we make predictions about *objects*. If I pick up a rock and throw it at a tree, the only constraints that come into play are those that describe the rock's physical properties, my own muscular capabilities, and my intuitive knowledge of physics: I run a mental simulation of the rock's trajectory and that simulation causes the muscles in my arm to fire in the correct sequence for the throw to succeed. The physical stance is how we interact with raw hunks of matter.[5]

The design stance is how we make predictions about *tools*. Instead of basing our predictions on the raw physicality of a thing, we base them on what the thing is supposed to do. Chairs are for sitting on, hammers are for driving nails, cars are for driving, laptop computers are for writing books. Adopting the design stance makes many aspects of life simpler. If I see a chair, I instantly know that there is a place for me to sit. I don't have to spend time carefully analyzing the physical properties of every object in the room in the hope that one of them will be large and sturdy enough to support me.[6]

Dennett's third stance—the intentional stance—is how we make predictions about *living creatures*. If I see a little girl playing in the park, I don't think of her as a mass of bone and muscle with a particular velocity (although that isn't an inaccurate way to think about her). Nor do I think about her as an automaton driven by its neural circuitry to execute a particular pattern of herky-jerky arm movements (although that isn't an inaccurate way to think about her, either). Instead, I think of her as a little girl pretending to be a butterfly. Just as the design stance abstracts away the physicality of a tool by replacing it with its utility, the intentional stance abstracts away both the physicality and the utility of a living creature and replaces it with a predictive model based on a mental landscape of ideas, beliefs, desires, and intentions.[7]

5. "Consider the physical strategy or physical stance; if you want to predict the behavior of a system, determine its physical constitution (perhaps all the way down to the microphysical level) and the physical nature of the impingements upon it, and use your knowledge of the laws of physics to predict the output for any input." Dennett, *The Intentional Stance*, 16.

6. "Sometimes, in any event, it is more effective to switch from the physical stance to what I call the design stance, where one ignores the actual (possibly messy) details of the of the physical constitution of the object, and, on the assumption that it has a certain design, predicts that it will behave as it was designed to behave under various circumstances." Dennett, *The Intentional Stance*, 16–17.

7. "Sometimes even the design stance is practically inaccessible, and then there is yet another stance or strategy one can adopt: the intentional stance. Here is how it works: first you decide to treat the object whose behavior is to be predicted as a rational agent; then you figure out what beliefs that agent ought to have, given its place in the world and its purpose. Then you figure out what desires it ought to have, on the same considerations, and finally you predict that this rational agent will act to further its goals in the light of its beliefs. A little practical reasoning from the chosen set of beliefs and desires will in many—but not all—instances yield a decision about what the agent ought to do; that is what you predict the agent *will* do." Dennett, *The Intentional Stance*, 17.

The intentional stance offers us a way for us to understand how living creatures navigate the world without trying to model them at either the physical or the design level. The little girl is *pretending* to be a butterfly because she *wants* to. We can tell she is *enjoying* herself because we can hear her laughing. Her arms are moving up and down because she is *imagining* that they are wings. The little girl's desires and beliefs and thoughts are, ultimately, the product of the weights of her synapses, just as the operation of her synapses is the product of particular chemical reactions, and those chemical reactions are the product of quantum effects at the subatomic level. But trying to understand her at any of those lower levels is far, far too complicated. So instead, we understand her with a far more tractable set of interpretive constraints.

Our understanding of the world necessarily includes an understanding of other human beings. This understanding of other human beings is functional—we have a set of interpretive constraints that make predictions about what other people are likely to do. These interpretive constraints do not simulate other brains at the neural level; rather, they generate a higher-level approximation of that low-level behavior. In other words, we believe that people have ideas, beliefs, desires and intentions because believing in those things creates a system of constraints that generates useful predictions about how people will behave.[8]

8. Although we can use the words 'belief' and 'desire' to talk about how we form expectations about others, the interpretative constraints that they correspond to may not necessarily be so tidy and accessible. In other words, I can predict your behavior without consciously having a well-articulated *theory* of your behavior, much as I can know how to weave through a pack of cars in a racing game without being able to articulate or even comprehend how I know such a thing. The process by which I arrive at my expectations of others is, for the most part, opaque to me. I find that I simply *know* what you will probably do—or, even more likely, I simply *act* as though I know what you will probably do without even noticing that I have formed an expectation. Or, as the philosopher Jane Heal writes, "When I want to know what you might think or decide, I try to imagine the world as it appears to you and explore some of the further states of affairs and requirements for action implicit in that world. If I am successful in this, I shall (in part) re-create your point of view, your trains of thought and likely decisions. I may thus come to some views on what you are likely to think or do, and I shall do so without calling on any detailed theory about how thoughts interact or what they give rise to. Where such use of the imagination gives me insight into what another is likely to believe or intend, it does so in virtue of the fact that I and that other share the capacity to think about the world in first-order ways rather than in virtue of my possession of a theoretical, second-order, representation of that capacity." Heal, *Mind, Reason, and Imagination*, 3.

And, indeed, if we stop to introspectively consider our own mental processes, we discover that the intentional stance also gives us useful answers about our own behavior. Even though I know rationally that my mental experience is the consequence of cascades of excitation through a weighted network of neurons, I *understand* my mental experience through a higher-level collection of interpretive constraints. I'm writing this book because I *want* to write it. I'm *thinking* about play while I'm typing it. I'm *hoping* that once it has been finished a lot of people will read it. The intentional stance gives me a computationally convenient set of interpretive constraints that account for (and make predictions about) my own mental experience.

Ludic Semiosis

When I see a bear, my neural cascade quickly converges on a set of bearish constraints that make predictions that match the sensations I'm receiving. Believing that there is a bear in front of me is generally the most effective way to resolve the crux triggered by the appearance of unexpected "bearish" sensations in my sensory flow.

However, things play out differently if, instead of seeing a bear, I hear you shout "There's a bear behind you!" I might resolve the crux by concluding that there is a bear behind me. Or I might resolve the crux by concluding that you are playing a joke on me. My understanding of the meaning of your shout depends a great deal on my understanding of *you*. When I interpret your shout, I do so parsimoniously; my epistemological cycle converges on an interpretation that minimizes the disruption to my overall system of constraints, including the constraints that encapsulate my understanding of you.

As a result, the sentence "There's a bear behind you!" can mean a number of different things:

There is a bear behind me.
You are playing a joke on me.
Someone in a bear costume is playing a joke on both of us.
The dim light is making you see things.
You have mistaken my large dog for a bear.
You are hallucinating.
I am hallucinating.

By way of the intentional stance, I have a predictive model of your behavior. This model operates by attributing to you a set of ideas, beliefs, desires, and intentions that accurately account for your actions. This model makes

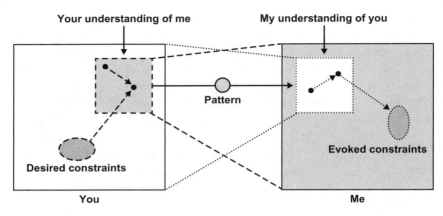

Figure 10.7
Reciprocal understanding during ludic semiosis.

predictions about the sorts of things you are likely to say from moment to moment. I then use what you actually say to make continuous tweaks to this model.

Furthermore, not only do I have a predictive model of you, you have a predictive model of me. And you use this predictive model when you are deciding what to say. The words you choose are the words you believe will shift my thoughts in a desired direction. They are the product of an iterative predictive process involving the internal constraints that encapsulate your understanding of me. (figure 10.7).

Of course, both your understanding of me and my understanding of you are interpretations. Our respective intentional models make predictions about each other's behaviors without replicating the actual neural machinery that is generating those behaviors. As a result, neither one of us can be completely certain of the accuracy of the predictions that these models make. You may believe from your understanding of me that I'll conclude that there is a bear behind me, but because of my understanding of you, I might arrive a different conclusion—that you're just playing a joke.

With this model of semiosis, there is no fixed relationship between signifiers and signifieds. The ludic sign isn't an atom of meaning, it's merely a tool for conceptualizing a transient causal linkage between pattern and constraint during a communicative event. If words sometimes appear to mean specific things, it's only because we often find ourselves in situations in which the reciprocal understanding of speaker and listener produces the desired evoked constraints. I know what a screwdriver is, and you know what a screwdriver is, and you know I know what I screwdriver is, and I know you know what a screwdriver is, and so when I ask you to hand me one, the communication produces the intended result.

Our ways of understanding of each other are situational and heterogeneous. I have a hodgepodge of constraints that I have built up from a lifetime of interactions with other people, and from my specific interactions with you. I don't have a monolithic, unified internal representation of you as a person, rather, I have an assortment of intentional strategies that are appropriate for different situations. Some of these strategies may be very simple—I don't need to understand you very well to successfully ask you to hand me a screwdriver—while others may be quite complex.

In some situations, my understanding of you may even include a simplified version of your understanding of me, and vice versa. You know that I know that you like to joke, so when you try to come up with something to say to warn me about the bear you realize that just saying "There's a bear behind you!" isn't good enough. So you say "I'm not joking! There really is a bear behind you!" instead. These recursive self-representations are an important element of many semiotic processes[9] (figure 10.8).

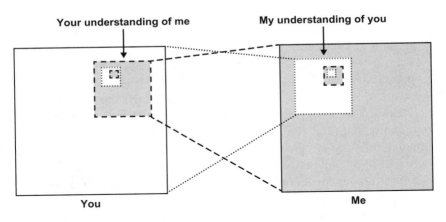

Figure 10.8
Recursive self-representation as an element of reciprocal understanding.

9. The idea of recursive self-representations allows this model of semiosis to encompass not only factual communication, but also illocutionary and perlocutionary speech acts. An illocutionary speech act is an utterance that brings about a state of affairs when spoken: "I now pronounce you husband and wife." A perlocutionary speech act is an utterance that produces a change in attitude in the recipient: "I love you." In both of these cases, the effect of the words on the listener transcends their informational content. For more information on performative speech, see Austin, *How to Do Things with Words* and Searle, *Speech Acts*.

The apparent paradox of a brain containing an infinite regression of self-representations is resolved by noting that each level of representation is simpler than the level above it, and that in practice we don't need an infinite number of regressions to make useful prediction about how people behave. The level of recursion depends on the nuances of the situation. A simple request may require no recursion at all; a complicated negotiation may involve both of us working through three or four levels of nested interpretive constraints.

It is also important to keep in mind that this entire process is unfolding in real time. The phrase "There's a bear behind you!" isn't generated or decoded as a unit, but rather as a stream of words and/or phonemes that play out over the course of a second or so. During any communication semiosis is continuous, working on fine-grained signifiers within a sequence in the order they are received. The terminal meaning of a communication isn't the result of a single monolithic attempt to account for the entire collection of patterns. Rather, it is a product of a long chain of tiny, fleeting microsemiotic events, each triggered by a subtle shift in the expected moment-to-moment unfolding of our sensory stream. Meaning accrues from the "piling up" of these tiny semiotic events; each act of microsemiosis builds on what has come before to incrementally produce a larger shift in our understanding of the world.

For the most part, all of this occurs outside of the sphere of our awareness. Unless we are being particularly careful about choosing out words, we're usually not conscious of the mental calculations required to generate an utterance. Similarly, when we hear someone speaking, the evoked meaning usually manifests itself so quickly and seamlessly that it feels like an inherent property of the words themselves, and not the non-deterministic outcome of a chaotic cascade of hundreds of tiny acts of microsemiosis.

What this model allows us to do is break away from the notion that communication is a deterministic process. Traditional semiosis encourages us to think in terms of coding and decoding: Signifiers are tightly tied to particular signifieds. We construct meaningful utterances by stringing together a collection of signifiers that encode the message that we want to transmit. The recipient of the message then decodes these signifiers to arrive at the intended message. Slippage between signifiers and signifieds, when it occurs, is treated as an aberration or a transgression, a breakdown or deliberate sabotage of the system. More important, there is no room in traditional semiosis for *structured* play. Signifiers may have the potential to set off chains of signification, but there aren't any tools for understanding the mechanics of how these chains unfold. It's like trying to understand chess by observing that the players are free to make moves without engaging with the rules that determine which moves they are free to make.

In ludic semiosis, there are two different systems of constraints in play. The speaker is navigating a functional model of the listener, exploring the anticipatory chains generated by different possible utterances to discover the one most likely to evoke a desired set of interpretive constraints. And the listener is navigating a functional model of the speaker, attempting to arrive at a new set of interpretive constraints that will cohere with their existing understanding. These two systems of constraints—the internal constraints of the speaker, and the internal constraints of the listener—do not *necessarily* form play spaces. As we saw in part I of this book, systems of constraints generate play only when they obey the heuristics. So often when two people communicate with each other there isn't any play going on, just a rapid convergence on an intended meaning.

However, sometimes one or both of these systems of constraints may have the necessary structure for play to occur. Sometimes, if the constraints are structured properly, the process of generating or interpreting an utterance will be experienced playfully. When this happens, the act of creation or reception becomes an end unto itself. It ceases to be merely a way to transmit a particular piece of information. It becomes art.

Semiotic Playgrounds

When we communicate, often the reason we do so is that we want another person to arrive at particular set of constraints—a particular way of understanding the world. When I say "Please hand me the screwdriver," it's because I want you to know that I want the screwdriver. When you say "There's a bear behind you!" you say it because you want me to know that there is a bear behind me. In situations such as these, we want the listener to quickly converge on an evoked meaning that is as close as possible to the meaning that we intend.

But sometimes the goal of communication isn't for the recipient to converge on a particular meaning as quickly as possible. Sometimes the goal of communication is to make the experience of convergence interesting *in and of itself*. When we read a poem or a novel (or listen to a song or a symphony, or watch a play or a movie) there might be an intended meaning that the creator of the experience hopes we arrive at, but the work is structured so that the path we take to get to that meaning is convoluted and indirect. The path is convoluted and indirect because navigating a well-constructed system of constraints is interesting and fun.

The parallels with gameplay should be obvious. In a game of soccer, the goal is to move the ball down the field and put it in the net. An efficient way to do this would be for players to take turns picking up the ball, walking over to the net, and placing it inside. But we don't play soccer in order to efficiently transfer balls into nets. Putting the ball in the net isn't an end unto itself; rather, it is a constraint that structures an interesting place space. Having the experience of navigating that play space is the point of playing soccer.

This is true of any aesthetic work. If I'm standing in a museum looking at a painting, there might be a particular interpretation that the artist intended for me arrive at. And I might arrive at that interpretation, or, because of my idiosyncratic engagement with the work, I might arrive at an entirely different interpretation, or even no interpretation at all. But I'm not looking at the painting in order to efficiently acquire new information about the world—to, metaphorically, put the ball in the net. I'm looking at the painting in order to have the experience of navigating the interpretive play space that it structures. The possibility of finding meaning within an aesthetic work can sometimes be an important part of the experience of engaging with it—it can direct our exploration by privileging certain interpretive moves over others. But the experience of engaging with an aesthetic work cannot be *reduced* to finding meaning, any more than a game of soccer can be reduced to a soccer ball sitting in a net. Aesthetic engagement, like all forms of play, is an end unto itself.

We experience an aesthetic work as a stream of signifiers. These signifiers are patterns that have been generated by our brains to provide a patchwork match for our undifferentiated stream of sensation. We arrive at those particular patterns through the piling up of tiny acts of microsemiosis as our brains try to parsimoniously converge on the nearest set of constraints that will account for our sensory stream produced by the work. These constraints are encoded by the strength of multiple synapses, and as the strength of these synapses changes, so does the path that cascades of excitation take through our neural network. This difference between one path of neural excitation and another is how our understanding of the work is physically embodied.

Because this is a dynamic process, our understanding of a work is continually shifting throughout our engagement with it. If I'm reading a book, each new word is decoded in light of what I have read before, and my overall understanding of what I have read before is then tweaked to account for the constraint imposed by my interpretation of the latest word. My current understanding of the book creates expectations about what sorts of words it will contain as I read further, and the way that the words that I actually do read meet or thwart these expectations produces shifts in my overall understanding as I move forward through the text.

Aesthetic engagement can thus be understood as navigation through an interpretive play space. During an encounter with an aesthetic work, we are invited to make sense of what we are seeing or hearing by forming interpretive constraints that both account for what we have already encountered and make predictions about what we will encounter in the future. If the work is dull or obvious we will quickly converge on a single set of internal constraints that make such accurate predictions that there are no additional interpretive moves for us to make. But if a work is interesting or deep, then we will find ourselves constantly seeking out new interpretive positions to account for the unexpected signifiers we are experiencing. The path we take through the interpretive play space of the work will be convoluted and indirect.

The result is a semiotic playground. An aesthetic work is a work that intersects with our pre-existing internal constraints in such a way that easy convergence on a single fixed interpretation is difficult. Instead, engagement with such a work is an active and continually unfolding process, where expectations (both small and large) are thwarted in order to trigger new cascades of anticipatory play. This process is dynamic even in situations in which the signifiers themselves are fixed. Each act of interpretation shifts the constraints that define our horizon of intent, our sense of what future interpretations are possible. Even with linear works, aesthetic engagement is necessarily active and playful.

The remainder of the book deals with the implications of this play-centered approach to understanding aesthetic experience.

III Stories

11 Playing without Winning

One difficulty with extending our model of play to non-game experiences is the question of how to handle goals. Games offer well-defined goals to work toward—for example, making it to the end of the level alive, putting our opponent's king in check, or scoring the most baskets. These goals act as global constraints on every horizon of intent—no matter what we are doing from moment to moment, we're always conscious of the effect that our actions have on moving us closer to victory or defeat.

In fact, several of our heuristics explicitly depend on the notion that some locations in a play space are marked as more desirable than others. In order for our actions to feel consequential, some outcomes need to be better than others. In bowling, knocking down all the pins is better than rolling a gutter ball. The difference between these two outcomes is one of the things that makes bowling interesting and challenging. If the goals were removed—if every outcome were equally desirable—bowling would feel empty and pointless.

Similarly, in order to feel satisfaction in achieving a desirable outcome, the outcome should be something we were trying to achieve. An abrupt and unearned victory isn't very enjoyable—satisfaction comes not from having won, but from having arrived at the result we were aiming for. The existence of explicit victory and failure conditions in rule-based games gives us a clear destination to work toward as we navigate their system of constraints.

But the function of predetermined goals as global constraints breaks down when we look at other varieties of aesthetic experiences. There isn't any way to win a novel. When we listen to a sonata, we don't feel as if we are working toward a particular resolution. It even breaks down with certain experiences that are commonly labeled as games—in *Dear Esther*, for example, reaching the lighthouse at the end doesn't involve overcoming any challenges or making any meaningful choices about which path to take.

How can works without explicit goals (or with trivial goals) function as play spaces? How can we feel a sense of consequence and satisfaction when we engage with these experiences if there isn't a particular outcome that we are working to achieve?

To answer these questions, we need to explore how it is possible to privilege locations within a play space without explicitly specifying them through a set of formal rules. For that reason, we're going to take a closer look at two types of play that manage to succeed despite a lack of emphasis on winning: childhood make-believe, and adult role-playing games.

The Experience of Make-Believe

Children learn how to play make-believe long before they learn how to play rule-based games. The Swiss developmental psychologist Jean Piaget identified three stages in the development of childhood play: practice play, symbolic play, and, finally, games with rules. At first, babies play only at simple imitation, mimicking facial expressions, gestures, and sounds. When they are a little older, this practice play expands to include physical experimentation, handling objects and interacting with the world. And then when they are toddlers, children graduate to symbolic play, making up imaginary scenarios and acting them out. Not until children begin to approach school age are they able to play rule-based games.[1]

One could argue that pretend play is more fundamental to human experience than any sort of rule-based game. Then why haven't we grounded our understanding of play in make-believe instead of rule-based games? We began by looking at rule-based games because their machinery of play is easier to see. Many of the elements that structure rule-based play spaces are tangible: We can buy a book that contains the official rules of chess, handle a billiard ball to understand its properties, pace out the dimensions of a soccer field, or read a strategy guide for playing *World of Warcraft*. Not all of the constraints that shape these play spaces are so explicit, but the presence of these exposed, rigid elements makes the entire structure easier to grasp.

The fact that the state of a game of chess can (mostly) be represented by the physical configuration of the pieces on the board makes it easier for us to see that chess *has* a state. But make-believe has a state as well, albeit one that is (mostly) hidden away inside the heads of the players. We began our exploration with chess instead of cops and robbers, not because games are somehow more fundamental than playing pretend, but because the

---

1. Singer and Singer, *The House of Make-Believe*, 52–53.

concrete example of the chessboard makes it easier to visualize abstractions such as game state and phase space.

Recognizing that make-believe has a state is important. Pretending functions through *doing*, not *being*. Pretending to be a princess is less about imagining that you *are* a princess, and more about *acting* (or imagining that you are acting) the way a princess acts. Maybe you are brushing your hair in front of a mirror, or giving orders to your subjects, or dancing at a ball with a handsome prince, but the experience of pretending is inevitably active. During make-believe, event follows event from moment to moment. What has come before defines the state, and that state determines what sorts of things are possible within the immediate horizon of intent. Because I'm dancing with the prince *right now*, I can't escape from the dragon, even though escaping from a dragon is a reasonable thing for a princess to do. In order to escape from the dragon I must arrive a location in the princess play space in which my escape makes sense within my current framework of active constraints. The play space of make-believe is a collection of potentialities afforded by the evolving circumstances of the players. To pretend is to navigate these potentialities freely, at the same time obeying the restrictions imposed by our imaginations.[2] Currie and Ravenscroft describe this process as follows:

The productivity of imagining can explain the productivity of pretence if we assume that imagination serves to update pretence. But it can do that without having to motivate pretence. It can do it as long as the pretender wants to retain the right kind of conformity between what he imagines and what he pretends. He imagines the [toy] elephant is wet, and forms the desire to pretend in a way that is in conformity with that imagining. Believing that the best way to pretend in conformity with that imagining is to pretend to dry the elephant, he forms the desire to do that. Thinking that the best way to do this is to rub the toy elephant with a cloth, that is what he does.[3]

If we look closely at make-believe, we discover that it obeys the same heuristics we developed to analyze rule-based gameplay. If we play the

---

2. "The agreements which participants in a collective daydream make about what to imagine can be thought of as rules prescribing certain imaginings. It is a rule of a certain joint fantasy that participants are to imagine traveling to Saturn in a rocket, or that they are to imagine of a particular stump that it is a bear. True, the agreements are made, the rules established voluntarily, and their prescriptions are relative to one's role as a participant in the imaginative activity in question. But they do prescribe. Anyone who refuses to imagine what was agreed on refuse to 'play the game' or plays it improperly. He breaks a rule." Walton, *Representation as Make-Believe*, 39.

3. Currie and Ravenscroft, *Recreative Minds*, 126.

same role repeatedly, it gradually becomes stale; buying eggs at an imaginary store is fun once or twice, but buying eggs at an imaginary store twenty times in a row becomes tedious. Our actions need to have a meaningful effect on the evolving state of the fantasy; if I point a stick at you and say "Bang," it's important that you clutch your chest and fall over dead. And what follows must have a predictable connection to what came before; it's bad if you do *nothing* when I shoot you, but it's also bad if you do a completely *unexpected* thing—breaking into song, for example, or standing on your head.

The particular trajectory we take through the make-believe play space can't be predetermined; pretending to explore a jungle isn't much fun if we plot out in advance everything that is going to happen. In order for the fantasy to function properly, we have to sometimes be caught off guard by spur-of-the-moment improvisation—an unexpected tiger attack, the ruins of a hidden temple, a treacherous rope bridge. But our improvisations should eventually converge on a satisfactory conclusion—we escape from the tigers, we discover hidden treasure, we grasp a conveniently located vine at the last instant before we plummet to certain doom.

Choice, variety, consequence, predictability, uncertainty, satisfaction—the same criteria that make a videogame fun also determine the play value of a session of make-believe. And the goal is the same: To structure an experience so that it consistently provides interesting horizons of intent that ultimately lead to either satisfaction or resolvable frustration—learning or doing. When children choose constraints for make-believe, they don't choose randomly. The different constraints are inevitably chosen to complement one another—to work together in order to construct an interesting space for exploration. Pretend play spaces are structured systems, not merely an accidental assortment of restrictions.

The Constraints of Make-Believe

The constraints of make-believe tend to fall into four broad categories[4]:

Roles To play a role is to pretend to be someone (or something) else—perhaps a fictional character, a real person, or a "type" (firefighter, mommy, cowboy, ninja, pirate). As was mentioned previously, the primary element

---

4. This way of understanding make-believe is an extension of a framework developed by child psychologist Greta Fein. See Fein, "Pretend Play in Childhood: An Integrative Review." Also see Singer and Singer, *The House of Make-Believe*, 64–67; Sutton-Smith, *The Ambiguity of Play*, 158–159.

of playing a role during make-believe is not to imagine that you *are* what you're pretending to be, but to *act* in a way that demonstrates your adopted identity. The role you adopt during make-believe places obvious limits on what actions are permitted and what actions are forbidden. If you're pretending to be a cowboy, you can ride around on a horse but you can't attack someone with a sword. Consequentially, the roles that children choose during make-believe tend to have distinct sets of stereotypical behaviors that provide clear moment-to-moment opportunities for action.

Characters   A character is an imaginary identity that exists apart from the players. A teddy bear may become a patient in a hospital. A baby doll may become a real baby. In some cases, a character may exist entirely in the player's imagination. The distinction between roles and characters is an important one. Whereas roles are defined by their *actions*, characters tend to be defined by their *identities*. Dolls at a tea party don't have to actually *do* anything to fulfill their function as guests. The mere fact that they are imaginary guests structures a range of possible actions that can be done to or for them. A guest is served tea in a cup. A guest is given a cookie on a plate. A guest is not attacked with swords.

Props   A prop is an imaginary object, often (but not necessarily) represented by a real-world object. A stick may become a gun. A glob of mud may become a cake. A hole in the ground may become a witch's cauldron. As with characters, props define a range of actions that are appropriate to do *to* them. But many props also suggest things to do *with* them. If I'm off on a treasure hunt, I may carry an imaginary shovel over my shoulder so I'll have something to dig with when I find it. And whether I have an imaginary shovel or an imaginary pickaxe determines what sorts of actions I'll be able to perform when I arrive at my destination.

Situations   A situation is a context for specific action. The players may be flying on a rocket to the moon, or exploring in the desert, or conducting an imaginary wedding. Each of these situations defines a range of tasks that are appropriate and a range that are inappropriate. As with roles, players tend to choose situations that offer broad yet well-defined sets of stereotypical actions. In the real world, most of us would probably prefer to spend an afternoon strolling on the beach than doing housework. But in terms of make-believe, housework is superior. Playing house offers a varied and evolving set of horizons; pretending to stroll on the beach doesn't.

A session of make-believe may or may not use all of these constraints, but it will always contain at least one of them. In the simplest forms of make-believe, the player may merely take on a role ("I'm an airplane!") or work through an evocative situation ("The floor is lava!"). However, more complicated scenarios can bring a variety of different constraints into play. Picture a group of children pretending to be pirates (role) armed with toy swords (prop) attacking an imaginary fort (situation) defended by stuffed animals (character).

Explicit goals are sometimes part of a session of make-believe, but they aren't essential. It is possible to construct a successful play space merely by choosing an interesting role or situation and seeing where the fantasy takes you. However, even without explicit goals, some locations within the play space are privileged over others. From moment to moment, there is constant pressure to make choices that sustain the fantasy—to seek out lines of action that reinforce the constraints that define the space. If I'm pretending to be a lion stalking a gazelle, the moment-to-moment challenge lies in find actions that express my "lion-ness." Doing becomes a mechanic for being.

This creates an interesting self-reflexive quality to pretend play. The constraints of make-believe exist to structure a field of potential action, but actions of make-believe are chosen so as to reinforce the validity of the constraints. In rule-based games, players often experience cruxes as their understanding of the game comes in conflict with how it actually unfolds. But in make-believe there is never any question as to how events will unfold—the players have absolute control over the success or failure of their actions. The challenge of make-believe lies not in resolving cruxes in our understanding, but in *minimizing* them. The unstated goal is to stay true to the roles, characters, props, or situations that structure the play space.

Imagine a little girl playing with dolls in a dollhouse. She has decided that the dolls are playing a game of hide-and-seek and the boy doll is hiding in the attic. Her goal is not for the mommy doll to find the boy doll as quickly as possible (even though that would be the goal in real game of hide and seek). Her goal is to move the mommy doll in ways that reinforce the fantasy that she has established. So the mommy doll looks under the doll bed in the doll bedroom and wonders aloud about where her little boy might be hiding. The little girl certainly has a horizon of intent— from moment to moment she is considering different moves within the play space. But rather than judging each move on whether or not it brings her closer to victory, she is using different criteria. A good move in doll hide-and-seek isn't one that helps the mommy doll find the boy doll, but one that strengthens the characters and situations the little girl has created. Within each horizon there are clearly better moves and worse moves, things to do and things to avoid, but there is no particular end state that the little girl is trying to achieve. Suppose the mommy doll never finds the boy doll, but instead gives up in make-believe frustration and the boy doll runs out and pretend-hugs her; that can be just as satisfying a conclusion as it the mommy doll had "won."

Make-believe gives us an excellent example of how a play space can be structured without imposing an explicit victory condition. The satisfaction of pretending comes not from winning, but from holding a subset of our constraints steady through a variety of different horizons. The mommy doll doesn't have to find the boy doll, but she does have to behave like a mommy throughout, just as the boy doll has to behave like a little boy.

Make-believe, for the most part, is a game that only children play. However, there are examples of adult games with strong fantasy elements. In a tabletop role-playing game such as *Dungeons & Dragons*, formal rules exist side-by-side with the softer constraints of make-believe. The players are working toward the explicit goals of staying alive, leveling up, and getting as much treasure as possible. But at the same time, they are playing characters and scenarios that possess an implicit structure that has to be sustained. Sometimes the most important moment-to-moment question faced by a player of a role-playing game isn't "How do I win this battle?" but rather "What would Sir Percival do in this situation?" Mediating this tension between alternate ways of privileging locations within the play space is one of the challenges of playing and designing role-playing games. And it has led to the evolution of a sophisticated body of critical thought about how these different modes of play function in practice.

The Roots of Role-Playing Games

Role-playing games evolved from table-top war games. Like all board games, table-top war games are systems of formal constraint. Their rules specify such things as how far a tank can drive in one turn and how much damage a line of redcoats will inflict when they fire off a musket volley. To play one of these games is to navigate these constraints in order to bring the state of the game to a particular terminal configuration—the enemy destroyed, the map conquered, the war won.

However, because the formal mechanics of these games are couched within a fantasy of recreating historical battles, they also provide an opportunity for make-believe. The appeal of a game such as *Waterloo* arises not only from the tactical challenges it presents, but also from the opportunity to imagine yourself as Napoleon for an afternoon. If you strip away all references to the real-world battle, the pure mechanics by themselves feel dry and empty. A strength-six unit repulsing an attack by a strength-four unit doesn't deliver the same thrill as Wellington's rifles breaking a charge by Ney's cavalry.

Role-playing games (RPGs) took this sliver of make-believe that existed within of all war games and amplified it. *Dungeons & Dragons*—the first RPG—was based on a war game called *Chainmail. Chainmail* was the creation of Gary Gygax, a Wisconsin game designer. Gygax's rules allowed players to re-create medieval battles such as Agincourt or Crecy using dice and miniature figures. It had rules for knights, catapults, and longbowmen—the sort of things you would expect in a medieval war game. But it also had at the end a curious appendix—a set of additional rules for fantasy elements such as dragons, elves, and wizards. The development of *Chainmail* happened to coincide with the explosion in popularity of J. R. R. Tolkien's book *The Lord of the Rings* in the United States, and Gygax and his gaming circle discovered that his rules for historical battles could (with a few tweaks) be used to re-create the fantasy battles described in Tolkien's books.[5]

However, Tolkien's fictional battles differed in an important way from historical battles—their outcomes were strongly influenced by the actions of particular heroic individuals. In general, war games tend to model soldiers in aggregate. A single marker on the board might represent a platoon, or a squadron, or even a whole battalion. The individual acts of heroism performed by real soldiers on real battlefields are abstracted away. In the real world, battles aren't won by the extraordinary actions of a single soldier, but by the concerted actions of dozens or hundreds or thousands. And any set of rules intended to simulate the event has to reflect this fact.

But in Tolkien's stories the outcome of battles often hinges on the singular actions of significant characters: Bard's lucky arrow shot in *The Hobbit*, Gandalf's arrival at Helm's Deep, Eowyn and Merry's stand against the Witch King. Any set of rules that attempts to capture the essence of these fictional battles has to accommodate this element of individual heroism. And, furthermore, these individual heroes are *characters*, with their own motivations and agendas. Gandalf isn't merely a piece of field artillery to be deployed in a location that will maximize his firepower; he is an individual with specific personality traits. What he does on the battlefield isn't structured solely by the formal rules that specify his movement speed and hit points, but also by additional set of soft constraints that limit what is believable for Gandalf to do as a character.

With this shift in focus away from group combat to individual heroics, it was a short step to get rid of armies altogether. Instead of the action being

5. Mackay, *The Fantasy Role-Playing Game: A New Performing Art,* 13–15.

limited to large-scale battles, the heroes could go off and have adventures on their own, as The Fellowship does in *The Lord of the Rings*. The formal rules might still be there to determine the outcome of a particular event, such as an arrow shot or a fireball spell, but the course of these adventures would be determined less by tactical advantage and more by narrative consistency. The players were still trying to move through a framework of constraints in order to arrive at a desired goal, but now those constraints included the roles they were playing, the non-player characters they met, the situations they found themselves in, the equipment they were carrying, and so on—in short, the constraints of make-believe.

The hard and soft constraints of a role-playing game aren't two separate and independent systems—they overlap and interact in interesting ways. For example, a common problem in children's make-believe is the question of who killed who:

"I shot you! Fall down!"
"No, I shot you! *You* fall down!"
"But I shot you first!"

Most role-playing games avoid this problem by using formal rules to resolve such conflicts.[6] At the same time, players may find themselves choosing actions that seem foolish or counterproductive within the context of the formal rules. Sacrificing yourself in battle to save your friends doesn't make sense if we view the game solely as a process of working toward a goal within a rule-based framework; after all, in most games there isn't a reward for dying. But in view of the soft constraints of the character's personality and his relationship with his imaginary teammates, dying may be the only reasonable course of action. In most role-playing games, the players navigate both sets of constraints simultaneously, floating between hard and soft limits depending on which seems most applicable to the current circumstance.

Since the invention of *Dungeons & Dragons* in the 1970s, hundreds of different role-playing games have been published commercially, and even more "home-brew" systems have been invented by dedicated hobbyists for the amusement of themselves and their friends. These games run the gamut from very strict formal systems that are only a small step away from

6. "Really to remove System requires that anything and everything that happens during play be mediated solely through the Social Contract, without any formalized method even to do that. I think that such play would be awfully difficult, requiring so much negotiation regarding how to play per unit of play as to be hopeless." Edwards, "Simulationism: The Right to Dream."

traditional board games, to open-ended dramatic experiences that are only slightly more structured than free-form make-believe. However, what they all share in common is the explicit use of both hard and soft constraints to structure their play spaces—the synthesis of rule-based gaming with the trappings of make-believe.

Agendas

An interesting body of theory concerning role-playing games emerged in the late 1990s in the discussion forums of The Forge, a website devoted to independent and experimental role-playing games. While some theorists have approached RPGs as cultural artifacts or semiotic systems, the contributors at The Forge were primarily interested in understanding the *experience* of playing an RPG. They were mostly players and designers themselves, and the questions they were trying to answer were practical ones: What do we get out of playing the game? Why are some games fun and others boring? And why can't we agree on which is which? The result is a body of work that is less concerned with the *significance* of RPGs and more with the *practice*, less concerned with what RPGs *mean* and more concerned with how RPGs function to *construct meaning*.

The culmination of the discussions on The Forge was a series of articles written by Ron Edwards, the moderator of the forum, and a talented designer in his own right. While acknowledging the contributions of others, Edwards was emphatic that his synthesis wasn't intended to be definitive:

Everything in this document in nothing more nor less than "What Ron Thinks." It is not an official Dogma for the Forge. It is not a consensus view of members of the Forge, nor is it a committee effort of any kind. It is most especially not an expectation for what you're supposed to think or believe.[7]

Despite these caveats, Edwards' writings do represent the best effort to take the multitude of different options and viewpoints expressed at the Forge and shape them into a coherent theory for how players experience role-playing games. And, as such, they provide a useful window into the general experience of play.

Edwards' overall framework can be expressed as a hierarchy (figure 11.1). To move from top to bottom in this diagram is to move from the general to the specific, from the abstract to the concrete.[8]

7. Edwards, "GNS and Other Matters of Role-playing Theory."
8. Edwards, "Narrativism: Story Now."

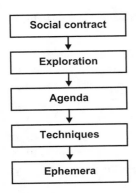

Figure 11.1
Edwards' hierarchy of RPG play.

Social contract The real-world context in which the game is played. It encompasses not only the game itself, but the relationships of the players outside the game, the logistics of causing the game to happen, and the significance of the game to the wider world.

Exploration The "shared imaginings" of the players. This is the game itself considered at the highest level of abstraction. It exists embedded within a particular social context, but can also be considered as a separate thing.

Agenda What each player wants out of the game. In traditional board games, sports, and videogames, the agenda is often, simply "to win." But role-playing games, with their emphasis on the soft constraints of make-believe, can appeal to a wider range of motivations. An agenda is a player's preferred "way of exploring" the shared imaginary space.

Techniques The particular rules or procedures, both formal and informal, that structure the exploration of the shared imagined space. Techniques are subordinate to Agenda because different systems of constraints facilitate different types of exploration.

Ephemera The actual actions of the players in the game. Ephemera are the "moves" that carry the players forward through the play space. They are the concrete expression of the possibilities afforded by the techniques.

In Edwards' hierarchy, playing a role-playing game is an experience embedded within a social context. A player approaches that experience with an agenda that shapes his exploration of the shared play space. The constraints (techniques) that define the shared space may satisfy or thwart this agenda, as the player executes a series of moment-to-moment actions (ephemera).

It is easy to see how the various hard and soft constraints structure the moment—to-moment actions of RPG players. The role you play determines the range of reasonable actions in a given circumstance. Roles are usually chosen that are likely to afford a wide range of interesting actions—it's more fun to play a thief than a shepherd. Situations are also typically chosen to provide interesting opportunities for player action—it's more fun to be sailing around on a pirate ship than stuck in a jail cell. The formal rules are designed to provide a satisfying mix of randomness and predictability, allowing the players enough structure to plan, but not so much that every action becomes a foregone conclusion. Players can succeed or fail, and in failing, learn from their mistakes. This all falls within the framework we have previously established for the structure of play.

However, Edwards' concept of agenda is something new.[9] We have looked at how the resolution of anticipatory play can lead to moments of satisfaction and frustration, but we haven't talked about how a game can satisfy (or frustrate) our expectations of the experience as a whole. Agenda is anticipation writ large. Why do we play a particular game in the first place? And what do we hope to get out of it?

These questions were of particular interest to the forum participants at The Forge because they were interested in understanding why some games succeeded in satisfying the needs of their players while others failed. More important, why the same game could succeed for one player and fail for another. Why might a game with a seemingly well-designed formal system, or a seemingly fruitful and compelling fantasy, still turn out to be frustrating for some players during the actual experience of play?

The forum participants eventually arrived at the idea that different players are playing for different reasons. They have different agendas that they bring to the table—different things that they are trying to accomplish during play. In our terms, we would say that they have different locations within the game's phase space that they are trying to work toward. And their satisfaction or frustration with the game overall is a function of the

9. New within the context of this book, that is. However, their roots of Edwards' ideas lie deep in the history of war-gaming. As far back as the 1950s there were arguments in the hobbyist press between players who approached war games primarily as *simulations* and players who approached them primarily as *games*. For an exhaustive discussion of how this early gamist/simulationist schism played out, see Peterson, *Playing at the World*, 297–303.

accessibility of those locations. Are they achievable? And does the system of constraints allow them to be approached systematically?

The designers and players at The Forge identified three different attitudes that players can adopt toward goals. These three different creative agendas define the expectations of the player toward the overall experience: What sort of ultimate satisfaction will the game deliver, and how will it go about delivering it?

Edwards' three agendas are gamism, simulationism, and narrativism. Gamist players are interested in working through challenges toward a predetermined set of victory conditions. Simulationist players are interested in preserving the coherence of certain privileged constraints. And narrativist players are interested in seeking out circumstances that maximize or minimize narrative possibility—they seek to avoid or achieve closure.

I'm going to rename these three agendas in terms of the effect they have on biasing positions in the player space:

Goal-oriented play The gamist agenda. Players work to arrive at a particular destination in the play space that is established in advance. This is the dominant agenda in most board games, most sports, and most videogames. Often this involves direct competition between players, or, even when they cooperate, an emphasis on differential levels of achievement.

Coherence-oriented play The simulationist agenda. Players work toward avoiding the disruption of certain privileged constraints. For example, a simulationist player may play through a recreation of the Battle of Gettysburg knowing in advance that the South is certain to lose. Moves that reflect "what really happened" are preferred over moves that deviate from historical accuracy. Coherence-oriented play is a common way to approach make-believe. When you are playing pretend, you usually aren't very interested in winning. Instead, most of the play comes from seeing where the particular foundational constraints you have adopted will take you.

Closure-oriented play The narrativist agenda. Players work toward situations that maximize or minimize the potential for anticipatory play. A narrativist isn't trying to arrive at a particular destination in the play space, but to move toward *any* destination that is ripe with possibility. Or, if the experience is drawing to a close, to find a nearby destination that minimizes future action and offers closure. When play ends, it isn't because victory has been achieved, but because he has arrived at a point where any future action feels pointless—the needs of the characters have been satisfied and the conflicts implicit in the situation have been resolved.

Coherence-oriented play and closure-oriented play are things that we haven't encountered before, so a bit more explanation is in order. Coherence-oriented play is the play of "what if." A set of privileged constraints is selected and then moves are made that preserve the coherence of those constraints, regardless of whether the outcome moves you closer to victory. The pretend firefighter rushes into a burning building because that is what a firefighter would do, the historical re-enactor holds his ground and fires his rifle, because that is what his counterpart did 150 years before. There isn't a single win condition that the player is trying to achieve; any outcome that avoids breaking the simulation is satisfying.

Closure-oriented play, in contrast, is directed toward keeping things interesting. It means seeking out situations with broader horizons of action, regardless of whether they move you closer to victory or sustain the coherence of the current play space. The pretend firefighter suddenly discovers that the burning building is being attacked by a giant octopus, the re-enactor gets bored with huddling in his trench and charges the enemy lines. It means avoiding closed off situations, and moving toward open ones. Or it means the opposite. When we are ready for play to end, we want to achieve closure, not avoid it. We want to shut down our chains of anticipatory play and arrive at a stable position in the play space where any future moves seem pointless. Thus, closure-oriented play can also be directed toward making things *less* interesting—toward wrapping up the game and bringing it to a clean conclusion.

While goal-oriented play works toward a specific end—a clear win condition—coherence-oriented and closure-oriented play are more open-ended. A scenario that begins with two characters falling in love can end in a wide variety of satisfactory ways—marriage, disillusionment, betrayal, suicide, joy, regret. The narrativist isn't working toward an outcome that has been chosen in advance; he is merely trying to discover *any* outcome that fulfills his desire for closure, preferably with many interesting twists and turns along the way. The simulationist also isn't working toward a particular outcome; he is trying to discover a sequence of events that feels true to the premise of the scenario and the personalities of the characters.

No one plays as a pure gamist, or a pure simulationist, or a pure narrativist. Rather, most people tend to have a dominant mode that they prefer, but drop selectively into the other modes as circumstances require. In Edwards' words,

Much torment has arisen from people perceiving GNS as a labeling device. Used properly, the terms apply only to decisions, not to whole persons nor to whole games. To be absolutely clear, to say that a person is (for example) Gamist, is only shorthand for saying "This person tends to make role-playing decisions in line with Gamist goals." Similarly, to say that an RPG is (for example) Gamist, is only shorthand for saying "This RPG's content facilitates Gamist concerns and decision-making."[10]

This quotation highlights the utilitarian underpinnings of the theory as it was developed at The Forge. The goal was to understand what players were looking for from games and what rule systems would meet those needs. There wasn't one set of criteria that could be used to separate good games from bad; rather, the very meaning of good and bad depended on the agendas of the individual players. A player with the wrong agenda could easily find himself frustrated in a group with other goals, even if the rest of the players were having a great time:

To a **gamist**, the other ways of playing can feel aimless. He is used to having a clear objective and working toward it. ("Are we going to sit around all day just talking? I want to fight something!")

To a **simulationist**, the other ways of playing can feel arbitrary. The goals are being imposed from outside the game, rather than being a natural outgrowth of the fantasy itself. ("But *why* are we trying to assassinate the Goblin king? What has he ever done to us? This doesn't make any sense.")

To a **narrativist**, the other ways of playing feel hollow. He doesn't just want to explore the play space and arrive at a predetermined destination; he wants to feel the sense of accomplishment that comes from creatively resolving the inherent tension in the original constraints. (*"Another* loot run in the local dungeon? Can't we go on a quest to rescue a princess or something?")

In practice, the motivations of a particular gaming group or player are never completely pure. While typically one agenda will dominate, the others will usually be lurking in the background. A gamist player may get most of his fun from slaying goblin hordes, but still enjoy the narrativist moment when the goblin king begs for his life. A simulationist gamemaster may design the lair of the evil wizard to include a realistic sewer system, but still make sure that the monsters that inhabit it present a fair challenge from the gamist perspective. And a narrativist group may spend an entire weekend role-playing events leading up to a duel between two characters, but still expect the fight itself to unfold with a simulationist approach to combat mechanics.

What is important for our purposes is that the three different agendas represent three different valuation strategies for assessing the worth of

10. Edwards, "GNS and Other Matters of Role-Playing Theory."

moves in a play space. Instead of every move being evaluated by whether or not it carries us closer to victory, we have two other ways to assign value:

Does this move maintain the coherence of a set of privileged constraints?
Does this move increase or decrease my opportunities for anticipatory play?

Besides being techniques for understanding how role-playing games function, coherence-oriented play and closure-oriented play are very useful tools for understanding how play operates in media other than games. For example, when we read a novel our moment-to-moment experience consists of a series of interpretive moves in response to the constraints imposed by the text. We aren't working to arrive at a particular interpretation that was established in advance. Instead, we are looking for lines of action that satisfy either a simulationist or narrativist agenda. We are seeking interpretations that minimize the disruption to our existing understanding of the characters and the plot. Or we are seeking interpretations that increase or reduce our opportunities for future anticipatory play—interpretations that move us toward or away from closure.

In the next chapter we are going to shift our attention from make-believe and role-playing games to theatrical performance. We are going to examine how the tools we have developed allow to analyze different theatrical techniques, and how it's possible for play to emerge even in very linear and tightly scripted experiences.

12 Performance

There are obvious similarities between theater and make-believe, but there are also significant differences. The most important difference is that theater is performed for the benefit of an audience. In a game of make-believe, each player is interested in satisfying his own agenda, or less commonly, the agendas of his fellow players. There is no consideration for whether or not the game is interesting to an outside observer. A child playing on the playground isn't worried about putting on a good show for his teacher standing nearby. His individual satisfaction as he navigates the space of make-believe is sufficient.

But an actor on a stage has a different purpose in mind. Though he may sometimes experience moments that are personally satisfying, his primary purpose is to execute a sequence of actions that will be interesting for the audience. His private experience is secondary. He might sometimes find himself feeling bored on stage, or frustrated, but those negative feelings are immaterial as long as he succeeds in delivering a successful performance.

Another significant way that theater differs from make-believe is that the outcome is determined in advance. An actor playing Hamlet knows that he is working toward the moment of his death following his duel with Laertes. He isn't free to chart his own trajectory through the narrative to arrive at a different outcome. In a role-playing version of *Hamlet*, the player might wind up fleeing Elsinore with Ophelia, or ambushing Claudius when he walked alone on the parapets, or succumbing to the machinations of Rosencrantz and Guildenstern, or any of a number of other plausible conclusions. A large part of the fun of a role-playing game (at least, if you are even slightly a gamist) is the satisfaction of steering your character toward a desirable resolution. The actor playing Hamlet knows that he is doomed to wind up stabbed and poisoned in Act V whether he wants to be or not.

In fact, not only is the outcome of a performance determined in advance; much of the moment-to-moment action is, too. Actors typically work from scripts that specify the words they speak and their entrances and exits. They spend time in rehearsal with a director to establish the staging of each scene—how they should deliver their lines and how they are to move in relation to the other performers. An actor on stage is subject to a very tight set of constraints on his actions, providing few opportunities for free movement.

Yet, despite all these limitations, theatrical performance still provides the possibility of play. Even within the narrow constraints established by the script, the actor is afforded a significant number of moment-to-moment creative choices. An individual performance is shaped not just by the mechanical execution of pre-determined dialogue and stock gestures, but also by improvisation—by spontaneous nuances of expression, timing, inflection, and tone.

Different performance traditions place a greater or lesser emphasis on the level of improvisation is expected within the construction of a performance. The Russian acting teacher Constantin Stanislavski made a distinction between two major schools of theatrical technique: "representational" and "experiential." The representational actor works out in advance every action he intends to execute on stage. His performance consists of skillfully replicating these actions in front of an audience. He doesn't allow himself to become emotionally engaged with his character; the internal stance he attempts to cultivate is one of emotional detachment. Only by "standing apart" from the role he is playing can he properly focus all his attention on sustaining the illusion that he is constructing for the audience.[1]

In contrast, the experiential actor approaches each performance as a fresh opportunity for creative discovery. Rather than working out every action in advance, the experiential actor prepares by developing a deep understanding of who his character is. Then, when he is on stage, he allows his performance to emerge organically. His actions aren't predetermined, and his attention isn't concentrated on skillful fakery. Rather, his attention

1. "At first [actors of the representational school] feel the part, but when they have done so they do not go on feeling it anew, they merely remember and repeat the external movements, intonations, and expressions they worked on at first, making this repetition without emotion. Often they are extremely skilful in technique, and are able to get through a part with technique only, and no expenditure of nervous force. In fact, they often think it unwise to feel after they have once decided on the pattern to follow. They think they are surer to give the right performance if they merely recall how they did it when they first got it right." Stanislavski, *An Actor Prepares*, 22.

is focused on sustaining his internal fantasy of the character. His actions are the spontaneous by-product of this sustained fantasy.[2]

In short, Stanislavski's experiential approach is an attempt to harness the power of make-believe to deliver a more effective performance. Instead of focusing his attention on putting on a good show, the actor concentrates on being true to the role he has adopted. His moment-to-moment actions aren't chosen for the effect they have on others, but on how well they satisfy the immediate horizon of intent established by these constraints. Paradoxically, by ignoring the audience and concentrating on his internal fantasy, the actor may wind up producing a more powerful effect. The emotions he portrays using this technique will tend to be less "stagy," more natural, and, one hopes, more capable of stirring similar feelings in the audience.

In reality, no performance is every entirely pure. Even the most dedicated experiential actor is still aware that he is on stage. He knows in the back of his mind that he is working to please the audience, even if a large part of his technique involves trying to ignore that fact. Similarly, even the most disciplined representational actor may sometimes inject a flash of spontaneity into the performance if the circumstance requires it, subtly changing his expression or inflection in response to an unexpected beat. The gap between the representational and experiential theatrical traditions is a continuum, not a dichotomy. It's a tool for recognizing the role of improvisation within the experience of theatrical performance.

Because improvisation is present to a greater or lesser degree in all theatrical experiences, these experiences can be analyzed with the framework we have already developed for analyzing games. We can treat the circumstances of the performance—the script, the director, the actor's preparation, the venue—as constraints structuring a playfield. And we can analyze an actor's interpretive choices—particularly the choices of an actor with a strong experiential technique—through the lens of the heuristics of play. Play gives us a convenient language to talk about the "doing" of a performance—about the mechanics of being actively present as a participant within the unfolding of a tightly structured fantasy. And it gives us a methodology for analyzing how particular systems of constraints can be more or less amenable to generating satisfying interpretive play.

2. "In our art you must live the part every moment that you are playing it, and every time. Each time it is recreated it must be lived afresh and incarnated afresh." Stanislavski, *An Actor Prepares*, 20.

The Experience of Performance

A typical theatrical performance begins with a script consisting of a sequence of dramatic beats. These beats may be stage directions, or lines of dialogue, or even phrases or single words. Each beat is a distinct moment that requires some action by one or more of the performers—saying something, moving in some way, displaying some emotion. Beats can always be performed in a variety of ways. Is a gesture broad or subtle? Is a line played for laughs or tears? Is it delivered with a wry smile or a disapproving frown? Are the words shouted to the back of the hall, or muttered so softly they can barely be heard in the front row?

Some scripts are tightly constrained—they give the performers very specific instructions for how they are to be performed. Others are loosely constrained—they only vaguely hint at what actions are possible. In improvisational theater, the script may consist of nothing more than a general scenario, or a vague suggestion for a character. The amount of freedom can vary not only from script to script, but also from beat to beat. Some lines may be very open—they may suggest a number of possible ways they can be performed—while others may be much more closed. Even with the tightest beat, however, it isn't possible for the script to specify every nuance of the performance; there is always some freedom left for the actor.

The collection of all the beats within a script forms a linearly directed phase space (figure 12.1). This phase space encapsulates all possible performances that are allowed by the script. In the process of constructing a performance, an actor makes choices within this phase space. Within the range of all possible ways of executing a beat, only one will actually be realized during a given performance. There may be a thousand different ways

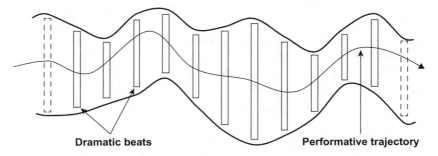

Dramatic beats   **Performative trajectory**

Figure 12.1
Dramatic performance as a phase space.

to speak the line "to be or not to be," but when the moment comes, the actor must, by necessity, pick one. This process of picking may be conscious or unconscious, it may be skilled or naïve, but it is unavoidable. As the play plunges forward in time, and the potential crystallizes into the actual, each beat must necessarily be performed in a specific way, resulting in a trajectory through the phase space of possible performances.

The challenge for an actor is to execute the sequence of beats in a way that is interesting to the audience. (What constitutes a beat that is "interesting to the audience" is a question that we will set aside for the moment.) Actions aren't picked randomly, or on a whim, but are selected to establish a coherent unfolding narrative. Stanislavski's two techniques—the representational and the experiential—offer two different ways of accomplishing this task.

In a representational performance, the realization of each beat is worked out in rehearsal. The actor thinks his way through the script, or experiments until he finds a sequence of actions that feels solid and powerful. He then strives to accurately re-create this sequence in front of the audience. Any play within a beat is exhausted during preparation. When the actor is actually on stage, his attention is concentrated on sustaining a fixed trajectory through the script's phase space by nailing each beat at it presents itself (figure 12.2).

There are several major challenges facing the representational actor. Even a short scene may contain hundred of beats, many demanding specific and precise actions in order to be effective. Sustaining that level of focus over the course of an entire play can often be beyond the reach of even the strongest actors. Furthermore, because of the involuntary roots of our emotions, some particularly subtle nuances of expression or inflection

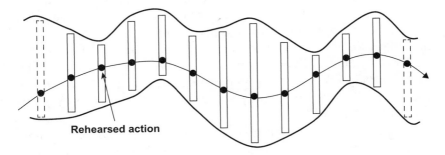

Rehearsed action

Figure 12.2
A representational performance.

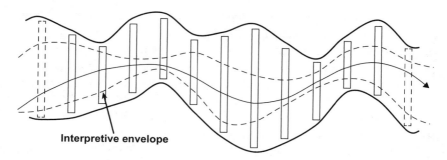

Figure 12.3
An experiential performance.

may be difficult to consciously evoke. In addition, representational performances have an inherent brittleness. Because they are worked out in detail
in advance, they don't provide as much flexibility for the actor to respond
to shifting dynamic conditions.

Stanislavski's experiential technique offers a different approach. Instead
of working out the specifics of each beat in advance, the experiential
actor prepares by developing a set of interpretive constraints that are
capable of structuring an on-the-fly improvisation as he moves from beat
to beat. At any moment, the actor isn't merely executing a rote action.
Rather, he is dynamically exploring an interpretive envelope of his own
construction—in other words, he is moving freely within a system of constraints (figure 12.3).

In order for this technique to work, the interpretive envelope must
accommodate the pre-existing structure of the script. The actor must analyze the script and "reverse engineer" a set of constraints that will ensure
that he hits each beat in an appropriate way. If a scene calls for him to
scream at his lover and throw her out of the house, he must, in advance,
invent a set of constraints—motivations, intentions, personality traits—
that will make those scripted actions feel like a natural unfolding of the
moment-to-moment evolution of the scene. The actor is actually playing
a subtle trick on himself; he is purposely constructing an internal play
space that will allow him to freely wander in the direction that the script
demands that he go.

There are certainly advantages to the experiential approach. Because
the performance is constructed dynamically, the actor is in a better position to respond to events around him—he can play off the actions of the
other members of the cast or the mood of the audience in a way that a

representational performer can't. And, because of his reliance on moment-to-moment emotional intuition, he may have access to nuances of performance that are inaccessible to an actor who is proceeding in a more conscious and methodical manner. The biggest drawback, of course, is the possibility of going off the rails. Whatever the limitations of the representational approach, it at least guarantees consistency from performance to performance. With an experiential performer the possibility always exists for his free movement will take him a direction that fails to deliver a satisfying experience for the audience.

Stanislavski's experiential technique had a huge influence on performance practice. Known popularly as "The Method," it was widely taught in the twentieth century by such well-known acting coaches as Lee Strasberg, Sanford Meisner, and Stella Adler. While individual teachers and performers may emphasize different aspects of Stanislavski's ideas, they all share a similar focus on playing a role not through rote execution of well-rehearsed forms, but rather through spontaneous reaction to the imagined situation at hand.

Many of the differences between different schools of method acting boil down to disagreements over the most effective way to construct the actor's interpretive envelope. Stanislavski himself introduced the concept of "emotion memory." When preparing for a scene the actor searches for an analogous experience in his own past that can be used as an emotional touchstone for the action he is portraying.[3] For example, an actor mourning the death of his lover on stage may structure his performance by concentrating on his memories of the death of a childhood pet.

Sanford Meisner rejected this approach, and maintained that Stanislavski had done the same late in his career.[4] Meisner advocated grounding a performance not in emotional memories but in imagined experiences chosen to be personally meaningful. Meisner taught his students to invent internal fantasies that stirred their emotions in powerful ways and use

---

3. Stanislavski, *An Actor Prepares*, 177–208.

4. "In the early days of the Stanislavsky System, Mr. S. was looking for true behavior, and if what he wanted was great pleasure, he asked where you look for the reality of great pleasure. His answer was simple: you remember a time when you were under the influence of great pleasure. That's called *emotion memory*. I don't use it, and neither did he after thirty years of experimentation. The reason? If you are twenty and work in a delicatessen, the chances are very slim that you can remember that glorious night you had with Sophia Loren. The chances are slight that you know the full pleasure of that kind of glorified sex. Am I making myself clear?" Meisner and Longwell, *Sanford Meisner on Acting*, 79.

those fantasies to constrain their actions during a performance. Rather than remembering the death of a childhood pet, the actor might fantasize about how he would feel if he came home to discover his girlfriend murdered.

Often these techniques demand conscious self-deception on the actor's part. For example, Strasberg taught his students to push their knowledge of the future events of the play out of their minds while they were performing. As actors, they might know what was destined to happen to their characters, but when they were immersed in the moment, that knowledge would be removed as a constraint.[5] Meisner, for similar reasons, encouraged his students to memorize their lines as mechanically as possible, without any sort of inflection or emotional content.[6] That way, when they arrived at a moment when a line was to be delivered, they would be forced to make an on-the-fly creative choice. An actor might know that every night he would deliver a particular line in a quivering rage, but he would push that knowledge out of his mind, so that in each performance the rage would come as a spontaneous overflowing emotion.

The point isn't to exhaustively catalogue all the different techniques that have been developed to help an actor prepare for a role. Rather, it is to illustrate the particular nature of the constraints that arise from these the techniques. In chapter 8, we explored the idea of interpretations—internal constraints that don't directly correlate with the external rules of the play space but that nevertheless have predictive value within the space. The internal constraints developed through these acting techniques do not necessarily correlate with the external constraints supplied by the script. However, they do structure the actor's experience so that his actions fall within the bounds that the script requires. In Strasberg's words,

> The actor is not limited to the way in which he would behave within the particular circumstances set for the character; rather, he seeks a substitute reality different from that set forth by the play that will help him to behave truthfully according to the demands of the role.[7]

Within this carefully prepared framework of interpretive constraints, the actor then improvises his performance. The goal is to make every action feel fresh and alive, even if it has been done a hundred times before. It isn't necessary for each performance to be radically different from the ones that preceded it—in fact, from show to show the performances will tend to be

5. Strasberg, *A Dream of Passion*, 108–109.
6. Meisner and Longwell, *Sanford Meisner on Acting*, 69.
7. Strasberg, *A Dream of Passion*, 86.

quite similar to each other—but it is important that each show feel like a
new experience for the actor into order for a sense of play to be preserved.

Performance as Play

The improviser has to be like a man walking backwards. He sees where he has been,
but pays no attention to the future.[8]

An actor operating within an interpretive envelope is limited not only by
the constraints that he worked out in preparing for his role, but also by
the specific performative choices he has made in the run-up to his current
beat. Each beat doesn't exist in isolation; it is part of a chain of beats that
are intended to form a coherent whole. So while an experiential actor may
try to trick himself into forgetting his character's future, he must stay constantly mindful of his character's past.

In any play space, what we are allowed to do from moment to moment is
a function of both the constraints and the state. The state determines where
we are in the overall phase space, and our location within the phase space
determines what constraints are currently active. These active constraints
define a horizon of intent, a set of moves that are allowed in the immediate
future. And the choices we make within this horizon determine our new
location within the phase space (figure 12.4).

As an actor makes choices during a performance, these choices become
part of the performance's state. The actor's opportunities for future action
are then bounded not only by what each beat allows, but also by his
memory of his previous performative choices. The unfolding state of the

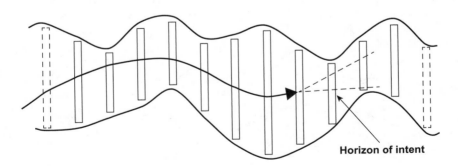

Horizon of intent

Figure 12.4
The horizon of intent during a performance.

8. Johnstone, *Impro: Improvisation and the Theater*, 116.

performance actualizes particular horizons of intent within each new beat. For example, if an actor puts a sarcastic twist on a line at the beginning of the scene, he may be forced to sustain that tone through the scene even if such an interpretation isn't required by the script.

In this way, the moment-to-moment performative choices that an actor makes are *consequential*. Every action triggers a shift in the state of the performance, opening up some future lines of action while simultaneously closing off others. The actor isn't interacting with an external system—this play of potentialities is take place entirely within his head. But the "moves" that he makes still matter. And not just to the audience; they matter the actor himself because of how they structure future opportunities for interesting action.

The consequentiality of performative choice is central to how theater functions as a play space. If we look at theater through the lens of our heuristics, it is obvious that each beat offers both choice and variety. There are a number of ways to perform each beat, and the beats don't repeat. However, it is less clear how a performance can offer an actor uncertainty or satisfaction. Each line is scripted in advance. And the actor has no control over the story's ultimate resolution. Realizing that every performative choice has consequences resolves this issue. The actor may have memorized every line in the script, but he can't be certain of the specific choices that he and his fellow actors will make during any given staging. During the forward plunge through the performance, he can project what will unfold a few beats ahead, but the piling up of interpretive nuance makes it difficult to anticipate further than that. Each performative choice shifts the horizon of intent for future beats, and these shifts accumulate as the performance proceeds. A small variation in how one line is interpreted can cascade into a completely different trajectory through the play space (figure 12.5).

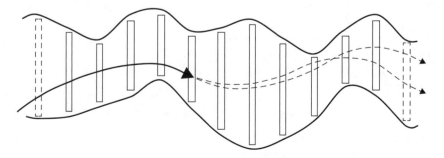

Figure 12.5
The consequence of performative choice.

Furthermore, although an actor may not have control over how the story ends, working toward a predetermined goal is only one way to privilege locations within a play space. Theatrical performance isn't suited to that kind of gamist play. Instead of working to make the story turn out a particular way, an actor can instead adopt a simulationist or narrativist agenda. He can work to find "moves" that hold a particular set of constraints constant throughout the experience—his understanding of his character, for example. Or he can work to find "moves" that open up or close off future opportunities for play—favoring interpretations that are fraught with dramatic implication, or that have a quality of finality and closure. In this way, different performative choices can feel better or worse to an individual actor—they can move him closer to or farther from a satisfactory personal resolution—without them having any effect on the way that the story will turn out.

Stanislavski devotes an entire chapter in *An Actor Prepares* to teaching actors how to structure a coherence-oriented performance.[9] He discusses how to break a scene down into manageable chunks and then within each chunk construct a compelling objective to move toward. The objective should arise from the actor's understanding of his role and the immediate situation of the scene, not from the overall structure of the script, or the demands of the audience. For example, "I want to find my lost friend" is a useful objective, whereas "I want to make the audience cry" is not. The actor isn't trying to "win" his performance by achieving his objective—in fact, often objectives will be chosen that are impossible to achieve within the context of the script. Rather, the actor is picking objectives that will provide a clear imperative to motion, that will structure his moment-to-moment horizons of intent so that they offer frequent opportunities for interesting and consequential performative choices. If your objective is "I want to find my lost friend" then a satisfying performance is a performance where every action sustains the coherence of that motivation.

A theatrical performance doesn't demand to be played the same way that a game does, but it does possess the potential to become playful if the actor approaches it with certain internal constraints. He must allow himself room to improvise from beat to beat, and sustain this spirit of improvisation even through repeated performances of the same material. He must "look backward" at previous beats, using his earlier performative choices to constrain his future actions. He must construct an interpretive envelope that allows him to anticipate the outcomes of his actions, at the same time

9. Stanislavski, *An Actor Prepares*, 121–137.

actively ignoring his foreknowledge of the play's plot. And he must adopt either a simulationist or a narrativist agenda. This means making choices that reinforce the constraints that define his character or situation, or making choices that open up interesting lines of future action, or (if the performance is drawing to a close) making choices that lead to a sense of stability and closure.

Ludic Semiosis and the Role of the Audience

When we analyze performance, it is important to distinguish between the experience of the actors and the experience of the audience. These two experiences inform and influence each other, but they are nevertheless separate and distinct. "The performance as viewed" isn't the same as "the performance as performed" (just as "the performance as performed" isn't the same as "the performance as scripted"). We must be careful not to fall into the trap of talking and thinking about "the performance" as though it were a single sort of experience for everyone involved.

Just as the actors' play space is constrained by the script, the audience's play space is constrained by the actors. The actors, through their performances, generate a stream of signifiers directed toward the audience. Spoken lines, nuances of inflection, facial expressions, body language—all of these things carry semiotic weight. To the audience it doesn't matter if the actors are enjoying themselves or not. It doesn't matter if a particular beat is an expertly executed bit of deliberate artifice, or a clever off-the-cuff improvisation. All that matters is that each new signifier in the stream works to structure an interesting unfolding interpretive space.

The signifiers generated by the actors do not form a complete play space in isolation. Rather, they do so by intersecting with the pre-existing internal constraints of the various audience members. Hamlet's soliloquy isn't interesting in and of itself, no matter how expertly delivered. It is interesting because it affords the possibility of interpretive play when combined with the knowledge, attitudes, and sentiments of the audience.

In ludic semiosis, communication is the product of reciprocal understanding. I have an internal model of you and you have an internal model of me. I generate utterances for you by testing patterns until I find one that shifts my model of you into the intended configuration. And you interpret my utterance by iteratively altering your model of me to account for what you have heard.

As we watch a performance, we develop an evolving understanding of the action on stage. Each new signifier we perceive modulates this understanding. We interpret the actions we witness by making minor abductive adjustments to our internal constraints, and then testing those adjustments by seeing if future actions conform to our expectations. Do the characters' actions agree with our understanding of who they are? Does the unfolding narrative progress logically from beat to beat?

If we hear an actor speak the words "to be or not to be," there are a number of different interpretations on which we can converge:

Hamlet is contemplating killing himself.
Hamlet is fascinated by death.
Hamlet is incapable of decisive action.
Hamlet is unhinged by grief.
Hamlet is overthinking his situation.
Hamlet likes to hear himself talk.
This actor is a horrible Hamlet.

The particular interpretation we arrive at will be the result of a cascade of microsemiotic events, tiny shifts in our internal constraints in response to each signifier as it arrives. The meaning of "to be or not to be" is not something contained within the words themselves. Rather, the words serve as the initiating trigger for the construction of a wide variety of different meanings depending on how each audience member understands the action on stage.

One interesting thing about "to be or not to be" is the curious slipperiness of its possible interpretations. If the goal were for the audience to arrive at a particular interpretation as efficiently as possible, there are less ambiguous ways to go about it. Instead of "to be or not to be," the actor could say something like "I'm overwhelmed by the thought of avenging my father. If I killed myself my suffering would end." But who would want to watch a play that consisted entirely of characters baldly stating their inner motivations?

This highlights a point that we touched on briefly at the end of chapter 10. The goal of an aesthetic experience isn't for the audience to converge as quickly as possible on an intended meaning. The goal of an aesthetic experience is to make the process of convergence toward meaning interesting in and of itself. The meaning of "to be or not to be" is ambiguous because ambiguity makes the process of interpretation non-trivial. It opens up a play space bounded by the constraints of the performance and our own preconceptions, and offers us an opportunity to make interpretive moves in order to reconcile the action on stage with our understanding of the situation.

Earlier in this chapter, we set aside the question of what makes a beat "interesting for the audience." But ludic semiosis now gives us a way to answer it. A beat is interesting for the audience if it triggers an opportunity for interpretation. An interesting beat will deliver a set of signifiers capable of initiating a non-trivial cascade of microsemiotic events. The beat must be somewhat ambiguous, in the sense that it doesn't quickly resolve to a single obvious interpretation. But it must be ultimately resolvable—it isn't so ambiguous or contradictory that convergence is thwarted.

This way of looking at aesthetic works can make them seem like puzzles—like ciphers asking to be decoded in order to reveal what they mean. But that is the case only if you approach them with a gamist agenda. If you start from the position that the work has a single correct interpretation and your goal is to find it, then, yes, it is exactly like a puzzle. But if instead you approach a work from a simulationist or narrativist stances, its "puzzleness" vanishes. You aren't trying to "solve" the experience and discover its one true interpretation; you are satisfied with arriving at any interpretation that allows you to experience a feeling of coherence or closure.

The necessity of structuring a successful interpretive play space for the audience has a profound effect on the actors. Just as the audience has an internal model of each actor, each actor has an internal model of the audience. Actions on stage aren't performed for their own sake, but in order to produce an effect on the people watching. An experiential actor may try to forget about the audience when he is immersed in the moment, but only because he is hoping that the emotional honesty of the resulting performance will be more affecting than the calculated craft of a representational actor. His reciprocal understanding of the audience is displaced from his performance onto his preparation—from the navigation of his interpretive envelope onto its construction.

The audience supplies constraints for the actor just as much as the script does. For example, even if an actor isn't personally interested in the simulationist agenda, the needs of the audience often force him to be. In order for the audience to successfully form expectations about a character, the character must feel consistent and coherent. That means that, as the actor moves from beat to beat, he has to hold a steady and continuous line. Each of his actions has to be directed toward sustaining a particular set of constraints—his conception of who the character is and what his motivations are. It isn't important that the audience grasp his character in exactly the way that he does—in fact, they almost certainly will not—but his character does need to be coherent enough to be graspable, and the demands of this coherence form a powerful constraint on what the actor is allowed to do on stage.

The audience's expectations of closure have a similar effect on what the actor does. Regardless of whatever interpretive envelope the actor is working within, he knows that the performance must end when it ends. Character arcs need to be resolved; loose ends need to be tied up. The energy of the ending scene of a performance is necessarily very different from the energy of the opening scene. This difference isn't written explicitly into the script—it emerges from the performers' intuitive understanding of the narrativist needs of the audience.

In the next few chapters, we are going to look much more closely at audience experience. Specifically, we're going to explore how interpretive play works when we replace the audience with a reader, and replace the actor with a text. The elimination of the performer as a factor in the experience should clarify some aspects of interpretive play. But it is worth keeping in mind that the critical framework we will develop to understand the moment-to-moment experience of reading applies to every type of received aesthetic experience—to stage plays, to rock concerts, to art galleries, to circus parades, to street theater, to sculpture gardens, and to the narrative elements of traditional videogames.

13   Narrative Play

Literary criticism often speaks of the "structure" of a novel, but story structure is very different from game structure. The literary concept of structure has to do with viewpoint, the treatment of time … and the way in which the story builds and releases tension. The structure of the story, however, creates a single unchanging narrative that the reader cannot alter. Narrative structure is one-dimensional, because you can follow only a single path through the story.[1]

This attitude is extremely common within game scholarship.[2] Games are non-linear and open, offering players the opportunity to move freely within their structure and make meaningful choices to arrive at a variety of different possible destinations. Books, by contrast, are linear and closed, forcing readers along a predetermined path toward an inevitable conclusion. The active nature of gameplay is contrasted with the passive nature of reading. A player is a participant, but a reader is merely a spectator. The player can influence the course of the game, but the reader doesn't have any control over the unfolding of the text. Information flows in one direction only.

This attitude is extremely common, but is it correct? A book is certainly a linear arrangement of signifiers. As we read, we step through these signifiers in a fixed order, deciphering them as we go. Every time we encounter a particular book, its contents will be the same. From start to finish, the characters will do and say exactly the same things, marching forward toward an unalterable resolution.

1. Costikyan, "I Have No Words & I Must Design."
2. This attitude is extremely common outside game scholarship as well: "[T]here are many current theories which give the impression that texts automatically imprint themselves on the reader's mind of their own accord. … Our concern will be to find means of describing the reading process as a dynamic *interaction* between text and reader." Iser, *The Act of Reading*, 107.

However, despite this rigidity, different readers can experience the same book in very different ways. A book that you find powerful and moving may seem dull and incomprehensible to me. And even if we agree about the quality of the work, we may find ourselves arguing over the interpretation of different elements: What is the motivation of the protagonist? What do the various events symbolize? What is the larger significance of the narrative? What does it all mean?

Now, some texts are certainly more open to interpretation than others. If I'm flipping through the owner's manual of my car to figure out how to change a fuse, the information I want is tightly bound to the words on the page. The manual says that the fuse box is under the left end of the dashboard. When I look there, that's exactly where it is. Furthermore, anyone else reading the manual will almost certainly come to the same conclusion. The words in the manual encode a specific piece of information: that the fuse box isn't in the trunk, or under the passenger seat, or mounted atop the roof—it's under the left end of the dashboard.

But if we examine other types of writing, we discover that the relationship between text and meaning can be considerably more idiosyncratic. These works may consist of a fixed sequence of signifiers, but the process of decoding those signifiers can produce different outcomes for different readers. You may believe that Westley and Buttercup live happily ever after at the end of William Goldman's novel *The Princess Bride*[3]; I may believe that they are ultimately captured by Prince Humperdinck's men and put to death. The book doesn't compel convergence on one interpretation or the other; it leaves the question open, allowing us to draw our own conclusions about Westley and Buttercup's fate from our understanding of the characters and the plot.

The openness of literary texts is what the ludic model of semiosis is intended to address. When we encounter to a string of signifiers, we work to discover a set of interpretive constraints that can account for them. The interpretation we arrive at through this process will be influenced by both

---

3. I have used *The Princess Bride* as an example several times in this book. I chose Goldman's novel partially because of its popularity—even readers who haven't read the book are likely to know the plot from having seen the movie. But I also chose it because *The Princess Bride* isn't merely an exciting adventure story—it's also a book *about* how exciting adventure stories work and the role that such stories play in our lives. It's a fiction that is simultaneously an intentional meta-fiction, and the double nature of the work makes certain observations about the experience it structures easier to make.

our starting constraints, and the cascade of microsemiotic events that occur along the way. Unless a text is intentionally structured to drive convergence toward one particular interpretation, it is likely that chance variation will generate divergent readings among a population of readers. This potential for divergent interpretation is, in fact, the very thing that makes stories interesting. If everything within a story is obvious and explicit, there is very little play for the reader. Instead of reading like a work of fiction, such a story will read like an owner's manual—full of information, but not terribly entertaining.[4]

The history of literary criticism is largely an argument over how to identify the correct interpretation out of a multiplicity of competing readings. Different critical schools have tackled this question in different ways, ranging from the theological hermeneutics of Thomas Aquinas to the self-referential approaches of the New Critics. My approach is somewhat different. I'm not interested in constructing an aesthetic system that distinguishes correct readings from incorrect ones. Rather, I'm interested in exploring the mechanics of how we navigate a text. It is a descriptive hermeneutics, not a prescriptive one. From this point of view, there is no such thing as a correct or incorrect reading; every reading, no matter how bizarre or idiosyncratic, represents the end result of some set of interpretive moves. Neither are there inherently good or bad texts; there are only texts that succeed or fail at structuring a play space for a particular audience.

In this chapter, we are going to look at the mechanics of how texts function as play spaces. Our attention will be specifically focused on texts that are structured for aesthetic effect—texts where the experience of reading them is as important as the information they convey. We are going to look at how engaging with a story can be understood as free movement with a system of constraints, and how the agendas we adopt determine what moves we make.

Narrative Constraints

Every game requires its players to supply some of the constraints that compose its play space, but narrative play relies particularly heavily on the pre-existing knowledge of its participants. We can't understand how texts structure experiences by examining them in isolation. Instead, we have to

---

4. "Indeed, if a literary text does organize its elements in too overt a manner, the chances are that we as readers will either reject the book out of boredom, or will resent the attempt to render us completely passive." Iser, *The Act of Reading*, 87.

consider how they operate as components of a larger encompassing system of constraints.[5]

For example, if a novel begins with a fire that leaves three children orphaned, we don't need the author to provide basic contextual information such as "Children need shelter" or "Children are cared for by adults" or "It's sad when someone you love dies." We already know these things before we begin reading, and we can immediately begin to explore the ramifications of the intersection between this knowledge and the situation described on the page: Where will they live? Who will take care of them? How are they feeling? And so on.

In fact, the bulk of the constraints that structure any narrative experience usually arise from outside the text. Even the simplest books usually require a significant body of pre-existing knowledge in order for a reader to engage with them. Consider, for example, the opening sentence of the children's bedtime story *Goodnight Moon*:

In the great green room there was a telephone and a red balloon and a picture of a cow jumping over the moon.[6]

Goodnight Moon is a book to be read aloud to preschoolers, and yet it begins with a literary allusion. The picture of a cow jumping over the moon refers to the nursery rhyme "Hey-Diddle-Diddle":

Hey-diddle-diddle, the cat and the fiddle, the cow jumped over the moon.
The little dog laughed to see such sport, and the dish ran away with the spoon.

If you had never heard the nursery rhyme, the picture on the wall would seem both significant and bizarre. Why a cow? Why a moon? How is one supposed to interpret this strange image? You would proceed through the story expecting some sort of answer to the curious questions the picture raises, an answer that would never come. However, for most readers (and their small listeners) the meaning of the passage is clear. The picture is an

---

5. "A literary work, even when it appears to be new, does not present itself as something absolutely new in an informational vacuum, but predisposes its audience to a very specific kind of reception by announcements, overt and covert signals, familiar characteristics, or implicit allusions. It awakens memories of that which was already read, brings the reader to a specific emotional attitude, and with its beginning arouses expectations for the 'middle and end,' which can then be maintained intact or altered, reoriented, or even fulfilled ironically in the course of the reading according to the specific rules of the genre or type of text." Jauss, *Toward an Aesthetic of Reception*, 23.
6. Brown and Herd, *Goodnight Moon*.

illustration of a famous nursery rhyme. The fact that it is hanging on the wall means that the great green room is a nursery. The author doesn't tell us this. She assumes that we already know it before we begin reading.

Goodnight Moon assumes we know a great many things about nursery rhymes, stuffed animals, dollhouses, the cycle of day and night, human sleep patterns, child rearing, and so on. *Goodnight Moon* can function as a story only because it plays off an extensive pre-existing matrix of constraints in the minds of its readers.[7] If we were to compare the relative amount of information contained in the text with the amount of extratextual information required to actuate it, we would discover that they differ by several orders of magnitude. *Goodnight Moon* is only 131 words long, but it would take thousands of words to explicitly state all the necessary background information that its intended audience implicitly knows.

This heavy reliance on the audience's conceptual background is one of the differences between stories and games. We expect that we will need to learn the rules of a game before we can begin to play. Games contain tutorials to teach us their rules, or have their rules explicitly written out for us to study. But with stories, this training step is omitted. We don't need to memorize "the rules of the story" prior to reading because stories assume we already have most of the constraints that we need in advance.

The very ubiquity of these extratextual constraints often renders them invisible. In fact, we tend to notice their presence only through their absence. The role of prior knowledge in constructing a narrative play space is most apparent when we try to tackle a work that assumes knowledge we lack. For example, Chaucer and Shakespeare can be difficult for modern readers precisely because their stories were originally directed at audiences who knew things that we don't: How should one behave on a pilgrimage to Canterbury? How important is family honor in Renaissance Italy? Discovering the play within a work that originated within an unfamiliar cultural context can be difficult unless we adopt an interpretive frame that approximates the frame of the work's intended audience.

The extratextual constraints that structure a reading experience can come from a number of different sources[8]:

7. "Given a truly impassive reader, all his beliefs suspended or anesthetized, [a poet] would be as helpless, in his attempt to endow his work with interest and power, as though he had to write for an audience from Mars." Abrams, *Literature and Belief*, 17.
8. These extratextual constraints are Jauss' horizon of expectations. They are the context in which a work functions (and perhaps modifies). See Jauss, *Toward an Aesthetic of Reception*, 21–45.

Canon   Our experience with a text is shaped by our prior experiences with other texts. We all carry with us a mental warehouse of applicable themes, characters, and tropes accumulated from years of interaction with other works. The features of a particular story are often understood, not in isolation, but in relation to how they play with or against similar features from other stories.

Genre   Placing a story within a genre communicates to the reader that certain conventions should be assumed, even if the text itself doesn't overtly communicate them. A mystery story will contain a puzzle. A science fiction story will contain an extrapolation of technology or culture. A romance story will contain two people falling in love. And so on. Regardless of how a genre story begins, we immediately begin seeking out interpretations consistent with the conventions of the genre.

Apocrypha   Unfamiliar texts can be rendered more readable by the inclusion of annotations that supply the reader with necessary context. Apocryphal constraints may be interwoven in the text as footnotes or marginalia, or exist as separate documents such as readers' guides or critical commentary.

Culture   We are all embedded within particular historical, social, cultural, political, and economic situations. These situations create normative assumptions that influence our reading of a work.

Life   Our experience with a text is also shaped by our prior experiences in life. Each of us possesses a wealth of knowledge and memory that conditions our expectations of what is realistic and believable. Emma Bovary's dissatisfaction with her provincial life will read very differently to a nineteen-year-old college student than it does to a forty-year-old single mother.

In addition to these major sources of extratextual constraint, a variety of minor considerations can contribute to our experience as well. Gérard Genette has identified the useful concept of the "paratext."[9] The paratext is the ancillary context that surrounds the text as the reader encounters it. What is the illustration on the front of the dust jacket? What is the reputation of the author? Who wrote the blurbs on the back? Is the story being read on a brand-new e-reader, or in a battered paperback? Trivial though they are, these minor details can subtly shape our interpretations. Even the physical environment of the reader can affect the reading. Reading a horror story in a deserted house on a windy night is a very different experience than reading the same story on a crowded subway train in the middle of rush hour.

9. Genette, *Paratexts: Thresholds of Interpretation*.

Considered collectively, these extratextual constraints intersect with the text to structure the reading experience. They bias the reader toward or away from particular interpretive moves. If the text includes the phrase "in the great green room," our resulting mental image will probably have green walls, whatever other features we choose. If it tells us there is "a picture of a cow jumping over the moon" on the wall, our extratextual constraints will probably tell us that there is not also a live alligator in the middle of the floor. Although any passage can conceivably be read an infinite number of ways, the textual and extratextual constraints strongly bias us against some readings. As we move forward to examine the experience of narrative play, we must always keep in mind that the text itself represents a relatively small part of the overall system of constraints in which the play is occurring.

Navigating Narrative Play Spaces

A story, like a script, can be thought of as a series of beats. The size of a beat is variable; it can range from a single word to a sentence, to a paragraph, or even to multiple paragraphs spread across several pages. Each beat represents a horizon of intent—it's a point where the ambiguity of the textual and extratextual constraints invites an interpretive move.

The nature of this convergence depends on the degrees of freedom provided by the text and the reader's extratextual constraints. At the most basic level this convergence is simply the imagining of the unfolding action in the mind's eye of the reader. The story gestures toward events that then acquire a specific solidity within our fantasy. For example, the words on the page may never describe the hero's clothing, but in our imagination, we see him dressed appropriately for the situation. A landscape that is hinted at with a few evocative details rises before us in voluptuous wholeness. Every text contains gaps; no matter how exhaustively an author describes a particular element there will always be nuances that remain unspoken and left for the reader to resolve.

For many stories, this basic level of interpretation may be sufficient to provide a satisfying experience. If I'm reading a mass-market thriller, my moment-to-moment interpretative choices will be mostly directed toward adding specificity to the exciting events that the text suggests. I'm primarily interested in knowing what happens next, not in the deeper motivations of the characters or the significance of the story as a whole.

But with other stories, our interpretive impulses may find deeper channels. For example, if I'm reading a mystery I may devote a great deal of attention the motivations of the various characters: Why is she lying to the police? Is he really in love with her or is he just trying to get his hands on her money? Why was the victim alone on that dark stretch of road in the middle of the night? And if I'm reading a piece of literary fiction, I may find myself thinking about how the events in story build toward larger thematic concerns: What is the nature of cruelty? What is our duty toward the less fortunate? Why are we here?

Roland Barthes gives names to these different types of interpretive move—he calls them the "proairetic" and the "hermeneutic" responses. The proairetic response is focused on translating the signifiers on the page into a coherent sequence of events, whereas the hermeneutic response is concerned with uncovering the "mystery," or the deeper secret that lies below the surface.[10] As we read, we often make moves on both levels. We are working simultaneously to figure out both what is happening and why it matters.

For the most part, this process isn't a conscious one. We don't sit pondering each interpretive act—rather, we plunge forward, making snap decisions about the meaning of the text and revising them as we go. Unless we make a particular effort, it is difficult even to be aware of the mechanics of what we are doing—the interpretations that we arrive at seem to leap unhindered into our thoughts while the discarded alternatives dissolve quietly into nothingness.[11] It's similar to how we experience immediate play during a videogame. When we jump to a new platform, we are clearly *deciding* when to press the jump button, but the act of deciding often lies below the threshold of our conscious awareness. We jump when we jump, and we read what we read, ignoring the mechanism by which that particular jump or reading was chosen.

As each beat is resolved by an interpretive move, our accumulated interpretations structure our expectation of future beats (figure 13.1). We can't be sure of the specific beats we will encounter as we read on, but we can perceive a shadowy chain of likely incidents stretching out ahead of us. Every time we interpret a new beat, our framework of anticipation shifts. Our mind races forward through our provisional expectations, tweaking

---

10. Barthes, *S/Z*, 19.

11. "The reader is no less immersed in a creative process that goes on largely below the threshold of awareness. He is conscious of the resulting images, ideas, states of mind, even physical states that are generated by his reading, but he is not aware of the individual responses or of much of the process of selection and synthesis that goes on as his eyes scan the page." Rosenblatt, *The Reader, the Text, the Poem*, 52.

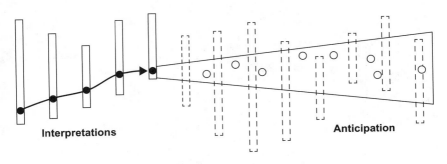

Figure 13.1
Narrative anticipation.

them to bring them into alignment with our new internal constraints.[12] For example, there is a beat in *The Princess Bride* where we discover that the pirate who kidnapped Buttercup is, in fact, her long-lost beloved Westley. She has just shoved him into a ravine. As he lies injured at the bottom, he utters the words that he spoke to her when he was courting her years before:

Down went the man in black.

Stumbling and torn and reaching out to stop his descent, but the ravine was too steep and nothing could be done.

Down, down.

Rolling over rocks, spinning all out of control.

Buttercup stared at what she had done.

Finally he rested far below her, silent and without motion. *"You can die for all I care,"* she said, and then she turned away.

Words followed her. Whispered from far, weak and warm and familiar. "As … you … wish … ."[13]

Their difference in station prevented the younger Westley from openly proclaiming his love, so "as you wish" were the words he used instead. No matter what Buttercup asked of him, he would always express his devotion to her by answering with those three words.

These three words set off an instantaneous cascade in the mind of the reader. The pirate is actually Westley! Old potentialities close off and new one open up. Is Westley badly injured? How will he get out of the ravine? Will he help Buttercup escape from Prince Humperdinck? Will true love

12. "Each sentence, each phrase, each word, will signal certain possibilities and exclude others, thus limiting the arc of expectations." Rosenblatt, *The Reader, the Text, the Poem*, 54.

13. Goldman, *The Princess Bride*, 146.

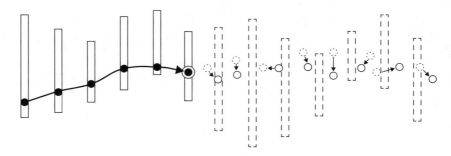

Figure 13.2
Wandering anticipation.

triumph after all? Our thoughts race ahead, considering and weighing the implications. One can almost hear the mechanical clatter as the blocky forms of our expectations settle into a new, stable configuration. Our anticipation of the future direction of the narrative is in constant flux, wandering between different potentialities in response to the new constraints imposed by each beat (figure 13.2).

Our awareness of this anticipatory play space is most acute when we encounter a beat that dramatically thwarts our expectations. The murder victim turns up alive, the hero's best friend betrays him, the love interest is actually a cross-dresser, the villain is a figment of the hero's imagination. When we encounter a plot twist, our sense of how the story will unfold is thrown into sudden disarray.

Plot twists work because we have expectations. If reading were purely a passive act, twists would have no power; we would accept each new evolution of the narrative as natural and inevitable, no matter how extreme or outlandish. But when we encounter a twist, we react with shock and surprise: "Wow, I didn't see *that* coming!" This is only possible because "seeing that coming" is an important part of the experience of narrative. The power of a twist lies in the separation between what we assumed the text would say, and what the text actually winds up saying. Brenda Laurel does a nice job of describing this distinction:

When we have no particular expectations, discovering new information is a simple and relatively unremarkable experience (oh, I see the door is over there; this character is a doctor; the husband and wife are having trouble getting along).

Discovery becomes more interesting when the new information is not what we might have expected—in other words, it is a surprise (What's that scruffy bum doing at this fancy party? Why is the house suddenly shaking? Will a higher interest rate give me a tax break?) Surprises have a higher potential of complication than do run-of-the-mill discoveries; that is, they often raise more questions than they answer. ... A far rarer and more potent form of surprise is what Aristotle referred to as *reversal*: a surprise that reveals that the *opposite* of what we expected is true. (That's not a man, that's a *woman*! The detective is actually the murderer! I thought that "formatting" would tidy my disk, not erase it!). Reversals can cause major changes in our understanding of what is going on and our expectations about what will happen next.[14]

Plot twists can't be accommodated by minor tweaks to our anticipatory framework. Because they lie outside our expectations, our only response is to completely revise the collection of interpretations that generated our expectations in the first place. In gameplay terms, a plot twist is a crux—an indication that our existing understanding is lacking and that a new understanding is required in order to proceed. The result is a collapse of our existing anticipatory framework, followed by a shift in our past interpretations, and the rebuilding of a new anticipatory framework around the new system of internal constraints (figure 13.3).

We usually use the word 'twist' to refer only to cruxes that alter our understanding of the *action* of a story. If the crux instead triggers a shift in our understanding of the *meaning* of the story, we are more likely to refer to it as a revelation or an epiphany. The sudden snap from one interpretation to another feels like moment of transcendence, a "breaking through" of some underlying truth that had previously been hidden from us. At these moments, the story's catalogue of incidents becomes weighted with significance. Our interpretation exceeds the words we have read, becoming a

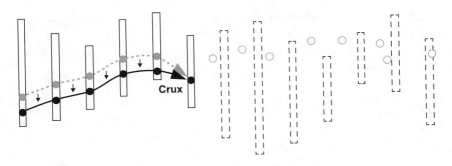

Figure 13.3
Collapse of anticipation triggered by a crux.

14. Laurel, *Computers as Theater*, 91.

wider and deeper understanding that ripples outward beyond the boundaries of the immediate play space.[15]

Reading any text thus becomes an oscillation between satisfaction and frustration. From moment to moment, we use our provisional understanding to form expectations about the action and significance of the story. Then, as we read further, the text confirms or falsifies these expectations. Falsification triggers a crux that we resolve by altering our understanding of the text. Jean-Paul Sartre describes this back-and-forth process eloquently:

> In reading, one foresees; one waits. One foresees the end of the sentence, the following sentence, the next page. One waits for them to confirm or disappoint one's foresights. The reading is composed of a host of hypotheses, or dreams followed by awakenings, of hopes and deceptions. Readers are always ahead of the sentence they are reading in a merely probable future which partially collapses and partially comes together in proportion as they progress, which withdraws from one page to the next and forms the moving horizon of the literary object.[16]

The back-and-forth continues until we reach the end of the story. At that point, we are left with a final interpretation that becomes, for us, the fixed meaning of the text. Step by step, as we moved through the narrative, we constructed a provisional understanding to explain what came before and anticipate what comes after. But when there is nothing left to read, this provisional understanding crystallizes. Without a continuous flow of new information demanding assimilation, we no longer experience the moments of discontinuity that trigger shifts in understanding.

When we talk about what a book means, we usually are talking about this terminal state of interpretation, this final crystallization of the complex system of internal constraints that we have built up during the reading process. But it is important to realize that this final understanding is a merely a lingering trace of the overall experience. The final position of the chess pieces on the chessboard tells us something interesting about the game that came before, but the experience of playing the game cannot be

15. "But when elements appear that do not fuse with or relate to what precedes either emotionally or in terms of 'sense,' there may be a retreat, a rereading, an effort to sense new guidelines within the context. ... As the text unrolls, there is not only the cumulative building up of effect through the linking of remembered earlier elements to the new ones. There is sometimes also a backward flow, a revision of earlier understandings, emphases, or attitudes; there may even be the emergence of a completely altered framework or principle of organization." Rosenblatt, *The Reader, the Text, the Poem*, 60–61.

16. Sartre, "Why Write?" (p. 50 in *What Is Literature?*).

reduced to its final position. Similarly, the terminal interpretation we arrive at for a text tells us something interesting about the process that produced it, but the process cannot be reduced to a single residual interpretation. Louise Rosenblatt sums up the experience this way:

> In broadest terms, then, the basic paradigm of the reading process consists in the response to cues; the adoption of an efferent or aesthetic stance; the development of a tentative framework or guiding principle of organization; the arousal of expectations that influence the selection and synthesis of further responses; the fulfillment or reinforcement of expectations, or their frustration, sometimes leading to a revision of the framework, and sometimes, if necessary, to rereading; the arousal of further expectations; until, if all goes well, with the completed reading of the text, the final synthesis or organization is achieved.[17]

Contrary to the model typically advanced within game studies, readers aren't passive participants. Rather, narrative play consists of an extremely rapid flurry of barely perceptible choices. As we leap from beat to beat, we choose a set of interpretive constraints to explain each beat's presence. These interpretative constraints generate expectations about the direction and significance of the story. Future beats either confirm or falsify these expectations, triggering either satisfaction or frustration. As we read, we oscillate between interpretation and expectation, between forming internal constraints that account for what has come before, and exploring the ramifications of these constraints to anticipate what will come next.

Privileging Interpretive Moves

Distinguishing good moves from bad is an essential element of any successful play space. In order for a choice to feel like a choice, it must make a meaningful change in the state of the game. If all moves are equally valuable, then choosing between them feels pointless. This is true for narrative play spaces as well. As we advance from beat to beat, we need a way to distinguish good moves from bad ones.

Now, we generally don't try to "win" the books we read. There isn't one predetermined interpretation that we are working toward as we advance through a text. But the gamist agenda isn't the only way we can privilege moves inside a play space. Coherence-oriented play favors moves that sustain the stability of our existing constraints; closure-oriented play favors moves that lead to interesting future horizons for us to explore. Thus, when we read a story, we don't have to be working toward predetermined victory

17. Rosenblatt, *The Reader, the Text, the Poem*, 54.

conditions in order to play. Instead, we can privilege interpretive moves by how well they preserve coherence or how well they avoid closure.

To illustrate how this works, let's take a look at the beginning of *The Princess Bride*:

> The year that Buttercup was born, the most beautiful woman in the world was a French scullery maid named Annette.[18]

What interpretive moves can we make in response to this beat? Two characters are mentioned—Buttercup and Annette. We are told that Annette is French, and a scullery maid, and she is the most beautiful woman in the world. When these textual constraints intersect with our prior extratextual constraints, they immediately begin to generate interesting expectations. Exceptional beauty isn't something we usually associate with scullery maids; it creates an instability that structures possible future trajectories— secret romances, a hidden past, scandal and intrigue. And, at the same time, we have a mystery. Who is this baby named Buttercup? What is the connection between her and Annette? Why is she mentioned at all?

Thus, we have the opportunity here for a variety of different interpretive moves. As we read this sentence, we aren't just internalizing its literal words; we are also converging on a system of interpretive constraints that will both explain its significance, and will structure our anticipation of the future unfolding of the text. Here are two possible moves we could make:

> Annette will lead a calm and uncomplicated life. Buttercup is a baby like many others; she has no connection to Annette

or

> Annette will lead a tumultuous and adventurous life. Buttercup is connected to Annette in some way.

Most readers will choose a move more like the second. This is because the second move is privileged within closure-oriented play. An adventurous and tumultuous life offers more opportunities for interpretive moves than a calm and uncomplicated one, and so we pick the interpretation that magnifies our possibility for future play.

It is important to keep in mind that when we make a closure-oriented move we aren't playing a game of "guess what happens next" with the text. We didn't make such a move because we think it is the *correct* interpretation, but because we think it is the *more open-ended* interpretation (figure 13.4). As it happens, after the opening sentence the next few paragraphs of

18. Goldman, *The Princess Bride*, 33.

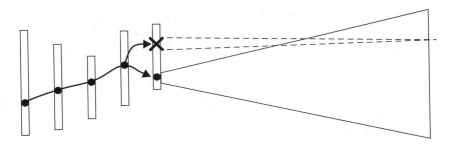

Figure 13.4
Privileging open interpretations.

The Princess Bride reveal that Annette does in fact lead a tumultuous and adventurous life, and that Buttercup is indeed connected to her in an important way. Correctly anticipating where the text is headed is certainly satisfying, but this is only because the text confirms our hope that future interpretive play lies ahead. We would not feel similarly pleased to discover that we had correctly guessed that the following paragraphs were dull and uneventful.

We generally aren't consciously aware of the expectations we have about a text, or of the mental processes by which we form them. When I read the opening sentence of *The Princess Bride*, I don't think aloud to myself "Well then, I expect that Annette will lead a tumultuous and adventurous life, and Buttercup is certainly connected to her in some way! That's my interpretive move for sentence number one!" My interpretation of the sentence exists not as a string of linguistic signifiers, but as a collection of interpretive constraints. If I'm interrogated about my understanding of the sentence, I can translate these weights into a string of signifiers for the benefit of others, but that translation step isn't a part of my normal reading process.

However, even though I'm not consciously aware that I have formed expectations, I know that they exist. I know they exist because I feel frustration when they are thwarted. If Buttercup were never mentioned again in *The Princess Bride*, it would nag at me. The text would feel broken and incomplete. The same would be true if Buttercup were mentioned, but if her connection to Annette were never explained. While we are playing with a text, we usually are completely unaware that we're doing so, but we can be certain that play must have occurred because of the interpretive constraints that linger afterward as its by-products.

It isn't possible to assign value to a particular interpretive move simply by staring at the words on the page. In order to determine a move's capacity for anticipatory play, we actually need to perform it; we need to discover where it takes us within the text's phase space. As we encounter each beat, we need to execute a rapid flurry of abductive probes along lines of potential consequence. We need to run a short distance ahead along different interpretive paths, testing each of them to see what play value it provides. The path where Buttercup is special offers us many branching pathways to examine, whereas the path where Buttercup is mundane offers us few, but in order to know this we have to actually explore both paths.

This is very similar to what happens when we play a game. When we play chess we engage in runs of anticipatory play, weighing the consequences of different moves in order to discover which ones will advance us closer to victory. When we are engaging in goal-oriented play, the final move we settle on it the one that produced the most advantageous board position during our flurry of anticipation.

In fact, it is useful to conceptualize the rules of chess primarily a mechanism for generating flurries of anticipation. We typically think of ourselves as playing chess in order to win, but (unless we're playing to win some prize) it would be more correct to say that the possibility of winning in chess exists to for the purpose of encouraging us to engage in elaborated chains of abductive exploration.

The same is true of texts that have been structured for aesthetic effect. When we read *The Princess Bride*, we are working to find interpretive moves that satisfy our desired for closure-oriented play. And, in order to identify these moves, we need to engage in elaborated chains of abductive exploration. But there is no external reward for discovering these satisfying interpretations. We don't get a prize for successfully guessing what the text means. Rather, the possibility of finding a satisfying interpretation is dangled before us in order to encourage us to engage in anticipatory play. This is the source of the wandering expectation that we identified earlier in this chapter. We have a sense of where the story is headed because we have explored the ramifications of different interpretive moves in order to determine which one to make.

When we are reading a story, closure-oriented play usually drives us to privilege interpretive moves that increase our anticipatory opportunities. However, as the story draws to a close, our attitude toward closure flips. As we recognize that we're nearing the end of the story, we begin looking for moves that will shut anticipatory play down. Instead of trying to avoid closure, we begin looking for ways to achieve it. We stop privileging interpretations that destabilize the situation and begin to privilege interpretations that drive our understanding to a final settled state.

For example, imagine how the passage where Buttercup pushes Westley into the ravine would read if it were the end of the story:

Buttercup stared at what she had done.

Finally he rested far below her, silent and without motion. *"You can die for all I care,"* she said, and then she turned away.

Words followed her. Whispered from far, weak and warm and familiar. "As … you … wish … ."[19]

When we encounter this beat in the middle of the book, we resist closure and interpret it to mean that Westley is alive. It's a moment when the narrative opens up with a profusion of possibilities. But if the story were to end this way, our reading of it would be quite different. We would seek closure; Westley would die from his fall. His whispered "As … you … wish …" would become a wistful farewell to his lost love instead of a hopeful revelation. The same passage will be interpreted as either hopeful or tragic depending on what sort of interpretive moves we are privileging as we read it.

We privilege different interpretations on the basis of whether they move us toward or away from closure. But we also privilege interpretations on the basis of whether or not they preserve the coherence of our existing constraints (figure 13.5). Given a choice between an interpretive move that triggers a crux and one that avoids one, we usually choose the latter. As we move from beat to beat within a text, we tend to favor interpretations that lie within our existing understanding of where the text is headed and what it means. Another passage from *The Princess Bride* illustrates this:

Dusk was closing in when Buttercup crested the hill. She was perhaps half an hour from the castle, and her daily ride was three-quarters done. Suddenly, she reined Horse, for standing in the dimness beyond was the strangest trio she had ever seen.[20]

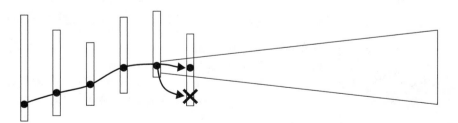

Figure 13.5
Privileging stable interpretations.

19. Goldman, *The Princess Bride*, 146.
20. Ibid., 82.

When we encounter this beat, we have an interesting interpretive move to make. Who are these three figures in the dusk, and what significance do they have to the unfolding of the story? Since this passage comes from fairly early in the book, we will look for an interpretation that opens up additional possibilities for anticipatory play. So the three figures can't just be three farmers walking home from the fields, or a trick of the light. They might be bandits—that would be interesting—or maybe messengers with some exciting news. But whoever they are, we expect that they will prove important for the course of the story, and probably will kick it off in a new direction.

However, our interpretation of the significance of the three figures is also constrained by our simulationist desire to maintain coherence within the narrative. We aren't likely to decide that the three figures are vampires or cowboys, even though such an interpretation would be entirely consistent with the literal text. While those interpretations would satisfy our desire to avoid closure, they would trigger a massive crux in our understanding of the world of *The Princess Bride*. Because of the simulationist agenda, we tend to avoid interpretations that radically disrupt our understanding, even if such interpretations offer interesting opportunities for anticipatory play.

As we explore a narrative, we balance these two competing mechanisms for privileging outcomes. We want to make interpretive moves that increase our future opportunities for play, but we also want to make interpretive moves that minimize the cruxes that we experience. And often the best move to accomplish the former isn't the best move to accomplish the latter.

In chapter 4, we looked at how play spaces are often structured to have multiple conflicting goals. The most interesting choices within a play space are often those where we have to choose from between different desirable outcomes. If navigating a text were simply a matter of always avoiding closure, or always avoiding cruxes, then choosing one interpretation over another would be relatively easy. But because these different agendas offer us competing ways to assign value to interpretive moves, the process of choosing becomes more challenging. Because we have competing criteria for what "best" means, we never are certain which interpretation is the best.

Not only do tensions exist *between* the agendas, they also exist *within* them. As we move through a text, our provisional understanding is a hodge-podge of interpretive constraints assembled on the fly from the microsemiotic cascades triggered by previous beats. We will have a provisional understanding of the arc of the plot, but we also have provisional understandings of other aspects of the story, such as the personalities of the individual characters, or the significance of the story as a whole. These different understandings will generally tend to cohere, but it is entirely possible for a beat to throw them in conflict with each other. For example, we may sometimes discover that sustaining coherence of plot requires us to abandon coherence of character, or that working to achieve thematic closure requires us to sacrifice closure on other levels.

When we read George Orwell's *Nineteen Eighty-Four*, we empathize with Winston and Julia and we want them to escape. But we also perceive the bleak argument that Orwell is making. We flicker back and forth between different interpretive strategies for the text—some that favor a happy outcome for the characters, some that favor a coherent critique of an authoritarian state. This instability culminates in the final horror of Room 101, where Winston and Julia are broken by their interrogators and betray each other. The ending of *Nineteen Eighty-Four* brings not pleasure, but grim intellectual satisfaction as we abandon our hopeful expectations in exchange for thematic completeness.[21] If we want to read *Nineteen Eighty-Four* as a commentary on the cruelty of totalitarian repression, then Winston and Julia need to be crushed by it. And when they are crushed, it validates that interpretation of the text.

There are a variety of levels on which interpretive play can operate:

Grammatical Is this word a misprint?
Syntactical What does this sentence mean?
Motivational What is this character trying to accomplish?
Logistical What just happened?
Thematic What is this story about?
Contextual Why did the author write this?

And there are many more. As we read a text, we seek out coherence and closure, but there are many, many ways for us to find it. We can read for character or plot or theme or political implication or cultural context or even for the pure music of the words themselves. But whatever interpretive

---

21. "Catharsis depends upon the way that probability and causality have been orchestrated in the construction of the whole; it also depends upon our uninterrupted experience of engagement with the representation. More than that, it is the pleasure that results from the completion of a form. The final form of a thing may be suspected from the beginning or unforeseen until the very end; it may undergo many or few transformations. It may be happy or sad, because the 'success' of the outcome in terms of the representational content is not nearly so potent as the feeling of completion that is implicit in the final apprehension of the shape of the whole of which one has been a co- creator." Laurel, *Computers as Theater*, 122.

system we set up in order to make sense of what we are reading, we will still be searching for either closure or coherence.

Umberto Eco makes a useful distinction between texts that are *open* and texts that are *closed*. An open work provides interesting play in conjunction with a large number of different extratextual constraints; a closed work works with only a few.[22] As we read an open work, we are invited to try out a variety of competing interpretive frames, many of which will generate interesting play spaces. In contrast, a closed work will generate play within only a few frames. It doesn't ask us to work to discover a good strategy for engagement, rather, it expects us to default to a familiar set of extratextual constraints and get on with it.

In gameplay terms, an open work is like a soccer ball, and a closed work is like a hockey puck. Both objects possess inherent physical properties that affect the play space that is organized around them. A soccer ball is more "open," in the sense that it works with a much wider range of rules than a hockey puck does. You can use a soccer ball to play soccer, or volleyball, or kickball, or water polo, or even, in a pinch, a passable version of hockey. In contrast, a hockey puck works with a much narrower range of rules.

Every text is intended to work within some default set of extratextual constraints. But as readers, we are free to construct any interpretive frame that we want. In the process of doing so, we may discover ways to play with a text that were unimagined by the text's creator, just as we may discover ways to play a game that were unimagined by the game's designer. A hockey puck may be intended to function with a very narrow range of rules, but that doesn't mean that we are forbidden from inventing entirely new rules that allow it to be played with in unexpected and interesting ways.

Some stories even invite a gamist approach to reading. The genre conventions of mysteries dictate that they will include a crime in need of solving, that the clues needed to solve the crime will be supplied over the course of the story, and that the correct solution will be revealed at the end.

22. "In fact, the form of the work of art gains its aesthetic validity precisely in proportion to the number of individual perspectives from which it can be viewed and understood. These give it a wealth of different resonances and echoes without impairing its original essence; a road traffic sign, on the other hand, can only be viewed in one sense, and, if it is transfigured into some fantastic meaning by an imaginative driver, it merely ceases to be *that* particular traffic sign with that particular meaning. A work of art, therefore, is a complete and *closed* form in its uniqueness as a balanced organic whole, while at the same time constituting an *open* product on account of its susceptibility to countless different interpretations which don't impinge on its unadulterable specificity." Eco, *The Role of the Reader*, 49.

Unlike most other types of stories, mysteries do have a well-defined victory condition for the reader to pursue. We may choose some of our interpretive moves according to how they satisfy our desire for coherence and closure, but we are simultaneously looking for interpretations that tell us *who did it*. Arriving at the correct solution before the final revelation feels like a victory. And it is a victory, in exactly the same way that solving any puzzle is a victory—we have successfully navigated a system of constraints to arrive at a privileged destination.

James Thurber satirized the gamist stance in his short essay "The Macbeth Murder Mystery." The piece describes a mystery fan who, desperate for something new to read, purchases a copy of *Macbeth* and attempts to solve it. She begins by rejecting both Macbeth and Lady Macbeth as the culprits, since according to genre convention the most obvious suspects "are the ones that are never guilty or shouldn't be anyway." She briefly considers Banquo, but when he turns up dead her suspicions settle on MacDuff:

My companion leaned toward me, her eyes bright, her teacup quivering. "Do you know who discovered Duncan''s body?" she demanded. I said I was sorry, but I had forgotten. "Macduff discovers it," she said, slipping into the historical present. Then he comes running downstairs and shouts, "Confusion has broken open the Lord's anointed temple" and "Sacrilegious murder has made his masterpiece" and on and on like that. The good lady tapped me on the knee. "All that stuff was rehearsed," she said. "You wouldn't say a lot of stuff like that, offhand, would you—if you had found a body?" She fixed me with a glittering eye. "I—" I began. "You're right!" she said. "You wouldn't! Unless you had practiced it in advance. 'My God, there's a body in here!' is what an innocent man would say." She sat back with a confident glare.[23]

The literary critic Edmund Wilson, writing contemporaneously with Thurber, took a much harsher stance toward mystery novels in a series of three scathing essays he wrote for *The New Yorker* in 1945. In the second essay ("Who Cares Who Killed Roger Ackroyd?"), he writes:

It was then that I understood that a true connoisseur of this fiction must be able to suspend the demands of his imagination and literary taste and take the thing as an intellectual problem. But how you arrive at that state of mind I do not understand.[24]

Wilson senses that a different approach is necessary to join the game, but he is so firmly grounded in his literary frame that the idea of adopting a gamist agenda is incomprehensible to him. He is confident he *knows* the right way to read. After all, he makes his living reading, and then writing

23. Thurber, "The Macbeth Murder Mystery."
24. Wilson, "Who Cares Who Killed Roger Ackroyd?"

about what he has read. The thought that certain stories might be inaccessible to his default critical stance baffles him. Rather than admit that his tools are inadequate for explaining how mysteries function as entertainment, he dismisses an entire genre as worthless. For Wilson, a mystery novel fails to structure an interesting play experience within his default set of extratextual constraints, and so he concludes that there is simply no play there to be had. He nudges the hockey puck fretfully with his toe, wondering how anybody ever manages to kick the damn thing downfield.

In the previous chapter, we constructed a framework to allow us to analyze stories as play spaces. To recap, here are the main elements of that framework:

- A story consists of a string of signifiers. As we encounter each signifier, it structures a horizon in conjunction with our internal constraints.
- We respond to this horizon by making an interpretive move. An interpretive move is an adjustment to our constraints.
- In making an interpretive move, we engage in anticipatory play. We evaluate the worth of possible interpretations by considering their consequences.
- We weigh each move according to how it satisfies coherence or closure. Does it minimize disruption to our existing constraints? Does it lead to more opportunities to play in the future?
- This process lies below our conscious awareness. It consists of a cascade of microsemiotic events that eventually converge on a provisional interpretation.
- Each new interpretive move becomes an internal constraint that structures our future horizons.

This model of narrative engagement deliberately avoids questions of quality. It makes no distinctions between good stories and bad stories, between interesting narrative experiences and dull ones. It makes no prescriptivist claims about how we should read, or how we should interpret. Rather, it is simply a descriptivist methodology for analyzing the process of reading and interpreting.

One consequence of this methodology is the recognition that all critical analysis takes place within the context of some assumed set of extratextual constraints. It isn't possible to make judgments about the meaning or quality of a work by considering it in isolation. The text itself supplies only some of the constraints that structure the narrative playfield—the remainder come from the reader, and many of those are transient products of the engagement itself. Thus, when we say "X means Y," what we usually mean is "X means Y to readers like me." We are saying that if you approach a work with a particular set of extratextual constraints it will structure a particular sort of playfield that will allow particular sorts of interpretive moves and those interpretive moves will leave behind a particular lingering trace of meaning. *Nineteen Eighty-Four* is a commentary on the cruelty of totalitarian repression only if we approach it with extratextual constraints that accommodate those interpretive moves. With different extratextual constraints, *Nineteen Eighty-Four* can become a thriller with an unsatisfying ending, or a tragic love story, or a trite piece of propaganda. And we have no way to elevate any one of these readings over the others, other than by arbitrarily privileging the particular set of extratextual constraints that allow it.

However, even if we aren't able to assign fixed meaning to a text that holds across all readers and situations, we can nevertheless analyze the play spaces it structures. We can examine how different extratextual constraints intersect with the text to structure particular interpretive moves. Does this way of reading of *Nineteen Eighty-Four* open up more opportunities for narrative play? Does it contribute to our broader understanding of the world as a whole? We may not be able to determine which reading is correct, but we can certainly say which readings are more fruitful or productive.

In order for this sort of analysis to work, we must make assumptions about readers other than ourselves. This is tricky territory. Every reader has his or her own default internal constraints, which are products of their lived experience and their earlier textual encounters. Sartre illustrates this point beautifully:

People of the same period and community, who have lived through the same events, who have raised or avoided the same questions, have the same taste in their mouths; they have the same complicity, and are the same corpses among them. That is why it not necessary to write so much; there are key-words. If were to tell an audience of Americans about the German occupation, there would have to be a great deal of analysis and precaution. I would waste twenty pages in dispelling preconceptions, prejudices, and legends. Afterwards, I would have to be sure of my position at each step; I would have to look for images and symbols in American history which would enable them to understand ours; I would always have to keep in mind the difference between our old man's pessimism and their childlike optimism. If I were to write about the same subject for Frenchmen, we would be *entre nous*. For example, it would be enough to say: "A concert of German music in the band-stand of the public garden." Everything is there: a raw spring day, a park in the provinces, men with shaven skulls blowing away at their brasses, blind and deaf passers-by who quicken their steps, two or three sullen-looking listeners under the trees, this useless serenade to France which drifts off into the sky, our shame and our anguish, our anger, and our pride too.[1]

A playfield structured by the intersection of reader and text will inevitably be idiosyncratic and unique. How, then, can we make any meaningful claims about the narrative playfields that others experience and the interpretive moves they make within them?

First, though it is true that each reader brings a unique set of extratextual constraints to bear, there is a great deal of overlap between readers from similar backgrounds. Sartre recognizes that if you are French and you lived through the German occupation you have internalized a certain set of extratextual constraints that most Americans didn't. The literary critic Stanley Fish has observed that it is possible to group readers into "interpretive communities"—collections of similar individuals from similar cultures who tend to approach works using similar strategies.[2] When performing textual analysis, we don't have to take every conceivable reader into account. Rather, we can construct a hypothetical reader who is representative of a particular interpretive community. I may not read *Nineteen Eighty-Four* exactly the same way that you read it, but if both of us are products of late-twentieth-century American culture it is likely that your reading will at least be recognizable to me and vice versa. We may not be able to assign a single fixed meaning to a text, but we can talk about likely meanings within particular interpretive communities.

Second, the act of reading itself drives our internal constraints toward accommodating the text. Whatever frame we possess when we begin reading, our interpretive moves modify our internal constraints. Since these modifications occur in response to the text, it is possible for two readers who began with very different internal constraints to converge on similar interpretations simply because they have both discovered the same "sweet spot" in how they can play with the text. Thus, although we can't assign fixed meaning to a text, we may discover that certain strategies of engagement reoccur in response to particular textual challenges.

What this means is that, although each of us will necessarily experience a text in his or her own unique and idiosyncratic way, our readings will not be completely *sui generis*. We will inevitably find points of commonality in the interpretive moves we make. And these points of commonality can

---

1. Sartre, "For Whom Does One Write?" in *"What Is Literature?" and Other Essays*, 71.
2. Fish, *Is There a Text in This Class?*

then allow us to grasp how other readers may legitimately arrive at interpretations that are divergent from our own, or even to learn how adjust our
own internal constraints so that we can play in new and different ways.

In the rest of this chapter, we will look at how a text can function to
create a satisfying play space. We will examine particular passages in *The
Princess Bride* using the heuristics of play that we developed in the first part
of the book. We will step through the heuristics one by one and observe
how they apply to the system of constraints that *The Princess Bride* provides.

This analysis assumes that the book is being approached with a workable
set of extratextual constraints. Any text can be made dull or frustrating if it
is read with the wrong extratextual constraints, just as any text (no matter
how poorly crafted or perverse) can form the basis of a satisfying experience
if it is read with the right extratextual constraints. Thus, as we explore the
various ways that this particular text can structure play, it is worth keeping
in mind that these effects do not emerge automatically, but rather as the
result of the novel's being read by a sympathetic reader.

Choice and Variety in Narrative

Choice in narrative is interpretive choice. We aren't able to choose what
words appear next on the page, but we are able to choose the meaning that
we assign to the words that do appear.

To hold our attention, a text must deliver a moderate number of
moment-to-moment interpretive choices. A story that explains everything
and leaves nothing to the imagination is likely to be dull. There have to be
some questions for us to answer: What is going to happen next? Why did
the protagonist do that? What does this all mean? But a story that leaves
too many things unexplained is frustrating—its fragmentary constraints
offer so many possibilities that it is difficult for us to converge on one interpretation. If we can't make *some* sense of what we are reading, there isn't
much opportunity for play.

However, as we have seen, merely providing the right number of
moment-to-moment choices isn't enough. The play value of a horizon
of intent is determined not only by how it functions in isolation but also
by how it relates to the other horizons that came before it. If we encounter
the same horizon over and over, it rapidly loses its play value. Repeatedly
making the same choice doesn't feel like choosing; we already know what
to do, so we just do it.

This applies to stories as well as games. Successive dramatic beats should
provide us with new horizons by advancing the plot, developing the

characters, or expanding on the theme. If a scene merely re-traverses familiar territory, telling us things we already know, our horizon remains static
and we find ourselves repeating the same interpretive moves.

Lack of variety typically manifests itself as belabored detail: long passages of excessive description, exhaustive elaborations of trivial actions, or
empty bantering or bickering that doesn't advance our understanding of
the characters. The result is as a "dead patch" in the story—a stretch during
which the interpretive horizon is fixed. At first the horizon will generate
normal anticipatory play; however, as the lack of variety persists, the horizon becomes exhausted and play stops. We may find ourselves thinking
"Come on, get on with it," or skimming paragraphs rather than reading
them closely, or skipping ahead.

This doesn't mean that all stories have to be action-packed. Rather, it
means that a story should take into account the accumulated interpretive
moves of the reader. As we proceed from beat to beat, we build up a provisional understanding of the text. We think we know what is going on,
and what the story means. But we need to be continually presented with
new beats that offer opportunities for us to tweak that understanding in
different ways. It isn't that our understanding has to be evolving continually; rather, it that we need to be continually offered opportunities for it to
evolve, even if we decline to follow up on them.

For example, near the beginning of *The Princess Bride* we learn that Buttercup treats the family farmhand with disdain:

The horse's name was 'Horse' (Buttercup was never long on imagination) and it
came when she called it, went where she steered it, and did what she told it. The
farm boy did what she told him too. Actually, he was a young man now, but he had
been a farm boy when, orphaned, he'd come to work for her father, and Buttercup
referred to him that way still. "Get me that, Farm Boy—quickly, lazy thing, trot now
or I'll tell Father."[3]

This beat is interesting when we first encounter it. A new character has
been introduced, and we must do some interpretive work to fit him into
our evolving understanding of the text. But once we have developed a basic
understanding of who Farm Boy is and how he relates to Buttercup, we
want the text to move on. If Goldman had followed up this paragraph with
five more pages describing in exhaustive detail dozens of different inci-
dences of Buttercup's being disdainful toward Farm Boy, we would begin
to get bored.

3. Goldman, *The Princess Bride*, 35–36.

In the world of *The Princess Bride*, Buttercup and Farm Boy have seen each other daily for years. Thus, it is entirely plausible that Buttercup has acted disdainfully toward Farm Boy dozens or even hundreds of times. But Goldman doesn't describe all those incidents—doing so wouldn't increase our understanding of the relationship between the two characters. Instead, he swerves off in a different direction, telling about how the village girls are jealous of Buttercup, explaining the geography of the kingdom of Florin, and introducing Count and Countess Rugen. When the story returns to Farm Boy, it is from an entirely different direction. The Count and the Countess are visiting Buttercup's father's farm. The Countess flirts with Farm Boy, and Buttercup, much to her surprise, feels jealous. This beat drives us to reassess our understanding of the relationship between Buttercup and Farm Boy. We have a new interpretive move to make within a fresh horizon.

When telling a story, it isn't sufficient to merely step through a sequence of events. Each event, as it is presented, must offer an opportunity to reassess our understanding of what has come before—it must offer an interpretive choice. And the interpretive choices must build on each other and grow as the story progresses. It isn't enough for us to decide over and over again that Buttercup is disdainful toward Farm Boy. We need for their relationship to change and evolve so that we have new decisions to make.

Consequence in Narrative

For a choice to feel meaningful, it must influence our future horizons. A game in which we aren't able to influence the outcome isn't very satisfying. Each move must affect what future moves are available to us. Similarly, as we read, our successive interpretive choices should feel as if they build upon those that came before. A story isn't merely a collection of disjointed incidents. Rather, each narrative beat functions as a link in a chain of meaning, and how we respond to each beat shapes our possible responses to future beats.

When a narrative beat isn't part of this chain, we say that it is gratuitous.[4] It's a bit of business whose resolution doesn't contribute to future play. It's literally "inconsequential"—it could be dropped without significantly

---

4. "Incidents are said to be 'gratuitous' if they have no causal relationship to the whole action; gratuitous incidents shed no light on why things have happened or why they happened as they did; they may also be the effects of causes that are not represented." Laurel, *Computers as Theater*, 74.

affecting our interpretation of the rest of the story. In contrast to a lack of development, gratuitous beats usually aren't boring. As we are experiencing them, they may seem just as engaging as the other parts of the story. But afterward we may find ourselves thinking "What was that all about?" or "That seemed pointless." To illustrate this point, let's return to *The Princess Bride*. Several pages after the Countess pays attention to Farm Boy, Buttercup has a revelation:

"I love you," Buttercup said. "I know this must come as something of a surprise, since all I've even done is scorn you and degrade you and taunt you, but I have loved you for several hours now, and every second, more. I thought an hour ago I love you more than any woman has ever loved a man, but half an hour after that I knew that what I felt before was nothing compared to what I felt then. But ten minutes after that I understood that my previous love was a puddle compared to the high seas before a storm. Your eyes are like that, did you know? Well they are. How many minutes ago was I? Twenty? Had I brought up my feelings up to then? It doesn't matter."[5]

The play value of this beat depends a great deal on the specific provisional understanding of Buttercup that we have arrived at in response to the beats that preceded it. For example, if we took Buttercup's disdain at face value, her sudden discovery of her love for Farm Boy will be experienced as a significant crux. This beat will trigger a backward ripple through our understanding of Buttercup's character—a thrilling realignment of the strategic constraints that form our grasp of the work. But if, on the other hand, we previously read Buttercup's disdain as a bit of self-delusion, this passage will be experienced as the satisfying culmination of a trajectory we had already anticipated. Whichever way we read those earlier beats, our previous interpretive moves were consequential. They altered the configuration of our playfield, and determined what new interpretive moves are available to us now.

After reading the passage reproduced above, most readers will probably understand that Buttercup loves Farm Boy (or Westley, as we discover his name to be). But, depending on the particular interpretive moves they made in response to earlier beats in the narrative, different readers will have taken different trajectories through the novel's phase space to arrive at this understanding.

In general, when we read a text that we know has been deliberately created to structure an aesthetic experience, we assume that each beat is consequential—that it exists within the narrative for a reason. Our assumption

5. Goldman, *The Princess Bride*, 47–48.

of consequentiality gives us confidence when we engage in anticipatory play. When we read that Buttercup is treating Farm Boy with disdain, that isn't merely a fact that we note and then drop. Rather, it remains a part of our active constraints. It lingers at the edge of our awareness, and we revisit it from time to time, using that understanding as a way to anticipate what happens next or to decide what meaning to assign to the text as a whole.

When a beat fails to structure future horizons, we feel frustrated. As inconsequential beats pile up, we try harder and harder to find a way to find a way to integrate them into a coherent anticipatory playfield. Eventually, a narrative that is too disjointed and diffuse will simply collapse into incoherence, and narrative play will cease.

Predictability in Narrative

As we play a game, we construct interpretations to explain our experience. These interpretations are the basis for anticipatory play. Only by understanding what came before can we predict what will come after. However, in order for this process to work, the play space must supply an experience that is both consistent and comprehensible. If events occur at random, or the relationship between cause and effect is uncertain, we may find ourselves unable to construct an interpretive framework, and anticipatory play may become impossible.

Similarly, the beats that make up a story have to be structured so that it is possible for us to integrate our understanding of them into a unified framework with predictive value. Partially, this is a matter of consequence—our understanding of earlier beats should structure the horizons of later beats. But it is also a matter of coherence. Interpretive choices don't operate in isolation. They do so as parts of a system of multiple constraints derived from our responses to multiple earlier beats.

In plain language, what this means is that the early parts of a story must work together to give us a sense of where the story is headed. That way, as we encounter each new beat, we have the constraints we need if we are to engage in anticipatory play. We can imagine different possible routes that the narrative can take, and we can use that information to help us converge on the most appealing interpretation of each beat.

About halfway through *The Princess Bride*, Buttercup and Westley flee into the Fire Swamp to avoid being captured by Prince Humperdinck. Before they enter, Buttercup is afraid:

Buttercup stared at the Fire Swamp. As a child she had once spent an entire nightmared year convinced she was going to die there. Now she could not move another step. The giant trees blackened the ground ahead of her. From every part came the sudden flames. "You cannot ask it of me," she said.[6]

By the time we read this passage, we have learned a number of things about the characters and the world. We know that Westley is uncommonly brave and resourceful, and that he and Buttercup are deeply in love. We know that the story has the form of a fairytale, with extravagant heroics and narrow escapes. We know that more than half of the story still lies ahead of us. Taken collectively, this knowledge allows us to anticipate what will likely unfold over the next few pages. Despite Buttercup's reservations, they will enter the swamp. There will be a dangerous traversal. Westley will rescue Buttercup, and perhaps Buttercup will rescue Westley. In the end, the two young lovers will emerge from the Fire Swamp unscathed. Even though we aren't consciously aware that we have these expectations, we know that they exist because we would be surprised if they were thwarted. If Buttercup and Westley were to die in the Fire Swamp, or if Westley were to abandon Buttercup and go on alone, or if it were to be revealed that the Fire Swamp was harmless, we would feel shocked and let down. We would find ourselves thinking "That's not how the story is supposed to go."

The Princess Bride itself offers a beautiful example of how this sort of predictive failure typically plays out. Besides being a fairytale, *The Princess Bride* is also a book about fairytales and how we read them and what we expect from them. The adventures of Buttercup and Westley are contained within a frame story of a young boy whose father is reading him *The Princess Bride* while he is sick in bed. From time to time, Goldman pulls back from the main adventure to describe how the boy and his father are responding to it.

Here is a passage from late in the book. At this point in the main story, Westley is being held prisoner by Prince Humperdinck and seems to be facing almost certain doom. In the frame story, the father hesitates about reading further. When his son angrily asks why, he explains reluctantly:

"Westley dies," my father said.
   I said, "What do you mean, 'Westley dies'? You mean dies?"
   My father nodded. "Prince Humperdinck kills him."
   "He's only faking though, right?"
   My father shook his head, closed the book all the way.
   "Aw shit," I said and I started to cry.
   "I'm sorry," my father said. "I'll leave you alone," and he left me.
   "Who gets Humperdinck?" I screamed after him.

6. Goldman, *The Princess Bride*, 157–158.

He stopped in the hall. "I don't understand."

"Who kills Prince Humperdinck? At the end, someone's got to get him. Is it Fezzik? Who?"

"Nobody kills him. He lives."

"You mean he wins, Daddy? Jesus, what did you read me this thing for?"[7]

In order for a story to function as a story, we need to feel as if we understand where it is headed. We make interpretive moves that structure chains of anticipatory play. Because of this anticipatory play, we have a sense of what might happen and what will not. We expect that Westley and Buttercup will not die in the Fire Swamp, that Westley will not die in Prince Humperdinck's dungeon, and that Prince Humperdinck will be punished for his evil deeds. We expect these things because we have caught glimpses of them as our thoughts have raced forward to explore the anticipatory play space of the text.

Predictive failures often manifest themselves as plot holes. We arrive at a beat without understanding how we could possibly have gotten there, given our previous understanding of the story. Westley is dead. How can that be possible? Nothing that came before prepared us for the words that we now see on the page. This triggers a massive crux—clearly, our understanding of the text was flawed in some way. But unlike a typical crux, a plot hole is so large and disruptive that it's difficult to achieve the necessary realignment of our interpretive constraints. We are abruptly unsure of everything—what the characters are doing, why they are doing it, how their actions fit with what we read before. Suddenly the whole story feels incoherent and arbitrary. Things are happening for no reason! We can't converge on a stable interpretation, and play collapses.[8]

Uncertainty in Narrative

Predictability is desirable, but it is possible to have too much predictability. If a play space is too predictable, we race ahead of our current horizon,

---

7. Goldman, *The Princess Bride*, 222.

8. Walter Scott's novel *Ivanhoe* contains a famous example of just this sort of collapse: the abrupt resurrection of Athelstane after many pages describing his death and battle and his funeral. The crux was so severe that Scott felt compelled to add the following footnote to future editions: "The resuscitation of Athelstane has been much criticised, as too violent a breach of probability, even for a work of such fantastic character. It was a *tour-de-force*, to which the author was compelled to have recourse, by the vehement entreaties of his friend and printer, who was inconsolable on the Saxon being conveyed to the tomb."

preemptively exhausting future horizons long before we arrive at them. We have already decided all our moves in advance, so there are no more interesting decisions to make.

If a character's motivations are too transparent, or if the consequences of a situation are too obvious, or if the significance of a passage is too explicit, reading what follows will be dull. As we read further, we aren't making new interpretive choices; we are merely re-traversing familiar terrain that we already thoroughly explored during our previous chain of anticipation.

Often a lack of uncertainty in narrative is attributable to overfamiliarity. Clichéd prose, stock characters, and formulaic plots limit play significantly. When we encounter a situation or a character that we have seen many times before, we don't spend much time exploring the ramifications. Rather, our expectations quickly snap to a default chain of anticipation. A beat that appears to be an opportunity for interpretive choice isn't such an opportunity after all.

But lack of uncertainty can also arise from prose that is too unambiguous and direct. In the parlance of screenwriting, dialogue that tells too much is said to be "on the nose." It is boring when characters bluntly announce what they are thinking or feeling. Rather than letting us gradually build up our sense of a character over the course of many scenes, on-the-nose writing delivers the author's intended interpretation in one large, predigested lump. It removes the uncertainty from our upcoming interpretive choices, preempting future play.

As we read a story, we want to have a strong idea of where it is headed and what it means, but we also want to feel as though that understanding is always in danger of being overturned. The whole time Westley and Buttercup are making their way through the Fire Swamp, each new beat that we encounter exists in tension with our expectations of how the story will unfold. We think we know what will happen to them, but Goldman has planted enough seeds of doubt so we aren't certain that our anticipation is correct. Each beat that meets our expectations confirms the correctness of our existing interpretive constraints, but subtle deviations from formula leave us feeling unsteady and drive us toward paying careful attention to each new sentence in order to shore up our uncertain understanding.

For example, almost immediately after they enter the Fire Swamp, Goldman tells us that the swamp isn't as bad as Buttercup and Westley had expected:

Westley led the way. Buttercup stayed just behind, and they made, at the outset, very good time. The main thing, she realized, was to forget your childhood dreams, for the Fire Swamp was bad, but it wasn't that bad. The odor of the escaping gases, which at first seemed almost punishing, soon diminished through familiarity. The sudden bursts of flame were easily avoided because, just before they struck, there was a deep kind of popping sound clearly coming from the vicinity of where the flames would appear.[9]

This is a surprising let-down, but it puts us on our guard. If the Fire Swamp isn't as dangerous as it has been built up to be, where is the story headed? We don't have to wait long to find out. Just as Westley comments on how unexpectedly safe the Fire Swamp is, Buttercup is abruptly sucked down into a patch of dry quicksand:

"[T]o tell the truth, I'm almost disappointed; this place is bad, all right, but it's not *that* bad. Don't you agree?"

Buttercup wanted to, totally, and she would have too; only by then the Snow Sand had her.[10]

On one level, this is exactly the sort of thing we were expecting. The heroes are in a dangerous situation, and we expect them to confront the danger and overcome it. But on another level, we weren't expecting this at all. Buttercup's sudden disappearance comes as an exciting surprise precisely because the story's previous positive beat subtly undermined our expectations.

Consider how much less interesting this situation would be if Goldman had made Buttercup's plunge into the Snow Sand more straightforward:

No sooner had Westley and Buttercup entered the Fire Swamp then they encountered the first of its many dangers. Buttercup stepped into a patch of deadly Snow Sand, and, in an instant, she plunged down into it, vanishing completely from sight!

On a purely functional level, this passage serves a similar purpose as Goldman's actual prose. It tells us that Buttercup has fallen in and Westley must rescue her. But it's also horribly dull. We knew something like this would happen, and now it has. There is no instability, no new interpretive choices for us to make, merely the blunt confirmation of our existing expectations.

This is how predictability and uncertainty can coexist within the same narrative experience. It isn't that a story has to be packed with continual twists and surprises; it's that we need to feel that the possibility of a twist or surprise is always lurking just around the corner. For a story to play out the way we expect it to is perfectly fine, so long as we are continually unsure whether our expectations are correct.

9. Goldman, *The Princess Bride*, 159.
10. Goldman, *The Princess Bride*, 159.

Satisfaction in Narrative

When we play a game, we want our actions to move us closer to some goal. If the rules consistently prevent us from reaching desirable configurations of the state, we will quickly become frustrated and stop playing. This is true for both the immediate and the anticipatory components of gameplay. It's satisfying to do something and achieve a desired result, but it's also satisfying to predict something and have that prediction come true.

When we read we aren't working toward a specific victory condition. Instead, we are working toward coherence or closure. Our goal isn't to win, but to minimize the disruption of our existing constraints, or to bring our understanding to a settled state.

The satisfaction of coherence is fairly straightforward: Does the text offer us a way to integrate all of our collective interpretive constraints into a larger system devoid of internal contradictions? Can we reconcile our understanding of the main character in chapter one with our understanding of the main character in chapter twenty? Do the thematic implications cohere with the unfolding of the plot? Does our understanding of the text agree with our understanding of the world?

The satisfaction of closure is a little more complicated. In order to achieve closure, we need to be able to settle on an interpretation of the work as a whole that removes the necessity for future anticipatory play. We need to be able to bring our understanding to a settled state—that is, a state in which we no longer feel compelled to make any additional interpretive moves. In order for this to happen, the text has to shut down any anticipatory chains that it has opened up.[11] When that doesn't happen, we say that the story has a loose end—a bit of play that never resolves itself. If a character or a situation causes us to form a set of expectations, we expect that eventually those expectations will be confirmed or falsified. If our expectations are confirmed, the satisfaction is immediate; if they are thwarted, a crux is triggered, setting off a flurry of fresh interpretive play to resolve it. But if our expectations are never resolved one way or the other, we are left hanging. We have arrived at the end of the story, but we are prevented from making the final interpretive moves that are needed to achieve closure.

11. "In drama—on the stage, in film, or even on television—discovering what is possible is a twofold source of pleasure for audiences. First is the stimulation to imagination and emotion that is created by carefully crafted uncertainty. ... Second is the satisfaction provided by closure when the action is complete, if the plot has been successfully constructed." Laurel, *Computers as Theater*, 67.

Goldman provides an excellent example of this in the ending of the frame story in *The Princess Bride*. When the father reaches the end of the story, his son is disappointed. It doesn't end the way he expected:

"And they lived happily ever after," my father said.

"Wow," I said.

He looked at me. "You're not pleased?"

"No, no, it's just, it came so quick, the ending, it surprised me. I thought there'd be a little more, is all. I mean, was the pirate ship waiting, or was that just a rumor like it said?"

"Complain to Mr. Morgenstern. 'And they lived happily ever after' is how it ends."[12]

But that isn't how it ends. The "real" ending of *The Princess Bride*, Goldman tells us, is far more ambiguous. The ultimate fate of the heroes is left deliberately unresolved. The father in the frame story offers his son the trivial move toward closure that is the traditional ending of all fairytales: "And they lived happily ever after." But the son senses that something more complicated is going on. *The Princess Bride* isn't a normal fairytale, and so the chains of anticipatory play that it sets up aren't so easily shut down. And the son is left unsatisfied by the resolution his father offers.

Of course, both the main story and the frame story in *The Princess Bride* are being told for the benefit of us readers. The boy and his father aren't real people responding to a real book; they are fictional characters, just as Westley and Buttercup are. The boy's response to the false "ending" of *The Princess Bride* is merely another beat for us to interpret, as the subsequent paragraph that describes the true "ending" of the main story demonstrates:

From behind them suddenly, closer than they imagined, they could hear the roar of Humperdinck: "Stop them! Cut them off!" They were, admittedly, startled, but there was no reason for worry: they were on the fastest horses in the kingdom and the lead was already theirs.

However, this was before Inigo's wound reopened, and Westley relapsed again; and Fezzik took the wrong turn; and Buttercup's horse threw a shoe. And the night behind them was filled with the crescendoing sound of pursuit ... .[13]

And, in fact, after that Goldman gives us yet another beat to consider, this time in the authorial voice:

Did they make it? Was the pirate ship there? You can answer for yourself, but, for me, I say yes it was. And yes they got away. And got their strength back and had lots of adventures and more than their share of laughs.

12. Goldman, *The Princess Bride*, 282–283.
13. Ibid., 282–283.

But that doesn't mean I think they had a happy ending either. Because in my opinion anyway, they squabbled a lot, and Buttercup lost her looks eventually, and one day Fezzik lost a fight and some hotshot kid whipped Inigo with a sword and Westley was never able to really sleep sound because of Humperdinck maybe being on the trail.[14]

What can we make of this welter of endings? We have three different narrators presenting us with three different problematic gestures toward closure: one that is too simple, one that is too ambiguous, and one that is detailed and specific but deliberately rejects closure. How do we bring our engagement with this text to a satisfying conclusion, so as to arrive at a stable state of affairs in which no more interpretive moves seem necessary?

One answer—*my* answer—is to accept the inherent ambiguity of the main story as a given and make my concluding interpretive moves in a different direction. This final set of beats emphasizes the tension between the tidiness of fairytales and the sloppiness of everyday life, in which even moments that seem like the beginning of "happily ever after" may be followed up by years of mundane troubles: lovers' squabbles, disappointments, worries, minor defeats. This tension isn't presented as a criticism of fairytales; rather, it is presented as a hopeful gesture, a celebration of the power of fairytales to offer us the satisfaction of closure even though we know in our hearts that such a move is always a bit of a trick.

And so, when I read the ending of *The Princess Bride*, I experience a feeling of completeness—not because my anticipatory play regarding the heroes has been cleanly drawn to a close (indeed, Goldman has deliberately denied me that), but because Goldman's calculated rejection of closure for the characters opens up the possibility of closure on a deeper thematic level. I can accept the unresolved tension between the different possible endings because my sharpened awareness of that unresolved tension (of the tension between stories and life, really) allows me to converge on a stable understanding of the book as a whole. I could continue to engage in anticipatory play about what Westley and Buttercup do after the final page, but what would be the point? Making more interpretive moves at that stage would only undermine the satisfyingly stable understanding of the text I've arrived at. I close the book, and the story (all the stories, on a variety of levels) is (for me) done.

This is how I read the ending of *The Princess Bride*. This reading is a description of a sequence of interpretive moves that I made within the play space formed by the text and by my own pre-existing system of extratextual constraints. It is quite likely that if you read *The Princess Bride* you made a

14. Goldman, *The Princess Bride*, 282–283.

different set of interpretive moves when you reached the ending. I make no claims that my reading is the proper reading. Rather, it is a possible reading—one potential way to engage with the text if you approach it with a particular set of interpretive constraints. It's exactly like a description of a particular set of moves at the end of a game of chess, a record of how one player arranged his pieces to achieve the satisfaction of checkmate. My reading exists in a necessary but indeterminate relation with the text. It is constrained by the text, but the text isn't reducible to my reading. The text allows this way of achieving closure, but doesn't compel it.

In order to function successfully as a play space, a text must offer the possibility of satisfaction—the possibility of arriving at a coherent and stable set of interpretive constraints that explain our encounter with it. However, there are a wide variety of different locations within a text's phase space that can satisfy these criteria. Sometimes we achieve closure because the author successfully ties up all the loose ends. But stories don't always have to have tidy endings; a story can, like *The Princess Bride*, offer closure on other levels instead.

The Non-Mimetic Elements of Narrative

The six heuristics presented above were developed to provide help in understand how to construct interesting play spaces, but they can also be seen as guidelines for constructing interesting narratives. (See table 14.1.) When we look at how they apply to narrative, we arrive at guidelines much like those that are typically taught to beginning writers. This particular critical approach is powerful not because it tells us something unexpected about how to write stories, but because it provides a useful framework for understanding *why* these guidelines exist in the first place. Why is it so important to keep advancing the plot? Why can't we use clichés in our stories? Why can't we introduce random and bizarre plot twists? Why can't we drop a major character halfway through a story and never mention him again? This play-based line of analysis helps us to understand the connection between the particular choices made by the author and the resulting experience of the reader. It suggests that many of the elements that we think of as constituting "good writing" are primarily mechanisms for shaping an interesting space for the reader's anticipatory play. It also helps explain another curious feature of stories: their *artificiality*. Stories don't unfold the way life does. That is strange, because at least since Aristotle it has been generally recognized that a significant part of the power of fiction is its mimetic capability—its capacity to hold a mirror up to the world:

Table 14.1

Heuristic	General principle	Application to narrative
Choice	Offer moment-to-moment choices.	Leave gaps to be filled by the readers' interpretive moves. Don't tell too much.
Variety	Don't repeat the same horizon.	Continually develop your plot, characters, and themes. Each narrative beat should offer a fresh horizon to explore.
Consequence	Actions should affect which future horizons are encountered.	Avoid gratuitous elements. Each narrative beat should influence the beats that follow.
Predictability	The outcomes of actions can be anticipated.	Avoid plot holes. What comes before should guide the reader toward what comes after.
Uncertainty	The outcomes of actions are not predetermined.	Avoid clichés, stock characters, formulaic plots, and on-the-nose writing. The reader should never be completely certain what will happen next.
Satisfaction	Desirable outcomes are attainable.	Avoid loose ends. As the story winds down, resolve the reader's chains of anticipatory play.

From childhood men have an instinct for representation, and in this respect man differs from the other animals that he is far more imitative and learns his first lessons by representing things. And then there is the enjoyment people always get from representations. What happens in actual experience proves this, for we enjoy looking at accurate likenesses of things which are themselves painful to see, obscene beasts, for instance, and corpses. The reason is this: Learning things gives great pleasure not only to philosophers but also in the same way to all other men, though they share this pleasure only to a small degree. The reason why we enjoy seeing likenesses is that, as we look, we learn and infer what each is, for instance, "that is so and so."[15]

We like our stories to be believable. If the characters are unrealistic, or the action is implausible, we quickly lose interest. This shouldn't be surprising. Our preference for accurate representation is a natural outgrowth of the prominent role extratextual constraints play in constructing the narrative play space. Since our knowledge of the world is a major component of the constraints that define our reading experience, the text must avoid contradicting this knowledge in order to preserve consistency. Mimesis satisfies our desire for coherence-oriented play.

15. Aristotle's *Poetics*, IV, 13–15.

But at the same time, many of the structural aspects of narrative are bizarrely *non-mimetic*. The typical way that stories unfold from scene to scene is very different from the messy and haphazard progression of ordinary life. Reality doesn't build toward a climax, for example, or provide foreshadowing, or exposition, or ironic juxtaposition. Much of the machinery of storytelling is, in fact, remarkably *unrealistic*. Aristotle himself was aware of this odd contradiction. Despite what he wrote about the value of mimesis, he also had this to say: "For poetic effect a convincing impossibility is preferable to that which is unconvincing though possible."[16]

Why do we tolerate this? What makes some departures from reality acceptable to us, and others not? I would argue that when we tolerate non-mimetic elements of narrative, it is because they are serving a ludic purpose. In other words, we want our stories to be believable, but we don't mind discarding believability when it gets in the way of constructing a successful play space.

Consider foreshadowing, for example. If a major beat is coming up, it's a good idea to drop a few hints to warn the reader. If the hero is about to be seriously injured in a car crash, the author might set things up by mentioning in passing how slick the road is, or that another driver is driving recklessly, or that the car is making a unusual noise. The reader accepts these ominous hints, even though they aren't realistic (in the real world, car crashes usually happen with no warning at all), because they soften the discontinuity created by the unexpected beat.

When something unanticipated happens in a story, we experience a crux. We discard our previous framework of expectation and assemble a new one that integrates the latest beat into our previous understanding of the story. But if the discontinuity of the unexpected beat is too extreme, we may find it impossible to integrate the old and the new. Instead of a resolved crux, we have a plot hole. We may accept the new beat and continue to read on, but the unity of the story is broken.

Foreshadowing is unrealistic, but it serves a ludic function. It lays the foundation for the resolution of the upcoming crux, allowing us to smoothly integrate our new knowledge with our existing framework of understanding. A story that sprung unexpected events on the reader with no foreshadowing at all would be more realistic, but less playful.

Just as it is important to foreshadow unexpected beats, it's also important *not* to foreshadow a beat that isn't going to happen. The usual term for this is "Chekhov's gun." The playwright Anton Chekhov famously

16. Aristotle's Poetics, XXV, 111.

wrote that if there is a gun hanging on the wall in the first act, it should be taken down and fired in the second.[17] If an author introduces an element that is particularly evocative, we form expectations for how it will figure later in the story. An interesting prop, a vivid character, an unusual setting, or a strange occurrence assumes a particular significance in our chain of anticipatory play. If the story never satisfies our resulting expectations, we feel disappointed and frustrated. The gratuitous business of the gun on the wall leaves us with unexplained loose ends when the story concludes.

Even the structure of Western narrative serves a ludic purpose. Most stories begin with an introduction that establishes the context and the main conflict, then progress through an escalating series of events that amplify and expand on the introduction until they arrive at the climax, where the central conflict is resolved. The climax is then followed by a stretch of falling action where the ramifications of the climax are explored, then by a dénouement, in which the various threads of the plot are tied off and brought to their natural conclusion. This "pyramid" structure (illustrated in figure 14.1) was described by Gustav Freytag in his 1863 book *The Technique of the Drama*.[18] Freytag was primarily interested in explaining the structure of classical Greek plays and analyzing how that structure influenced German plays of the nineteenth century, but his framework also can be applied to folk tales, romance novels, and literary fiction.

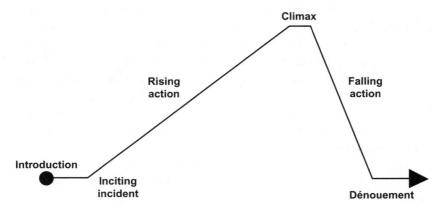

Figure 14.1
Freytag's plot pyramid.

17. Rayfield, *Anton Chekhov: A Life*, 203.
18. Freytag, *Technique of the Drama*, 114–140.

In a "pyramid" plot, the introduction establishes a minimal set of constraints so that play can begin. Often this consists of supplying us with some basic information about the main character's personality and situation. How much exposition is needed to accomplish this will depend on the background of the intended reader. The more familiar the setting and the hero are to the audience, the less work the author has to do to set the stage.

The introduction concludes with the "inciting incident"—a narrative beat that establishes the central conflict. The inciting incident creates an instability in the situation described in the introduction, and immediately suggests a variety of lines of anticipation for us to explore. At that moment, the story opens up and we begin to play in earnest, our imaginations ranging forward to explore the implications of the central conflict.

What follows is a long stretch of rising action. During this phase of the story, we work to avoid closure. Moving from beat to beat, we seek out interpretations that will open the story further, increasing our opportunities for play. As incident follows incident, we are guided toward the construction of a set of constraints that will allow us to resolve the central conflict. Part of this is mere logistics—moving the characters into the proper configuration in time and space. But just as important is how the characters change as the action plays out. The rising action isn't merely about getting the characters to be *where* they need to be; it is also about getting them to be *who* they need to be.

At the climax, the accumulated interpretive constraints we have built during the rising action allow us to resolve the instability of the inciting incident. With the primary impetus to explore removed, we enter a shorter period of falling action. Now, instead of avoiding closure, we seek it out, working through the ramifications of the new state of affairs created by the climax. Our horizons are shorter, and instead of trying to increase play we look for ways to reduce it. This culminates in the dénouement, in which our constraints settle into a new stable state that resists further exploration or elaboration.

Now, there are other ways to tell a story besides Freytag's pyramid—for example, the author can start in the middle of the action, without any introductory exposition, and leave it to the reader to puzzle out the identities and situation of the characters as he goes. There doesn't have to be an inciting incident; rather, the reader can be left to explore the potentialities of the initial situation without any clues to a particular direction of interest. Instead of building in a rising arc, the incidents of the plot can be arranged as disjointed episodes, or in a long, slow decline from an initial crisis. A story can end without a climax, leaving the reader uncertain as to how the conflict will resolve itself. If a story does have a climax, it can terminate abruptly without falling action or dénouement.

However, each of these approaches interferes with the reader's ability to play in some way—either by disrupting anticipation, or by eliminating consequence, or by denying satisfaction. The Freytag pyramid is ubiquitous in Western popular fiction because it is a particularly useful way to establish a robust and flexible play space.

This is not to say that the Freytag pyramid is the only way a successful plot can be constructed. For example, many Chinese and Japanese stories use the *kishōtenketsu* form, which is derived from traditional four-line Chinese poetry.[19] A story in this form begins with a presentation of the topic (*ki*) that is similar to the introduction in the Freytag pyramid. However, instead of this initial state of affairs being disrupted by an inciting incident, the story moves into a section of extended elaboration on the topic (*shō*). This elaboration is brought to an abrupt end by an incongruous twist (*ten*) that at first seems completely unrelated to what has come before. But this incongruity is then resolved by a conclusion (*ketsu*) that explains the juxtaposition between the *ten* section and the rest of the story. (See figure 14.2.)

In the *kishōtenketsu* form, the development of the topic resembles the rising action section of the Freytag pyramid, but without its directedness. Instead of exploring the consequences of a particular destabilizing inciting incident, the *shō* section is a more open-ended exploration. The reader is still encouraged to engage in anticipatory play, but his anticipation is directed less toward particular future events and more toward a broader understanding of the potentialities of the current situation. This sets the

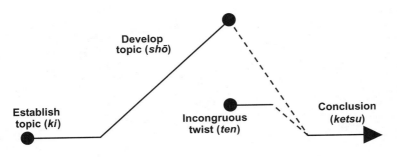

Figure 14.2
Kishōtenketsu plot structure.

19. Maynard, *Japanese Communication*, 158–162.

stage for the large disjunction of the *ten* section. So large a crux would feel like a major plot hole if we encountered it in a more directed narrative. But because our expectations are less specific, the appearance of an incongruous beat is less jarring. Since the reader isn't preoccupied with a central problem, the *ten* section can more easily open up a much broader field of play for him to explore. Essentially, the *kishōtenketsu* form sacrifices some of the anticipatory play triggered by the instability of an inciting incident in order to pose a more interesting problem of thematic coherence for the reader. It's a different way of structuring a story, but one that still adheres to the heuristics of play.

Both the Freytag pyramid and *kishōtenketsu* are non-mimetic—that is, they are at odds with how events normally unfold in our day-to-day lives. We tell stories using these non-mimetic forms because they serve a ludic purpose. They allow us to engage in long chains of satisfying anticipatory play with the proper balance of predictability and uncertainty. These forms (and other literary devices, such as foreshadowing and red herrings) work to structure an idealized epistemological playground—a mental space in which we can move easily through our natural cycle of knowledge construction and application. The heuristics of play explain why these forms and devices exist. They explain why certain familiar ways of structuring narrative are effective, and why certain common rules of composition exist.

As we play a game, read a book, watch a movie, or listen to a symphony, we are continually engaging in interpretive play. We construct new internal constraints that agree with what has come before, and we use those internal constraints to anticipate what will come after. These constraints are both explanations and predictions. They are a means of understanding a thing, without being a replication of the thing understood.

And when the experience is over—when we put down the controller, or close the book, or walk out of the theater—interpretive play stops. But it doesn't always stop right away. If the experience was compelling, we will keep playing in our minds even though the external stimulus has been removed. Many gamers will be familiar with the maddening experience of lying awake in bed after a late-night gaming session, mentally sifting through the potentialities of imaginary scenarios. When we leave a good movie, we often want to talk about it with our friends, trying to sort out who did what to who and what it all meant. A powerful book can haunt us for days after we finish it as its full ramifications gradually dawn on us.

This "winding down" process is a natural outcome of closure-oriented play. We are seeking a stable position within the phase space of the experience, a horizon of intent with no more meaningful moves. When we arrive at that point the work feels complete. We can set it aside and move on to something else without feeling the tug of unexplored potentialities. Sometimes this winding down may coincide with end of the work, but there is no reason it has to. If the work is particularly open, or its conclusion particularly abrupt, we may not find closure until long after our direct engagement ends.

However, eventually, we will stop playing. Either we will arrive at closure or we will give up as a result of frustration, fatigue, or the distractions of life. The postmodern conceit of "unlimited semiosis"—the infinite deferral of arriving at a fixed interpretation—is a theoretical construct that bears little relation to how we actually engage with real works. Life and attention aren't unlimited. Although theoretically the open nature of texts might allow infinite wanderings, our actual experiences will always be finite.

Indeed, without practical convergence on provisional meanings, reading itself wouldn't be possible. Semiosis—"meaning-making"—occurs not just at the level of the work but also at the levels of the chapter, the paragraph, the sentence, and the word. In Umberto Eco's words,

The meaning of a given word or of a given thing being another word or another thing, everything that has been said is in fact nothing else but an ambiguous allusion to something else. In this sense the phantasmagoric content of every expression is a secret, or an enigma that evokes a further enigma.[1]

Infinite deferral of interpretation, if it actually occurred, would prevent us from advancing beyond even the first word of a text. In order for us to read at all, the infinite regression of nuance suggested by each word must be rejected in favor of a more limited provisional understanding. As we move forward from word to word, we cut short our elaborated chains of semiosis as soon as we discover an interpretation that is provisionally sufficient.

When we eventually reach the end of the text and stop playing, our internal constraints settle into a final, fixed configuration. These terminal constraints are a condensation of the understanding that we amassed as we moved through the experience. They are the product of a long chain of speculation and validation, of provisional interpretations created and then discarded. As the work reveals itself, the confirmation of various expectations drives us toward prioritizing the strategies that generated those explanations. Our final interpretation consists of simply those constraints that survived this winnowing process. They become, for us, the meaning of the work—the explanation of why it unfolded as it did. Meaning is the residue of experience.

When we assign a meaning to a work, it often feels as though we have decoded a secret message from its creator. It's as though the meaning lay hidden inside the work all along—like buried treasure—and through careful excavation we have brought it out into the light. Indeed, art appreciation and literature appreciation are often taught to students as though this metaphor were true. Students are trained to be treasure hunters, to dig inside works to reveal what lies underneath: the powerful underlying

1. Eco, *The Limits of Interpretation*, 27.

messages and themes that transcend the literal meaning of the canvas, screen, or page.

The theory that a work of art has an inherent meaning is deeply rooted in Western culture—so deeply that sometimes people have difficulty perceiving it as a theory at all and not as the natural state of things. It goes all the way back to Plato, who argued that works of art are copies of copies—reproductions of a physical world that was itself was a reproduction of an invisible realm of ideal forms that lay beyond.[2] When we engage with a work of art, it's as though we are looking through two layers of smudged glass, dimly glimpsing the hazy outsides of Truth behind. Reading (or looking, or listening) then becomes a matter of being able to "ignore the smudges"—to look past the superficial aspects of the work and perceive what lies hidden inside it.

According to Plato, this "looking through" is easier in the case of great works, because the artist is directly inspired by the gods, not by worldly things. The greatest works are first-order reproductions of the underlying Truth, and are therefore more powerful and effective in moving and instructing us. The main point for Plato, however, is that all works, whether good or bad, ultimately trace their significance to their being first-order or second-order encodings of the underlying Truth. And they succeed or fail to the extent that the Truth is communicated successfully:

> For in this way, the God would seem to indicate to us and not allow us to doubt that these beautiful poems are not human, or the work of man, but divine and the work of God; and that the poets are only the interpreters of the Gods by whom they are severally possessed.[3]

In the Middle Ages, the idea of interpretation as decoding was further reinforced by the scholastic approach to biblical exegesis. The Bible, being divinely inspired, was thought to be a window on the mind of God. Not only was the text thought to be literally true; it was also believed that through careful interpretation the scholar could discover the truth hidden in metaphor or allegory or allusion. Aquinas writes:

> The author of the Holy Scripture is God, in whose power it is to signify his meaning, not by words only (as man also can do), but also by the things themselves. So, whereas in every other science things are signified by words, this science has the property that the things signified by the words have themselves also a signification. Therefore the first signification whereby words signify things belongs to the

---

2. Plato's *Republic*, Book X.
3. Plato's *Ion*. See *Critical Theory since Plato*, ed. Adams, 15.

first sense, the historical or literal. That signification whereby things signified by the words have themselves also a signification is called the spiritual sense, which is based on the literal and presupposes it.[4]

In both the classical and scholastic senses, the truth behind a text was unitary. There might be a multiplicity of incorrect readings, but only one correct reading, one divinely inspired meaning that constituted the essence of the text. As the medieval age gave way to the modern, this assumption of unitary meaning lingered on, even though the philosophical and theological frames that inspired it no longer had any currency. When we are confronted by a challenging work of art, many people's first response is still often "What does it mean?" We may no longer believe that a text was divinely inspired, but we still read as though it were, searching for a Truth that lies beneath the literal words on the page.

This search for coded meaning reached its apogee with the advent of the New Criticism in the early years of the twentieth century. The New Critics were responding to earlier critical approaches that had sought to anchor the meaning of a text through external evidence. (What was the author's original intent? How was the text an expression of his psyche, or an example of cultural moment in which it was written, or a significant stitch in the grand tapestry of literature?) The New Critics did away with all this. Instead, they argued, criticism should focus its attention primarily on the work itself. Instead of looking for external evidence of the meaning of a text, the reader should simply pay close attention to the words on the page, observing how, through metaphor and allusion, they indirectly suggest the underlying truth of the piece.

The approach of the New Critics is exemplified by this passage in R. P. Blackmur's essay "A Critic's Job of Work":

A great part of Blake's meaning is not open to ordinarily well-instructed readers, but must be brought out by the detailed solution of something like an enormous and enormously complicated acrostic puzzle. … The same sort of work, the adduction of ultimately self-evident facts, can be done and must be done in other kinds of poetry than Blake's. Blake is merely an extreme and obvious example of an unusually difficult poet who hid his facts on purpose. The work must be done to the appropriate degree of digging out the facts in all orders of poetry—and especially in contemporary poetry, where we tend to let the work go either because it seems too easy or because it seems supererogatory. Self-evident facts are paradoxically the hardest to

4. Aquinas, *The Nature and Domain of Sacred Doctrine*, "Tenth Article: Whether in Holy Scripture a Word May Have Several Senses?" in *Critical Theory Since Plato*, ed. Adams, 118–119.

come by; they are not evident till they are seen; yet the meaning of a poem—the part of it which is intellectually formulable—must invariably depend on this order of facts, the facts about the meanings of the elements aside from their final meaning in combination.[5]

This method of "close reading" is still taught to students today. Every year thousands of undergraduate papers are written on topics such as the theme of light vs. dark in *Great Expectations*, or how the whale in *Moby-Dick* represents God, or the thematic significance of the play within a play in *Hamlet*. As a method for encouraging students to look beyond the superficial, close reading is a useful tool. But as a means for uncovering the "true" interpretation of a text, it sowed the seeds of its own destruction. For, as many glib undergraduates have discovered over the years, one can find evidence for almost *any* reading if one digs deep enough. The more closely one examine a text, the more ambiguous it becomes. Under the microscope of close reading, seemingly obvious interpretations dissolve away into contingency and confusion.

Wolfgang Iser writes:

The split between present-day art and traditional norms of interpretation has a historical reason which often manages to escape the attention of modern critics. The continued application of a norm that involves scrutinizing a work of art for its hidden meaning, shows that work is still regarded as a vehicle through which truth can have its perfect form. [6]

The endgame of the Western interpretive tradition is *deconstruction*—using close reading of a text to expose contradictory interpretations. Rather than being a smudged window onto a hidden truth, the deconstructed text is a hall of mirrors, an endless maze of fragmented reflections. We may pause before one of these reflections because we find it appealing or useful in some way, but there is no textual justification for our destination. The meaning we arrive at is a pragmatic or aesthetic choice, not a necessary convergence:

If totalization no longer has any meaning, it is not because the infinity of a field cannot be covered by a finite glance or a finite discourse, but because the nature of the field—that is, language and a finite language—excludes totalization. This field is in fact that of freeplay, that is to say, a field of infinite substitutes in the closure of a finite ensemble. This field permits these infinite substitutions only because it is

5. Blackmur, "A Critic's Job of Work," in *Selected Essays of R. P. Blackmur*, ed. Donoghue, 41.
6. Iser, *The Act of Reading*, 12.

finite, that is to say, because instead of being an inexhaustible field, as in the classical hypothesis, instead of being too large, there is something missing from it: a center which arrests and [grounds] the freeplay of substitutions.[7]

In other words, a text provides an opportunity for endless exploration, not because it is itself infinite, but because it lacks a "center," a single fixed interpretation that can be discovered through careful close reading.

The realization that art and literature do not encode fixed hidden truths is one of the dominant themes of late-twentieth-century critical thought. Depending on how we read a text, look at a painting, or play a game, multiple different interpretations may emerge. Not only will these different interpretations not converge on a single divinely inspired meaning; they may contradict one another, telling different readers, viewers, or players different things simultaneously. This indeterminacy is an unavoidable outcome of play. If we are each allowed to find our own way through a text, we will each arrive at our own destination.

Interpretation is a recursive process. As we make our way through the phase space of a work, each new horizon offers us a range of interpretive paths. The path we choose opens up new potentialities, simultaneously closing off others. Our provisional response to the contingencies of the moment shapes what further responses are possible as the work continues to unfold. Some interpretive strategies may lead us to horizons within the phase space that are particularly interesting—that offer particularly fruitful opportunities for continuing play. But it is important to realize that this fact doesn't make these strategies more "true" or "correct."

Thus, asking "What is the meaning of a text?" is the same as asking "What is the correct way to play with a ball?" Both texts and balls offer constraints that structure our encounters with them. Their properties make some sorts of play easier and other sorts of play harder, and in this way they privilege some strategies of engagement over others. However, the meaning that emerges from the encounter isn't something that is extracted from the object itself, but rather a distillation of strategies that proved effective in response to the challenges posed. By throwing a ball against a wall and watching how it returns, we formulate a model of the ball's behavior—a model that is validated when we catch the ball on the rebound. By anticipating the unfolding of a story, we formulate a model of motivation and intent—a model that is validated when the unfolding matches our expectations. We systematize what has already happened to predict what is yet

7. Derrida, "Structure, Sign and Play in the Discourse of the Human Sciences," in *Writing and Difference*, 291.

to come. But the value of our strategy of engagement rests entirely on its predictive strength, not on its one-to-one correspondence to the object of our attention. Different models may "explain" the bounce of the ball or the course of the story equally well. And in this way, they are all equally true.[8]

This way of looking at things has profound implications for how stories transmit meaning. If all ways of understanding a work are equally true, then how does an author go about "saying" anything to his audience? How does he ensure that the meaning that emerges is the meaning that he intended, and not some idiosyncratic misreading by a perverse reader? The answer is that he can't, any more than a game designer can force a player to play his game in a specific way. An author can structure the experience to be more *amenable* to some forms of engagement than others. He can construct his playfield so that some strategies are more likely to emerge than others. But he can't force the reader, viewer, or player into making a specific series of moves without destroying play.

This indeterminacy doesn't imply, however, that aesthetic works are meaningless, or that all meanings that we choose to assign to them are equally valid. Though the rules of a game don't force the player to make a specific sequence of moves, they still forbid a large range of actions. If you are playing chess, you can't suddenly decide that snatching a pawn up off the board and throwing it at your opponent is a valid move. Similarly, though a story may allow us a wide degree of latitude in interpreting the motivation of its protagonist or the significance of its underlying themes, it also limits how far afield our imagination can range. We can debate whether or not Hamlet experiences homosexual attraction toward Horatio, but not whether or not Hamlet is a raccoon. The constraints supplied by the work bound the scope of our interpretive play without driving it to a predetermined conclusion.

Thus, although a creator may not have absolute control over the meaning of his work, he isn't completely powerless. All sets of constraints bias experiences so that some types of play emerge more naturally than others. You can play baseball on an ice rink, but not easily—the physical properties of the space work against you. Similarly, when we tell a story we can encourage exploration in particular directions by structuring the narrative beats so that they offer less resistance to particular interpretive moves. The

8. "We know that a text is not a line of word releasing a single 'theological' meaning (the 'message' of the Author-God) but a multi-dimensional space in which a variety of writings, none of them original, blend and clash." Barthes, "The Death of the Author," in *Image—Music—Text*, 146.

reader may not take us up on this offer. He might deliberately work against the grain of the text, or strike out in an unexpected direction toward an unanticipated destination. But the offer remains, as a source of resistance and challenge and as an artifact to be analyzed and understood.

Portability and Significance

The value that we assign to a work is often tied to the portability of its terminal constraints. Does the understanding we have arrived at apply only to the work itself, or can it be applied to other works or to day-to-day life?

When we read a novel, most of our interpretive moves are limited in scope to the work itself. We construct models that explain the events on the page and allow us to anticipate where the story is headed, so we understand that Catherine loves Heathcliff, that the *Pequod* is a whaling ship sailing from Nantucket, and that Daisy is responsible for Gatsby's death. But these basic interpretations are entirely confined to the world of the story. They allow us to makes sense of what is happening, and to play with the potentialities of the narrative as we move from beat to beat, but they have no further relevance once the story ends.

But some interpretations linger with us. At the end of *The Lord of the Rings,* Frodo discovers that the experience of destroying The Ring has so changed him that he can't return to the life he had before. There no longer is a place for him in the world, and he decides to go with Gandalf into the West, leaving Middle Earth forever. Understanding this moment doesn't just tell us why the story ends the way it does; it also tells us something larger about the nature of duty and sacrifice, about how even victory can break us, about how living in contentment may require a certain blindness to horrors. None of these interpretations are inevitable, but they are easy for even a casual reader to stumble upon, and they add a depth and significance to the work that lifts it above being simple escapist fiction. The understanding that emerges from an attentive reading of *The Lord of the Rings* is portable—it applies not just to the work itself, but to our general grasp of the world and life within it.

Depending on how we engage with it, any work can be a source of an understanding that extends beyond itself. But some works provide better starting points than others. For example, most Hollywood blockbusters are intended to be relatively self-contained experiences—quick diversions that provide a few hours of interpretive play that leaves no lasting trace behind, no lingering constraint with the potential to generate interesting future horizon. But sometimes a summer movie can transcend the limitations of the genre to resonate with an individual or an audience in a way that generates meaningful and portable constraints. When this happens, the movie ceases to be mere diversion and becomes something more significant.

Most games are good at encouraging us to form interpretations, but, as with Hollywood blockbusters, the interpretations they encourage tend to be local in scope. We internalize the rules, learn the layout of the levels, and develop strategies and tactics, but very little of this understanding is portable—it doesn't transfer well to domains outside the game. Understanding how to drift our go-kart though turns or which kind of gun is most effective against zombies might, at best, transfer to another similar game, but this knowledge doesn't have the same potential to transform our lives the way that understanding Frodo's sacrifice has.

This phenomenon is explained in part by the implicit assumption of the gamist agenda by designers and players. From the gamist perspective, everything in a game has significance only as a mechanism for advancing or retarding progress. If I shoot a prostitute in the head in *Grand Theft Auto*, the act has no meaning except as a targeting challenge. The tug of winning encourages me to structure my interpretive moves along purely utilitarian lines—everything in the game becomes a means to an end.

Gamers sometimes respond to criticism of the medium by saying "It's just a game! We aren't shooting prostitutes in the head because we hate women—we're shooting prostitutes in the head because doing so provides in-game challenges and rewards." It's like bowling in a bowling alley where there are faces painted on the pins. You knock down the pins because knocking down the pins is a desired outcome in the framework established by the rules. The fact that the pins are decorated with human faces is immaterial, merely an incidental bit of decoration; it has no bearing on the moves being made within the goal-oriented gamist frame.

However, this defense of games is a trap. By insisting that our in-game actions and interpretations have meaning only as tools for achieving victory, we close ourselves off to the idea that games can be an expressive medium. In order for a game to have the power to stay with us, our understanding of it must transcend the immediate necessity of winning. We must discover strategies of engagement that are broader, deeper and more lasting—meanings that we can apply in situations beyond the immediate context of the play space.

In most mainstream games, gameplay is designed as a self-contained experience. The rules are structured to provide an entertaining challenge as we work toward a well-defined goal. They aren't designed to serve as the basis for interpretive play. The result is a strange lack of connection between our actions and the role that we supposedly are playing. For example, snooping around and vandalizing things aren't heroic activities, but nevertheless many games encourage the hero to wander into strangers' homes and smash random objects to find treasure. There are good gameplay reasons for this—it's fun to explore and find rewards—but it also adds an element of absurdity to the characterization of the protagonist.[9]

However, when gameplay does align with narrative play the results can be powerful. In *Ico*, for example, we spend most of the game escorting a helpless girl to safety. We lead her by the hand from room to room, help her climb over high walls, call to her when she is lost, and protect her when she is attacked by shadow creatures. We are told almost nothing about the relationship between these two characters; our understanding of who they are and what they mean to each other emerges almost entirely through how they interact during gameplay. The rules encourage us to act as though we care for her, and by acting as though we care we discover that we actually do.

This scenario reappears in comically stripped-down form in *Portal*. In *Portal*, it isn't a girl we are asked to protect, but a *crate*—the "weighted companion cube." As we carry it with us, we discover ourselves developing a curious emotional attachment to it. We are a team—it protects us from energy blasts, and we take it to places where, as an inanimate object, it could never go on its own. Our shared adventures create a bond. Thus, when we do as we are told and incinerate the cube at the end of the level, we feel an unexpected twinge of sadness. The game, through careful use of gameplay, has made us care about the fate of a box.

Rainbow Six penalizes the player for harming innocent bystanders. *God of War* rewards it. And *Grand Theft Auto* offers a mix of penalties and rewards, depending on the situation. Each of these constraints creates a different moment-to-moment gameplay challenge. But, more important, each also situates us in a different moral universe. *Rainbow Six* is about the triumph of discipline and duty over chaos and nihilism. *God of War* is about vengeance, fate, and rage against the gods. *Grand Theft Auto* is about clawing your way to the top in an amoral, corrupt world. The rules for how we are expected to act toward bystanders in each of these games don't just shape our gameplay experience; they also shape our understanding of the protagonist's moral compass.

The game designer Brenda Romero has created a series of board games collectively titled *The Mechanic Is the Message*. Each game is a unique piece

---

9. The game designer Clint Hocking has coined the term *ludonarrative dissonance* to describe this problem.

of conceptual art addressed toward a different human tragedy: the Trail of Tears, the African slave trade, the English invasion of Ireland. The games are visually evocative—for example, the board for *Síochán Leat* consists of burlap covered with tufts of grass-like fabric, creating the illusion of Ireland's rolling green hills—but they are intended to be played, not just looked at. As the title of the series says, the message of these games lies in their mechanics. The interpretive constraints that players form as they navigate the play spaces of these games are intended to be portable, to linger after the game itself is over.

Romero's best-known game, *Train*, is about the Holocaust—more specifically, about the logistics of transporting 6 million Jews to the death camps. The board consists of three railroad tracks laid across a shattered windowpane. The object is to load small yellow pawns into boxcars and move as many of them as one can along the tracks to their final destinations. Initially, players aren't given any context for these actions—the game presents itself simply as a logistical challenge. Only when the first boxcar arrives and the "Auschwitz" card is revealed does the metaphoric significance of their earlier moves become apparent. It's a monstrous, horrible topic for a game, and at first glance, it may seem to be a callous trivialization of one of history's great atrocities.

What makes *Train* a work of art is how its rules are constructed. Romero has created a set of rules that are deliberately broken. They contain strange contradictions and ambiguities. Players are forced to come up with their own negotiated interpretations as they play. Some interpretations of the rules can even make the game unplayable—for example, a player can block the tracks, endlessly draw cards without ever loading any passengers, or allow some pawns to escape by deliberately derailing his own train. The mechanics of *Train* invite its players to look for ways to sabotage the play space—to subvert the ugly pantomime in which they are participating.

The power of *Train* arises from how uncomfortable the sabotage feels. When we sit down to play any game, we implicitly agree to abide by a set of social constraints. We agree to follow the rules, to make a good effort to win, and to work with the other players to sustain the integrity of the play space. If a player doesn't abide by these constraints—if he cheats, or refuses to take the game seriously—we feel betrayed and frustrated. And so, if we care about what other people think, we try to be good players when we play. We try to avoid subverting the spirit of the rules. We try to avoid being spoilsports.

But sitting down to play *Train* puts you in a situation in which there is tension between being a good person and being a good player. It's a game about the seduction of complicity, about how the mere existence of a set of rules structures an unspoken expectation of compliance. When we sit down to play with others, we try not to be spoilsports, but *Train* dares us to do just that. The meaning of *Train* (at least, the meaning I take away from it) is the horrifying realization of just how insidious our desire to play along is. Breaking *Train* feels like a betrayal of the other players, even though the game deserves to be broken.

I refuse to play *Train*. I have studied the rules and watched other people play, but I will not sit down at the table myself. The reason I will not play is that I know that I would immediately sabotage the experience, and that would be letting myself off the hook too easily. I hope that I'm the sort of person who would refuse complicity in real life, but my lingering doubt makes it impossible for me to make the necessary moves in *Train* with a clear conscience. It would feel cheap and self-congratulatory. If I had been an employee of Deutsche Reichsbahn in 1943, would I have had the courage to interfere with the running of the trains? I hope I would have, but I fear I wouldn't have. And so, I play *Train* by not playing *Train*. It's the only honest move I feel free to make.

Train achieves its effect through its mechanics. You can't experience *Train* by treating it as a piece of visual art. You have to read its rules and explore the anticipatory space that they structure. You have to alter your strategic constraints to accommodate the play space that is laid out in front of you. *Train* offers a meaning that is portable, but it's a meaning that isn't stated overtly. It's a meaning that emerges only when one engages with *Train*'s system of constraints.

Mixing Gameplay and Narrative Play

Many people have argued that games and stories are different sorts of things. You can have one or the other, or alternate between them, but you can't have both simultaneously, and any attempt to combine the two will always contain discontinuities—to engage with the story, we must stop engaging with the game and vice versa. To this way of thinking, games that include stories will always remain a hybrid form, incapable of achieving the artistic unity of a symphony or a novel or a painting. Jesper Juul articulates this position quite plainly:

Computer games and narratives are very different phenomena. Two phenomena that fight each other. Two phenomena that you basically cannot have at the same time.[10]

10. Juul, "A Clash between Game and Narrative."

I disagree. I think that the apparent incongruity between games and narrative is merely an artifact of a particular essentialist argument about the nature of games. If we define games to be fundamentally "interactive," then a linear narrative can't function like a game. If we define play as a sequence of transactions—doing things that evoke a response—then reading a linear arrangement of words can't be playful.

One of my goals with this book has been to call this point of view into question—to illustrate that the apparent discontinuity between games and stories is caused, not by some fundamental difference, but rather by an accidental misalignment of our interpretive frames. By erecting a new framework for talking about play in general, and by situating both games and stories within that framework, we can understand how these two seemingly disparate experiences can integrate with each other. We can understand how gameplay and narrative can be combined into a unified aesthetic whole.

It is easy to fall into the trap of thinking of narrative as a linear, deterministic experience. After all, reading involves moving step by step through a fixed text; we don't have any control over what the words are, or in what order we encounter them. But whereas the mechanics of reading are linear and deterministic, the experience that results from those mechanics is not. Even as we march linearly through the text, our imaginations are simultaneously ranging forward and back across the play space the text evokes. The same book can lead different readers to a variety of different interpretations. Even when two readers arrive at the same destination, often they got there by different routes.

Telling a story is the process of systematically creating new constraints in the minds of the audience. Each dramatic beat opens up or closes off avenues of anticipatory play; a well-written story holds the attention of the reader by continually offering fresh horizons of intent. Different storytelling media construct these new constraints in different ways. When we read a book, our system of constraints is generated entirely by the words on the page. But when we watch a movie or a play, the sources of our constraints are much more varied. The dialogue, the action, the costumes, the set design, the score—every aspect of the overall experience influences the structure of our narrative play. Though most traditional forms of narrative lay out these constraints in a linear, deterministic way, there is nothing essential about this approach. There certainly will be some internal dependencies within a work—some things must come before some other things. For example, you can't have a big dramatic escape unless the hero has been captured. But often there is room for flexibility in the order in which less significant narrative constraints are presented. We may need to know that jailer is a drunk, the window of the cell overlooks the ocean, and the hero has a hacksaw blade hidden in his boot, but the order in which these constraints are established can be switched around without significantly altering how the story plays.

When we play a game, the rules are part of the overall experience. They define our gameplay, obviously. But they also influence the structure of our narrative play. How our character moves, the challenges he faces, the way enemies and allies respond, the physical layout of the levels—all of these gameplay elements also serve to constrain our interpretive moves. A game in which you blast everything in sight (such as *Quake*) plays differently than a game in which you sneak around (such as *Thief*). But it also tells a different story—a story about being in a position of strength instead of a position of weakness.

Gameplay constraints are narrative constraints. And, by the same token, narrative constraints are gameplay constraints. Our actions in a game are limited less by what the rules actually are than by what we believe them to be. If we believe that a wall is an impassible barrier, we will avoid walking through it, even if in fact it isn't collideable. A narrative beat can't change the rules of a game, but it can change our beliefs about the rules. If we are invested in the fantasy that the game provides, we will tend to choose actions that sustain that fantasy. If I am told that I'm playing a bad guy, I will tend to act like a bad guy. If a non-player character is sympathetic or appealing, I'm more likely to go out of my way to help or defend him. We attribute to enemies goals and motivations that make narrative sense, even if they aren't reflected in their simple in-game behavior. And we try to see story arcs carried through to completion, even if doing so moves us no closer to victory.

The challenge of integrating narrative and gameplay isn't a matter of mixing two fundamentally incompatible experiences. Rather, it is a matter of understanding how ludic constraints can serve narrative purposes and vice versa. It's a matter of understanding how narrative play unfolds and how the structure of a game must make accommodations for that unfolding.

The first and most important consideration is that narrative play needs its own time and space to unfold within. There is an upper limit on how many things we can simultaneously attend to. Our ability to focus is a pipe of fixed diameter—there is only so much that can pass through it at once. If we pay attention to too many things, we will not have any mental capacity left focus on something new. If we want to pay attention to something new, we have to stop paying attention to something old.

Many games ask us to split our attention between immediate tactical challenges and long-term strategic challenges. The more we have to scramble to keep alive *right now*, the less time we have to think about what we are going to do next. If a game is going to ask us to make strategic decisions, it must provide us the mental space to do so. It should have either periodic lulls in the action or an overall slower pace of immediate challenges so that we have time to engage in anticipatory play.

But narrative play is also a type of anticipatory play. In order for a story to be satisfying, we need to have room to explore. We need to be able to range forward and back across the possible ramifications implied by the narrative constraints. If a game mixes narrative and gameplay elements, the player must have the necessary mental space to engage with the story. If every moment of the experience is packed with interesting and challenging gameplay decisions, there is no room for narrative play.

An extreme example of this approach is the game *Dear Esther* by The Chinese Room. *Dear Esther* strips gameplay down to the absolute minimum. You are exploring a deserted island. As you wander, you trigger spoken memories of your relationship with Esther. These recollections are fragmentary and ambiguous—you never learn exactly what passed between you and Esther. All you can do is assemble a rough sense of the relationship from the words you hear and the juxtaposition of those words with the scenery of the island. There is very little gameplay. Moment-to-moment choices are reduced to occasional decisions about which path to walk along. Sometimes several minutes go by without any gameplay whatsoever. But this lack of gameplay means that we are able to devote our full attention to the narrative. Instead of concentrating on what we need to do to win, we are able to explore long chains of narrative anticipation. We are able to spend time thinking about the words we're hearing and the sights we're seeing, and to do the hard and satisfying work of trying to understand what we have experienced.

But few games are as minimalist as *Dear Esther*. In games that demand more intense gameplay, one way to make room for the story is to simply suspend gameplay during narrative beats so the player can focus on the story without the distraction of jumping, dodging, and shooting. This is the classic "cut scene" approach—long stretches of gameplay punctuated by non-interactive narrative bits to advance the plot. Though this technique certainly resolves the question of whether or not the player has enough mental bandwidth for anticipatory play, it creates a new problem: loss of context. When we play, our horizon is defined by our active constraints. As the state of the game changes, our active constraints change too. But although our active constraints can evolve during play, it is better if they don't change too abruptly. In order to establish a coherent horizon, our constraints need to remain relatively stable relative to the tempo of play. If one set of rules is suddenly replaced with a completely different one, the resulting discontinuity will trigger a collapse of play. Our previous framework of anticipation will disintegrate around us as we struggle to get our bearings within a completely new context. This is why players so often want to skip cut scenes. When deeply immersed in a game, we are holding a large collection of active constraints in our heads. A cut scene asks us to temporarily set that complicated structure aside and replace it with an entirely new one. This abrupt context switch can leave us frustrated and disoriented, particularly if the game has encouraged us to engage in long chains of anticipatory play. We badly want to keep plotting and planning, to keep sifting through the interesting potentialities of the game's state. But in order to attend to the story, we have to abandon not only our ongoing play but also the entire framework that makes the play possible. A cut scene feels like not merely suspension of play, but a transgression of the play space itself.

What this means is that if narrative play is going to be satisfying it should be integrated within the overall experience. It isn't something that can be abruptly picked up and put down again. When we encounter a narrative beat, the necessary interpretive constraints should be close at hand and should be closely related to the strategic constraints that structured our recent gameplay moves.

Complicating things further, switching between gameplay and narrative requires not only a change of context but also a change of agenda. The gamist agenda privileges outcomes that move us closer to well-defined victory conditions, whereas the narrativist agenda privileges outcomes that increase or decrease our sense of closure. When we are deeply immersed in gameplay, our thoughts are dominated by winning; each move has significance only to the extent that it advances us toward our goal. As a result, narrative elements tend to feel pointless. Even if we do establish a narrative framework, the interpretive moves we make inside that framework don't help us win. Contemplating how tragic it was that my buddy was shot by a sniper during a simulation of D-Day doesn't kill any Nazis or move me farther up the beach.

This is a difficult problem to address, because its roots lie in the attitude of the player, rather than in the content of the game itself. If a player approaches a game primarily as an opportunity to work toward victory, he is never going to be very interested in its story, no matter how compelling it is. Simply by calling an experience a "game," we steer players toward the gamist agenda and a particular goal-oriented mode of engagement.

We can't force players to ignore their gamist tendencies. However, if we want to encourage players to engage with our story, it helps to create situations in which their actions are interesting in and of themselves, not merely as stepping stones to victory. When we give players opportunities to explore, observe, and experiment with a minimum of challenge, we open the door to closure-oriented play. Not every player may be willing to walk through that door, but we can at least suggest that there might be other interesting ways to experience a work than by trying to conquer it. One way to do this is by making winning trivial. For example, consider that thatgamecompany's game *Flower*. In *Flower* you play a gust of wind. As you move through each level, you use the joystick to control in what direction you are blowing. When you blow across a closed flower bud, it blooms, shedding a few petals that swirl along behind you. As you trigger each flower, the world changes around you, becoming greener and more lush. Now, there are certainly goals and challenges in *Flower*. In order to progress from level to level there are certain flowers that you have to make bloom. Steering requires a little bit of effort—you can miss a bud and blow past it. And in later levels there are obstacles to avoid—downed power lines that give you a jolt if you touch them. But there is no time limit, and no consequences for failure. If you miss a bud on one pass, you just turn around and try again. If you touch a power line you don't lose a life, you just get knocked back a little. As a result, although it is possible to adopt a gamist attitude toward *Flower*, such an approach isn't very satisfying. Success comes so easily that there isn't a lot of goal-oriented play to be had. This lack of challenge actually has the effect of opening up the player to a different sort of experience. If I don't have to concentrate on surviving to reach the end of the level, what other things can I concentrate on? *Flower* sets up an interesting space for interpretive play. It offers the player a chance to meditate on life and death, fertility and decay, fear and bravery. But this meditation is possible only because *Flower's* mechanics don't impose a large number of gamist demands.

Star Trek's holodeck is sometimes held up as an ideal to which interactive narrative should aspire.[11] Inside the holodeck, the players' adventures take place within a seamless virtual environment. The "players" aren't bound by the limitations of a two-dimensional screen or a handheld game controller. They can "play" through a Sherlock Holmes adventure simply by

11. See Murray, *Hamlet on the Holodeck*.

wandering around inside a simulacrum of nineteenth-century London and doing what Holmes would do. That is an interesting vision of the future of entertainment, but (technological considerations aside) would such a set up actually work as a narrative experience? The problem with the holodeck is that in order to engage with the virtual world, the player must pretend to be the character that he is playing.[12] That's fine if you are playing a stock figure such as Sherlock Holmes. But how does the holodeck tell a story about a new character? How does the player know what to do if constraints of his role aren't already firmly established before he steps into the simulation?

Pretending to be someone else can be fun, but it isn't easy, particularly if your actions aren't scripted in advance. Some people enjoy improvisation as entertainment—historical re-enactors, fans of tabletop role-playing games, cosplayers—but in general its appeal is narrow. And the participants usually spend a significant amount time preparing for each play session. It isn't the sort of thing most people can jump into spontaneously the way you can pick up a book or a videogame controller.

A holodeck would be a great place to play laser tag, or to act out your sexual fantasies. But it would be a lousy place to tell a story, because there is no mechanism for establishing the internal constraints that define the protagonist. It resembles a storytelling medium within an episode of *Star Trek* only because we are watching actors working from a script—a set of constraints. In the real world, such an experience would feel aimless and pointless.

The "myth of the holodeck" is important because it directly relates to the challenges we face when we try to tell stories with games. For most traditional stories, the personality of the protagonist strongly structures the field of narrative play. Who the hero is determines what he might believably do and consequentially influences our anticipation in powerful ways.

When we play a game, our sense of the protagonist's identity is a product of the actions we perform. Gameplay constraints are also narrative constraints. The more freedom the game affords us in choosing what to do, the more fluid the identity of the protagonist becomes. This is problematic. If we want to tell a story with much depth or subtlety, the personality of our

12. "The entertainment value of the experience depends on how the interactor relates to her avatar: will she be like an actor playing a role, innerly distanciated [*sic*] from her character and simulating emotions she does not really have, or will she experience her character in the first-person mode, actually feeling the love, hate, fears, and hopes that motivate the character's behavior, or the exhilaration, triumph, pride, melancholy, guilt, or despair that may result from her actions?" Ryan, "Beyond Myth and Metaphor: The Case of Narrative in Digital Media."

protagonist must mesh with the other constraints of the plot. *Hamlet* isn't just a story about some random individual thrown into the midst of court intrigue. It's a story about a very specific character, whose particular quirks cause the plot to unfold in interesting and meaningful ways. If we want to achieve "Hamlet on the Holodeck," the player must become complicit in the construction of the protagonist. Not only must he know the particulars of the role he is supposed to play; he also must want to play it.

As with the adoption of a non-gamist agenda, we can't force this sort of engagement on the player. But we can make it easier for a sympathetic player to find his way into his role. Just as the early levels of a game should gradually introduce the player to the gameplay constraints he will need for the rest of the game, so can they also should introduce him to the narrative constraints that will define his character. The player should learn who he is by what he is asked to do, and then (if he is invested in the story) uses that knowledge as the basis for narrative play.

For example, in the game *Shadow of the Colossus*, a player is asked to kill a series of sixteen giant monsters—the colossi of the title. The mechanics of accomplishing these killings defines the character of Wander, the protagonist. We learn who he is through what he does, and by extension we learn more about ourselves as we pretend to be him.

What makes Wander's actions—our actions—significant is how the colossi are portrayed. Unlike most videogame enemies, they aren't overtly hostile toward the player. Up until the moment they are confronted, they mind their own business, slowly lumbering through the landscape. The player is clearly the aggressor, seeking out the huge beasts and slaughtering them. From a goal-oriented perspective, the colossi are set up as obstacles to be overcome. From a closure-oriented perspective, however, this overcoming carries moral weight. We are told at the beginning that killing these creatures will save the princess, but no explanation of why this should be so is offered until near the end. For most of our play experience, we act out the role of a butcher. We have no animosity toward the colossi—they are merely a means to an end. Our utilitarian destruction of these awesome beasts thus becomes a significant constraint on the interpretive moves we can make in response to the work.

Establishing the protagonist is an important step in the construction of a narrative play space. In order to engage in anticipatory play, we have to be able to imagine how the main characters will respond to plot beats. The early gameplay in *Shadow of the Colossus* sets up Wander's character for our future narrative play. The game uses the implicit meta-goal of the gamist agenda ("overcome obstacles and win") as a hook to draw us toward a successful set of narrative constraints.

Designing a platforming game requires finding the right balance between predictability and uncertainty, so the player knows where to go while remaining unsure of how to get there. The resulting experience is a mix of anticipatory and immediate play—we alternate between imagining possible paths through the level and executing skill-limited actions to navigate those paths. If the path is too obvious or the jumps are too easy, we quickly become bored. But if the path is obscure or the jumps nearly impossible, we just as quickly become frustrated. This is why platforming games tend to avoid "blind jumps"—jumps in which we can't see our landing zone in advance. Even if landing a blind jump is so easy that it presents no risk at all, it interferes with our anticipatory play. We are being asked to choose an action with no sense of its possible ramifications. Are we jumping onto a hanging vine or the mouth of a crocodile? We don't know until it's too late to choose differently.

Designers sometimes try to make a story more interactive by letting players influence its course, either through explicit decision points or through cumulative tallies of significant actions. However, often these narrative branches are "blind jumps." We don't have enough information to anticipate the ramifications of our choices. Sometimes we are making a significant choice without even realizing it. We are clearly steering the narrative in some new direction, but what direction is it? Such awkward attempts to let us "play" a story can have the opposite effect: They can kill off the natural anticipatory play that emerges when we engage with a text. Rather than increasing our interpretive freedom, blind jumps curtail it. When we can glimpse where we are headed, and the consequences of our actions are clear, we feel free to explore. But when every action is fraught, we become wary. We avoid experimentation. More important, we avoid analysis—why bother trying to understand a system that can change in unexpected and arbitrary ways?

Closely related to the idea of the blind jump is the idea of the false choice. Whereas a blind jump is an action with unknown consequences, a false choice is an action that appears to have a consequence, but doesn't. No matter which course of action we pick, we always wind up at the same destination.

When we talk to another human being, we aren't merely transmitting data. We also expect our words to have an effect on the listener's mental state. If I say to you "I'm hungry," I'm probably not just idly passing information along. I'm probably also trying to evoke feelings of guilt or obligation: "I'm hungry, and it's your fault," or "I'm hungry, and it's your responsibility to fix that." But when we talk to a character in a videogame, this sense of shaping the mental state of another is usually missing. Often we are just triggering canned responses. If we pick "I'm hungry" off a dialogue menu, a non-player character may inform us that there is a diner down the street, but we will not have altered his attitude toward us—he will not be worried, or annoyed, or resentful, or guilty. Our future interactions with him will take place as though the exchange had never happened.

Often game characters function simply as crude vending machines for exposition. Push the buttons in the right order and you will learn some useful information about the story. Push them in the wrong order and you will wander aimlessly through a forest of empty banter. In neither case is there much play to be had. Merely making a dialogue interactive doesn't make it fun. If a conversational choice doesn't shape the thoughts and feelings of the listener, it feels false. And unless that choice influences the course of future play, it feels gratuitous.

Narrative play follows the same rules as gameplay. Interactive narrative beats must obey the same heuristics: choice, variety, consequence, predictability, uncertainty, satisfaction. When we are asked to make a narrative choice, that choice must have predictable and meaningful consequences. We need to be able to anticipate where in the play space of possible narratives that choice leads us.

There is a glimmer of this sort of narrative play at the beginning of *Fable II*. The player is given five training quests that teach the fundamentals of gameplay. However, each quest can be resolved in either of two ways, one clearly "good" and one clearly "evil." How you resolve these quests determines how the starting area will look for the rest of the game—is it a cheerful working-class neighborhood, or a filthy, crime-ridden slum? You are presented with clear choices that have obvious consequences, and the results of those choices shape the story space in interesting ways, opening up some narrative paths while simultaneously closing off others. (The narrative play in *Fable II* is not without its flaws. There is no granularity to this choice. You are offered only two alternatives—good and evil. Worse, the promise of this early section isn't sustained in later parts of the game.)

Of course, as with any sort of choice within a play space, the outcome of a narrative choice shouldn't be entirely certain. We should have a general sense of where a choice will take us (so that choosing feels meaningful), but there should be a degree of uncertainty so that we don't race too far ahead in the narrative. If we know *exactly* what is going to happen next, playing through it will feel dull. Any anticipation we have of where a story is headed should be tempered by doubt. To be fully engaged with narrative play, we need to be continually reassessing our understanding of what is happening and how the story is likely to unfold.

If we are given the opportunity to make a choice within a narrative, we need to be able to steer that narrative toward a desirable resolution. This is perhaps the most challenging restriction of all. In traditional narrative, finding a satisfying resolution is merely a matter of converging on a set of interpretive constraints that achieve closure. We work to find a way to understand the ending in a way that accommodates all that came before while removing the possibility of future anticipatory play. I may not be happy about Winston Smith's fate in *Nineteen Eighty-Four*, but I can still take satisfaction in arriving at an understanding of his fate that neatly encapsulates my encounter with the novel.

But once we introduce narrative choice, we also introduce an expectation of control over narrative outcome. If I can choose what Winston Smith does, I expect to be able to alter his fate—to steer him toward the ending that I want rather than the ending that Orwell wrote for him. If the structure of the experience thwarts my attempts to achieve the outcome I desire, ultimately I feel frustrated.

Paradoxically, introducing choice into a narrative can narrow and limit a player's experience. If I know that nothing I do can change the outcome of a story, my play experience will be primarily a narrativist one. I will move freely from beat to beat, seeking out ways to understand what has come before and to predict what will come next. I will work to avoid or achieve closure, even though the challenge of doing so may require me to range far afield from my pre-existing understanding of myself and the world. But if I can control the outcome of a story, my play experience will be primarily a gamist one. Early on, I will settle on a resolution that feels comfortable to me—that meshes nicely with my pre-existing knowledge of the world. And then I will work within the constraints provided to achieve that goal. Though theoretically I have been given greater freedom to explore, in practice my trajectory through the phase space of the story will be far more constrained. I will be less likely to come to any broad or surprising insights about the characters or myself. As I proceed step by step through the narrative, I will tend to favor choices that parsimoniously reinforce my preexisting understanding.

We can boil all these observations about mixing narrative and gameplay down into a set of principles. These principles can be thought of as a set of best practices for the design of play spaces that mix these two different types of play. Alternatively, they can be considered a manifesto—a set of criteria that we should aspire to meet it we want to create games that have a deep narrative effect on their players:

- Telling a story is the process of creating a system of constraints that supports narrative play.
- Gameplay constraints are narrative constraints, and vice versa.
- Narrative constraints need not be introduced in a fixed order.
- Narrative play takes time.
- Abruptly switching between different sets of constraints will collapse the play space.
- The gamist agenda works against narrative play.
- The player must understand the constraints that define his character and the world.
- Narrative choices should have foreseeable consequences.
- Current narrative choices should affect future narrative choices.
- Narrative choices should allow the player to move toward a desirable resolution.
- Narrative choice encourages gamist play.

In 2010, the film critic Roger Ebert wrote an article titled "Video Games Can Never Be Art." The main thrust of his argument was to equate games with the gamist agenda:

One obvious difference between art and games is that you can win a game. It has rules, points, objectives, and an outcome. Santiago might cite a immersive game without points or rules, but I would say then it ceases to be a game and becomes a representation of a story, a novel, a play, dance, a film. Those are things you cannot win; you can only experience them.[13]

But game developers have already moved past this narrow conception of what constitutes a game. They have created many things that we call "games" (for lack of a better term) that aren't intended to be encountered through the gamist agenda. Rather, they are designed to be coherence-oriented or closure-oriented experiences—interactive situations that players move through and contemplate in the course of their movement. And these experiences aren't merely shadows of the sorts of experiences one can have in other media; they have their own unique qualities and textures. Playing a game such as *Flower* (which Ebert ridicules as "a greeting card" without having played it) immerses you in a particular system of closure-oriented constraints. Navigating that system and discovering a way to account for the significance of the moves you make within it can be profoundly moving. And it can't be replicated in any other medium.

13. Ebert, "Video Games Can Never Be Art."

Interpretation, based on the highly dubious theory that a work of art is composed of items of content, violates art. It makes art into an article for use, for arrangement into a mental scheme of categories.

That's Susan Sontag, in her 1964 essay "Against Interpretation."[1] In the previous chapter, we spent a great deal of time looking at how we use art to construct meaning. But we don't typically approach works of art with interpretation as our primary goal. Rather, we are looking to be diverted, or entertained, or moved, or challenged. Along the way, we may construct provisional interpretations to help us engage with the work, but these tactical choices are directed primarily toward sustaining play. The meaning that emerges after the work is done is merely a residue of these tactics, a lingering trace of our pragmatic improvisation.

Thus, if we declare that the primary function of art is to tell us something, we immediately find ourselves working against the grain of the experience. It's like playing *God of War* to learn how to smash skeletons. If you play *God of War*, you certainly learn a lot about smashing skeletons, but no one would make the mistake of thinking that acquiring that knowledge was the point of playing. Your skeleton-smashing knowledge is merely an incidental by-product of your primary experience.

Assigning meaning to a work is always an act of closure. It's the end of play. It takes something that is open and dynamic and reduces it to something closed and static. Such a reduction may help us to get a handle on the work, but it's always a lessening and a distortion. The work ceases to be a playground offering a multitude of potentialities and becomes merely a signifier. Or, as Iser writes, "in discovering the hidden meaning, the critic has, as it were, solved a puzzle, and there is nothing left for him to do but congratulate himself on his achievement."[2]

1. In *Against Interpretation and Other Essays*.
2. Iser, *The Act of Reading*, 4.

This reductionist impulse is hard to avoid. We live in a culture that values meaning. Experiences that resist interpretation are suspect. They are shallow, self-indulgent, decadent, wasteful. This is what lies at the heart of Raph Koster's critique of unchallenging play: If a game isn't teaching us something new, if we aren't moving toward some useful understanding, then we are wasting our time playing it. And it's a critique that has also been leveled at abstract art and absolute music, either by claiming that such works are empty, and therefore pointless, or by claiming that their meaninglessness is a sham, and despite their apparent emptiness they contain deeply hidden signifiers that can be pried loose if only we attack them with the proper critical tools. It is often easier to dismiss a meaningless work, or to attempt to redeem it by attaching a meaning to it, than it is to embrace meaninglessness.

Hans Ulrich Gumbrecht addresses this attitude in his book *Production of Presence: What Meaning Cannot Convey*:

The institutionally uncontested central position in the humanities of interpretation—that is, of the identification and of attribution of meaning—for example, is backed up by the positive value that our languages quite automatically attach to the dimension of "depth." If we call an observation "deep," we intend to praise it for having given a new, more complex, particularly adequate meaning to a phenomenon. Whatever we deem "superficial," in contrast, has to lack all these qualities, because we imply that it does not succeed in going "beyond" or "under" the first impression produced by the phenomenon in question (we normally do not imagine that anything or anybody might desire to remain without depth).[3]

The problem with privileging interpretation is that it directs our attention away from our immediate engagement with a work and toward the aftermath of that engagement. It's a denial of "presence"—our sense of being immersed inside an evolving now. By focusing our attention primarily on the meaning of a work—the traditional approach of Western critical thought—we marginalize our actual experience—the fluid and unstable play that necessarily precedes and prefigures the construction of meaning.

It has been said that writing about music is like dancing about architecture.[4] When we listen to music, we certainly play within the framework the

---

3. Gumbrecht, *Production of Presence*, 21.
4. Tracking down the origin of this quotation has been difficult. The earliest cites point to comedian Martin Mull as its originator of this particular formulation of the idea, although it has existed in various other forms dating back to 1918. for more information, see the entry in the blog *The Quote Investigator* from November 8, 2010 (http://quoteinvestigator.com/2010/11/08/writing-about-music/).

performance provides. We construct interpretive constraints that explain the patterns of notes we hear and allow us to anticipate what will be coming next. We alternate between satisfaction and surprise as the melody confirms or thwarts our expectations. But the understanding we construct is almost entirely self-referential. The previous notes may suggest an impending crescendo, and we may feel a rush when that anticipation is satisfied. But the understanding that allowed us to form that anticipation isn't portable. It isn't something that we can use afterward in our daily lives, and it may not even be particularly applicable to other pieces of music. It is a provisional tactic for dealing with the immediate constraints presented by the performance itself. Thus, if we try to analyze music as a medium for transmitting meaning, we find ourselves oddly confined to the periphery of the experience. We can talk about the formal structure of a composition, or how people use a piece within a social context, but the actual experience of listening lies tantalizingly beyond our interpretive grasp. We can sense that something personal and complicated and interesting has transpired, but the traces that linger with us afterward are difficult to articulate.

Games pose a similar problem. A game exists in the playing, just as music exists in the listening. Our movement from horizon to horizon shapes the construction of a set of internal constraints that represent our understanding of the game. But often this understanding is both ineffable and nonportable. We can *feel* the threat of the zombies lurking around the next corner, the momentary gap that is about to open in the defensive line, the pattern of falling jewels that will set up the perfect combo, but the interpretative constraints that generate these expectations are difficult to talk about or apply afterward. As with music, a great deal of the worth and power of the experience comes not from what it means, but from the fleeting presence effect it produces.

Instead of analyzing a work to discover its meaning, it can be more helpful to look at the play it allows. What moves does it make easy, and what moves does it make hard? What does it assume about our extratextual constraints? How does it encourage and thwart our expectations? The construction of meaning then becomes not the purpose of the activity, but merely a feature of it. Gumbrecht writes:

What [Niklas] Luhman highlights as a specific feature of the art system is a simultaneity of meaning and perception, of meaning effects and presence effects—and if this is not too much of a subject-centered perspective to be applied to Luhman's philosophy, I would venture to say that what he found to be specific to the art system may well be the possibility to experience (*erleben*) meaning effects and presence effects in simultaneity. Whenever it presents itself to us, we may live in this simultaneity as a tension or an oscillation. Essential to the point that, within this specific constellation, meaning will not bracket, will not make the presence effects disappear, and that the—unbracketed—physical presence of things (of a text, of a voice, of a canvas with colors, of a play performed by a team) will not ultimately repress the meaning dimension. Nor is the relation between presence effects and meaning effects a relation of complementarity, in which a function assigned to each side in relation to the other would give the co-presence of the two sides the stability of a structural pattern. Rather we can say that the tension/oscillation between presence effects and meaning effects endows the object of aesthetic experience with a component of provocative instability and unrest.[5]

This is the tension between doing-dominated play and learning-dominated play—the oscillation between the satisfaction of having our expectations confirmed and the collapse and reconstruction of our internal constraints after a crux. Sometimes we pause to form new constraints to refine our understanding of the system, but often we are simply immersed in moment, doing for the sake of doing, looking for the sake of looking, listening for the sake of listening. The aesthetic experience isn't a means to an end; it is an end unto itself—an opportunity to be *present* in a world that is challenging and comfortable and comprehensible. We don't play to learn; we play to play.

The Cascade of Play

We have already seen that we can create systems of constraints in which one person's actions shape the play space for the other participants. Multiplayer games are designed so that my choices influence your horizons and vice versa. But, more significant, one person's play can generate an entirely different system of constraints for an entirely different group of players. An actor on stage may be playing within the constraints of script, but his actions and words become the basis for the interpretive play of the audience—a completely different sort of game. Unlike the reciprocal relationship that exists between players in a multi-player game, the relationship between a performer and the audience is strongly asymmetrical. The influence flows mostly (but not entirely) one way, and the performer's game offers very different challenges and very different sorts of fun than the audience's.

In fact, we can envision a cascade of play experiences flowing one into another (figure 16.1). At the beginning of the chain is the play of the

5. Gumbrecht, *Production of Presence*, 107–108.

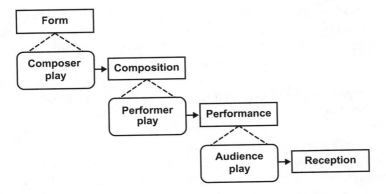

Figure 16.1
The cultural cascade of play.

composer, author, or designer working within the constraints of the form. These constraints are things like genre conventions, authorial intentions, audience expectations, budgets, deadlines, and other practical and creative strictures. For me, designing a game or writing a story has always felt like solving a puzzle. There is some place I believe I'm trying to get to, and there are some obstacles that stand in my way, and the creative process is a twisty exploration of the implications and potentialities of the phase space. Part of the fun of creation is the wandering, the discovering of an unexpected solution to a difficult problem, the arrival at a destination that I never envisioned at the beginning of the project.

The output of the composer, author, or designer is a system of constraints for the next stage in the cascade—a score, a screenplay, or a design document. The performer plays within the playground constructed by the composer. A musician in an orchestra, an actor on stage, and a texture artist on a videogame development team are examples of play at the performance level. The free movement of performers is different from the free movement of composers, with different constraints and different goals, but it is, similarly, play.

The output of the performer is also a system of constraints, but one intended for an audience—people sitting in a stadium, walking through a museum, or sitting on a couch at home. Their play is the play that I have talked about the most in this book—gameplay, narrative play, the way that we go about engaging with any work of art. Just as the play of the composer is different from the play of the performer, so the play of the performer is different from the play of the audience. At each stage of the cascade, different systems of constraints are being navigated; however, each represents an opportunity for play.

This strictly linear model of the cascade is, of course, a simplification. For example, a large portion of the audience for a production of *Hamlet* will already be familiar with the play. Their system of constraints will be shaped by both the performance and the composition. Or a game designer may use his knowledge of his target audience to alter some aspects of his design. The flow from composition to performance to reception indicates the dominant direction of the cascade, not its absolute structure.

Not every one of these stages is always present. In the cascade of a novel, for example, there is no performance; the author's composition directly supplies the constraints for the reader's reception. Furthermore, though each stage offers an opportunity to play, there is no guarantee that that opportunity will be acted upon. Depending on what effect you are trying to produce for the next stage in the cascade, the composition and performance stages can easily become work. No matter how much an actor might prefer to lose himself in his role, the necessities of the audience may force him to take a more pragmatic approach, deliberately hitting certain beats to achieve a particular effect.

In the process of writing this book, some days have been effortlessly fun; others have been mechanical slogs. It feels like a gift when writing becomes play, but the demands of producing a coherent finished product for the next stage in the cascade often trump the authorial desire to enjoy the process. It isn't always possible to resist the temptation to have fun while writing, even at the expense of the finished product. "Self-indulgent" prose is the product of a writer who is more interested in his own play than in the reader's play.

The play spaces at each stage of the cascade are structured not only by the constraints supplied by the previous stage but also by the extratextual constraints supplied by the participants. Audience play at a musical performance is a function not only of the notes sounded by the performers but also of the physical construction of the venue, the behavior of the crowd, and the expectations and background knowledge of individual listeners. Successful play depends on a good match between the constraints supplied by the previous stage and the constraints supplied by the circumstances of the encounter.

The interrelations between various stages of the cascade can even be used fill in the gaps when direct information about an event has been lost. The music historian Elizabeth Randell Upton[6] has used this technique to

---

6. The similarity in last names isn't a coincidence. She happens to be my wife.

help reconstruct the lost performance context for medieval songs. In many cases, all that survives of these works is a piece of parchment with notes written on it. There is nothing in the historical record to indicate where, when, why, or even how the works were performed (for example, whether there was instrumental accompaniment for the singers). But since the composer himself knew the conditions under which his work would be realized, the historian can look for features within the composition that were intended to mesh with the lost constraints of the performers, the venue, or the audience.[7] Studying the surviving score is like studying the shadow left on a wall where a painting once hung—it can't tell us everything about what was lost, but it can provide faint clues to cultural practices about which the historical record is silent.

Play takes different forms depending on the cultural constraints that the participants adopt to structure their play spaces. A performance of a Noh drama is different from a performance of a Shakespeare play because the audiences and the performers are operating within very different sets of cultural constraints. Each play, each performance, has been designed to mesh with a particular receptive tradition. A Noh drama performed for an audience that is expecting Shakespeare will not function properly as a play space—there will be odd gaps in the collective constraints that will produce stretches of boredom or confusion. In order for a Shakespeare-oriented viewer to successfully engage with Noh, he has to alter the constraints he brings with him to the experience (and vice versa). He has to learn new strategies of engagement that will combine with the performers' actions to form a successful play space. The play space that he discovers may not exactly match the play space of the performance's original audience, but then, because of the idiosyncratic nature of reception, there wasn't a single "original play space" for the original audience either. There was only a diffuse cloud of closely related play spaces, each structured by the particular aesthetic frame of an individual audience member.

Without being aware of it, each of us possesses a default aesthetic frame—a reflexive way of engaging with the challenges of any work of art. This default set of constraints is the product of a lifetime of reading books,

7. "A composer was likely to have known in advance which singers would perform his music, and so could accommodate those singer's voices when writing a particular piece of music. Similarly, a composer was likely to have known the conditions under which a particular piece of music would be performed, and could respond to those expected performance conditions as well. Recognizing such details as historical evidence allows informed speculation into the social settings for these performances." Upton, *Music and Performance in the Later Middle Ages*, 67.

listening to music, playing games, watching movies, and living. These naïve extratextual constraints are the lingering traces of successful strategies from our previous engagements—ways of looking, listening, playing, and interpreting that worked well enough in the past to suggest that they are portable to other domains.

These constraints are reflexive, but they aren't unalterable. In fact, they are continually in flux by necessity. Engagement with a work—playing with a work—always involves testing our current strategies of engagement against the challenges that the work presents. Does my current aesthetic frame explain the features of the work before me? Can a parsimonious adjustment of my aesthetic frame accommodate this experience? Our aesthetic frames are constantly changing. (If they were incapable of changing, they would be incapable of functioning as aesthetic frames.) Change happens at all levels of the cascade. Engaging in composer play changes your composition aesthetic. Engaging in performer play changes your performance aesthetic. Engaging in audience play changes your reception aesthetic. And this effect can extend across all the stages of the cascade. Designing a game changes how you play other games. Listening to other people perform music changes how you perform it. Navigating a play space composed of your internal constraints changes those constraints. They adapt as we struggle to meet the challenges of what we are experiencing.

And sometimes the constraints change as a result of specific actions we take that are external to the play space. If I am trying to learn how to shoot a film, I may begin by reading books on cinematography. Rather than learning my camera-handling technique entirely on my own through trial and error, I can start by adopting a set of internal constraints that have worked for other filmmakers in the past. I can construct a new aesthetic frame for myself around a pre-existing grammar of shots and cuts.

Reading a book on cinematography is like reading a strategy guide for a videogame. It gives you a strategic understanding of a play space without having to go through the laborious steps of discovering the understanding for yourself. The affordances and restrictions the book supplies allow you to immediately begin playing the game at a higher level. They allow you to skip past the early floundering stage and move directly to a mode of engagement in which the moves you make with the camera feel productive and satisfying.

We study art, literature, or music not merely to learn about individual works but also to use our encounters with those works to learn new strategies of engagement. We learn new ways of looking, new ways of listening, new ways of playing, new ways of interpreting. These new internal

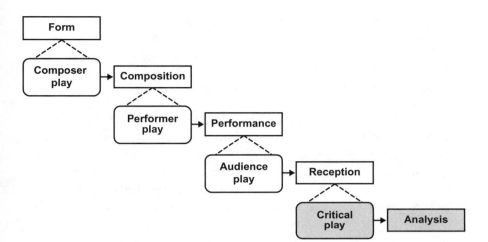

Figure 16.2
Critical play within the cascade.

constraints give us a wider selection of tools to choose from when we attempt to grapple with an unfamiliar experience. They make it more likely that we will be able to discover a set of constraints that will intersect with a future work to structure a successful play space.

Critical Theory as Play

It is even possible to extend the cascade of play beyond the audience's reception of the work. The audience's reception can itself be treated as a set of pre-existing constraints, and we can assemble an aesthetic frame that lets us use those pre-existing constraints as the basis for a new field of play (figure 16.2). In other words, instead of playing with the work itself, we can play with the audience's response to the work—how are they using it within a broader economic, social, or cultural context. This is the realm of a significant fraction of twentieth-century critical theory: Marxist criticism, feminist criticism, gender studies, postcolonial studies, and so on. Each of these critical approaches supplies a body of constraints that can be applied to a receptive act so that we can explore the significance of the act within a wider context. For example, we can investigate what Lara Croft's character in the *Tomb Raider* games tells us about the construction of feminine identity, or why the film *The Wizard of Oz* is significant within the gay community, or how Rudyard Kipling's poems reinforced the British conception of empire.

A critical discourse is a set of rules for a particular sort of game. Ideally, a critical discourse should be able to mesh with a variety of different receptive acts to structure a successful play space. A discourse is more useful if it is more portable—that is, if it can be successfully applied in a wide range of circumstances. A theory that can be used to interpret one receptive act isn't as powerful as one that can be used to interpret thousands or millions.

Critical play is commonly directly toward receptive acts, but it can also be directed toward the other stages of the cascade. We can also construct discourses that allow us to play with compositional acts or performative acts, and these constraints allow us to play in ways completely different from how a naïve performer or audience member would play. For example, we can analyze a musical composition as a mathematical structure instead of encountering it as a sounding phenomenon. Or we can appreciate a game as an ironic commentary on other games instead of treating it as an opportunity to make a series of challenging button presses. Some aesthetic works are even intentionally designed to mesh with a particular critical discourse. Marcel Duchamp's *Fountain* and René Magritte's *The Treachery of Images* are works of art that are also works *about* art; they are particularly good a structuring an interesting set of critical moves when they are encountered from within a particular conversation about the nature of art.

The moves we make within this sort of critical play space are similar to the moves we make when we engage with a narrative text. We search for strategic constraints that can parsimoniously account for features of the receptive act while minimizing disruption to the discourse itself. We move toward closure—all features of the receptive act must be accounted for within the critical discourse. Simultaneously, we seek coherence—the chosen critical discourse must itself remain constant.

It is interesting to consider critical play as a process. It has its own presence effects, for example. How it feels to be inside a moment of critical engagement is different from how it feels to be inside a moment of naïve reception. Just as we have a tendency to privilege our interpretations over the process of reception that produced those interpretations, we also have a tendency to privilege the results of critical analysis over the process by which those results were achieved. The presence effects of scholarly engagement (the quality of "being inside" the process of critical analysis) are rarely discussed. This omission means that the specific moves we make to arrive at our critical conclusions remain unexamined, as does the way those moves are subtly influenced by our drive toward play.

Critical play is still play. How we engage in critical play is guided by the same heuristics that determine the shape of all successful play spaces. In order for a critical discourse to be successful, it must mesh with a work in ways that obey our heuristics. If it doesn't, the discourse will offer moves that are either boring or frustrating—provisional interpretations that are either obvious and trivial or contradictory and confusing. And the play space will collapse.

What does it mean for a critical discourse to obey the heuristics of play? A successful critical discourse will offer a moderate number of possible interpretive moves at any moment in time. For example, if I'm operating within a Marxist critical discourse, my interpretive moves will be limited to considerations of the economic, political, or social function of a work of art. The constraints of the discourse will rule out a multiplicity of other possible interpretive moves—considerations of beauty or transcendence, for example.

The set of possible interpretive moves within the discourse must vary from moment to moment, and the effects of each interpretive move must affect what other interpretive moves are possible in the future. For example, Elvis Presley's performance of black music for a white audience can be interpreted as either a popularization of African American culture or an appropriation of it, and which interpretation we choose constrains the future interpretations in our analytical chain.

Furthermore, our choices are more interesting if the discourse offers competing valuation strategies. Discourses that offer simple, clear answers to interpretive challenges—"all Japanese role-playing games are crap," for example—don't provide much play value. Interesting discourses generate horizons that contain multiple plausible interpretive moves. Settling on a particular interpretation, then, involves an elaborated chain of anticipatory play: "If I choose this possible interpretation what are the ramifications? How does it reshape the play space for future interpretive moves that I might want to make? Might this other possible interpretation maybe be a better choice?"

Our ability to weigh the value of different interpretive choices thus depends on our ability to form coherent chains of consequence within the constraints of the discourse. For example, suppose we are negotiating the choice between "Elvis popularized black music" and "Elvis appropriated black music." Each of these moves has foreseeable interpretive consequences. If we are hoping to arrive at a terminal interpretation that portrays Elvis as a positive force in twentieth-century popular entertainment, then "appropriated" is a problematic choice—it increases the challenge of future interpretive moves that we will have to make in order to sustain coherence. More important, we *know* that it's a problematic choice when we make it.

Choosing "appropriated" opens up a whole new set of interpretive challenges because we can anticipate the consequence of that choice. Now our new playfield is centered on the tension between reconciling two apparently contradictory statements: "Elvis appropriated black music" and "Elvis was a positive force in twentieth-century popular entertainment." This new playfield can exist only because our discourse supported the anticipatory chains of consequence necessary to identify the tension.

Of course, this tension exists only because cultural appropriation is a negative act within the discourse we have chosen. It is certainly possible to construct competing discourses in which cultural appropriation is either a neutral or a positive act. (In fact, such discourses were common when Elvis was performing.) Within such a discourse, the tension described above wouldn't exist, and no critical play would be required to resolve it. A move that is interesting and challenging within one discourse can be obvious and dull within a different discourse.

Our interpretive moves must have predictable consequences, but they also must preserve a degree of uncertainty. If all the ramifications of an interpretive move become immediately obvious in a single quick cascade of anticipation, then there is no play to be had in exploring them further. Critical play thus favors constraint sets that are dense enough to thwart perfect anticipation of the ramifications of our interpretive choices. In order for a discourse to be interesting, we must be surprised from time to time by the consequences of our interpretations.

And a discourse should be satisfying. It should allow us to chart a trajectory of interpretive moves such that we are able to arrive at a desirable destination. Of course, what constitutes "desirable" depends on the weight we assign to the different agendas. If we are primarily interested in goal-oriented play, a satisfying discourse is one that allows us to construct a justification for a particular pre-existing position. If we are primarily interested in closure-oriented play, a satisfying discourse is one that allows to achieve closure—to account for all features of our subject. If we are primarily interested in coherence-oriented play, a satisfying discourse is one that is robust enough to resist modification despite the challenges posed by the encounter.

In reality, any critical encounter is always mediated by all three agendas to some degree. We usually have some favored interpretation toward which we begin working (even if we later abandon it). We usually try to avoid leaving glaring loose ends unaccounted for (even if we recognize that absolute closure isn't possible). And we usually try to preserve the integrity of our preferred discourse (even if we are open to modifying it if we need to).

And because the three agendas themselves represent competing high-level valuation strategies, interesting discursive moves often occur in situations in which the demands of one agenda are in conflict with the demands of another.

The process of weighing the relative worth of different interpretive moves isn't something we are consciously aware of doing. We aren't capable of attending to the low-level mechanisms that lead us to choose one interpretation over another. Every move in an episode of critical play is the product of a ramified cascade of microsemiotic events—a fleeting ripple across a multiplicity of hypotheticals followed by a rapid convergence on a single dominant strategy. All we are aware of is the result of the process. We suddenly realize that we know what something means, the knowledge crystallizing before us as a fait accompli.

Our satisfaction with the results of our inquiry is a function of the process underlying it. The quality of any experience of critical engagement is governed by the play value of the horizons that we navigate below the level of our conscious awareness. The understanding that emerges from a critical encounter is the residue of this journey, the lingering afterimage left behind by the lightning-quick flicker of our provisional interpretive moves and *ad hoc* strategies. We are blind to the contingency of this understanding—blind to the degree to which our certainties about the world are by-products of this non-deterministic ludic process.

We know things that are satisfying to know. And when something is satisfying to know, it feels *true*. Discourses that invite truth claims are particularly seductive to us because a truth claim is a particularly satisfying way to achieve closure. We are similarly attracted to discourses that exhibit stability in a wide variety of circumstances, as well as to discourses that allow us to work toward some desirable goal (an increase in status, for example). A discourse that allows us to satisfy all three agendas simultaneously is very seductive indeed.

This may seem to be a fancy way of saying "We believe what we want to believe." And it is, to some extent. But it's more than that. Belief itself is a property of brains that have evolved to enable knowledge-generating behaviors. Our brains condense sensory experience into constraints that are capable of making correct predictions about the future. Thus, it would be more accurate to say "We believe what our knowledge-generating algorithm tells us we should believe."

This knowledge-generating algorithm isn't magic. It doesn't have direct access to truth about the world. Rather, it cobbles together a heterogeneous set of *ad hoc* rules in response to the contingencies of our moment-to-moment experience. Our beliefs are products of that process—fragmentary, provisional, limited. But although our knowledge-generating algorithm may not be magic, it isn't complete rubbish. This fragmentary, provisional knowledge is the only sort of knowledge there is. We can think only with the brains we have; we have no choice in the matter. Everything we know—the most immediate truths about our surroundings, the most esoteric discoveries of science, the most sublime insights of art—is a product of this contingent process.

The heuristics of play guide the unfolding of this process. They impose a structure on our mental experiences, steering us toward situations that allow us to slip smoothly through repeated iterations of the epistemological cycle. This includes the choices we make during moments of critical engagement. We are drawn toward modes of critical engagement that obey the heuristics of play.

This observation allows us to make several interesting claims about discourses. First, a discourse can be satisfying without being true. A satisfying discourse is merely one that allows us to make interpretive moves that obey the heuristics of play. Satisfying moves feel true when we make them; they feel like correct insights into the nature of the world. However, our knowledge-generating algorithm provides a route only to provisional utility, not to ontological certainty. What this means is that it is entirely possible for us to construct discourses that provide very little useful insight into the nature of the world but nevertheless feel utterly true. So long as the discourse allows to continually make satisfying interpretive moves, it doesn't matter whether or not those interpretations have any significance outside the discourse itself.

Furthermore, because of the seductiveness of play, we tend to actively seek out discourses for ourselves that allow us to make these kinds of satisfying moves. The result is the retroactive justification of our naïve critical choices. For example, if I see a painting that I like, and I want to analyze my aesthetic response, I will seek out a discourse in which my liking of the painting is justified. I will work to construct a critical frame that intersects with my naïve receptive act to structure a successful play space. Such a play space will permit me to make a sequence of interpretive moves that culminate in closure, simultaneously minimizing cruxes that contradict my initial response. If my analysis is successful, all the questions raised by my liking of the painting will be answered, and the trajectory that led me to arrive at that point of closure will have been interesting to follow. And, as the result of the process, my justification of my aesthetic response will feel true and correct.

In chapter 1, we looked at the problem with definitions—the tendency to treat definitions as essential statements about the nature of reality rather than as tools for structuring discursive fields. This tendency is a product of the process I just described. Defining our terms is the first stage of critical play. The meanings we attach to various signifiers determine how they constrain our interpretive moves within the resulting play space. We seek out definitions that structure critical play spaces that are interesting to navigate—spaces that obey the heuristics of play—and that allow us to make the sorts of moves that we want to make. In fact, because so much of critical play is anticipatory, many of our most meaningful interpretive moves will be definitional. Often the challenge is not to successfully navigate an existing discursive field, but to structure our discursive field so that our desired navigation of it becomes satisfying to accomplish.

I defined play as "free movement within a system of constraints." That definition made certain sorts of interpretive moves possible. It structured a discursive field that allowed me to make the sorts of interpretive moves that I wanted to make. It allowed me to navigate a trajectory that left behind as its residue a particular way of understanding play and our engagement with the world. The rules of a game aren't chosen because they are true or correct; they are chosen because they allow for interesting moves that, one hopes, leave behind a lingering trace of internalized constraints that prove meaningful to the player.

Our critical faculties are drawn toward discourses and topics that offer the possibility of surprising interpretive moves—satisfying trajectories that culminate in coherence and closure. This view of scholarship isn't intended as a criticism. As I mentioned in my discussion of presence earlier in this chapter, I consider the prioritization of interpretation over experience as merely a consequence of the Western cultural tradition. We assign value by considering the residual understanding scholarship produces, rather than considering the presence effects that it makes possible. This is so even though the course of the scholarship may have been determined largely by its presence effects. By dismissing the unexamined utilitarian claims of scholarship and recognizing it as a form of aesthetic engagement, I am neither rejecting it nor attempting to denigrate it. I'm merely constructing a discursive frame for understanding scholarship as a human behavior.

We analyze what we find interesting or useful to analyze. We have no other way to proceed—the process is governed entirely by the knowledge-generating algorithm encoded in our brains. Just as knowledge exists only as an embodied property of human brains, so does "interesting-ness" and "useful-ness." There is no such thing as an "interesting question" or a "useful answer" considered apart from the functioning of the epistemo-logical cycle and the heuristics of play. All scholarship—all forms of crit-ical engagement in both the sciences and the humanities—unfolds as a sequence of aesthetically satisfying moves within a ludically structured dis-course. We trust that these moves will produce a lingering understanding that will have some portability beyond the immediate considerations of navigating the play space, but we have no way to ensure that outcome. All we can do is enjoy the ride.

Meta-Critical Theory as Play

Most of the time, of course, we make do with no critical theory at all. We like what we like and are interested in what we find interesting, and we don't bother to justify our likes and interests. Even when do bother to jus-tify our likes and interests, we don't bother to justify our justifications. For example, if I say "I like *The Princess Bride* because it plays with the idea of storytelling" I probably will not go on to analyze why playing with the idea of storytelling is something worth liking.

This is how aesthetics has manifested itself through most of human history—a vast sea of composer play, performer play, audience play, with a thin foam of critical play riding atop it. In fact, the cascade functions just fine even if critical play is completely absent. We can compose music with-out having any knowledge of Schenkerian analysis, we can put on a show without studying method acting, and we can play a videogame without reading *A Theory of Fun*. Doing any of those things may make the earlier stages in the cascade easier or more interesting, but critical analysis isn't an essential part of the process.

Similarly, we can engage in critical analysis without having a theoretical justification for our critical frame. We can say interesting things about Elvis Presley's promotion and/or appropriation of black culture without bother-ing to ground our discourse in something deeper. The fact that our dis-course allows us to say interesting things is grounding enough. It is a tool that demonstrates its utility through application.

However, if we *do* want to look more deeply at how discourses function, we need to add one final step to the cascade: meta-critical play (figure 16.3). Meta-critical play is similar to critical play in that consists of a sequence of interpretive moves made within a play space structured by a discourse. But instead of intersecting with a receptive act (as critical play does), this discourse intersects with the analytical output of critical play. If critical

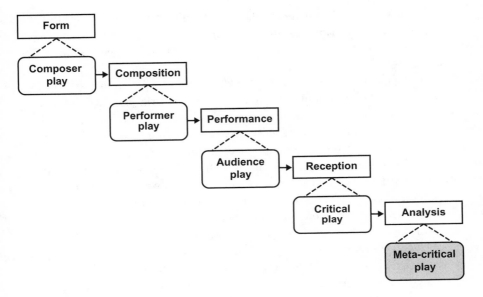

Figure 16.3
Meta-critical play within the cascade.

play is "talking about art," then meta-critical play is "talking about talking about art."

Meta-critical play is the situation you find yourself within at this very moment. You are operating within a discourse that has been designed to mesh with the concept of critical analysis so that you can make interpretive moves in relation to it. These interpretive moves unfold one by one in response to the beats on the page—these very words. The result is an evolving provisional understanding—a set of strategic constraints—that can be used to structure elaborated chains of anticipatory meta-critical play.

Meta-critical play is rare. We usually make and consume art without stopping to analyze what we are doing. When we do stop to analyze what we are doing, we usually don't stop to analyze our analysis. Because of this, our critical discourses tend to be couched in essentialist terms. They make foundational claims about the nature of art and then draw aesthetic conclusions on the basis of those claims: Art is an imitation of nature. Music exists to glorify God. Drama serves a ritual function. Novels serve the politics of their times. Games are interactive. These foundational claims are situated outside the circle of critical play. Indeed, their very fixity is what makes critical play possible; they form the rigid set of constraints we move within.

In fact, sometimes these constraints are so familiar and rigid that we forget that they are negotiable (as all rules are). The idea that we can manipulate the rules of our critical systems—play with them—can feel strange and unsettling.

The apparent solidity of a critical discourse is typically a function of its being applied to a limited number of artistic works and receptive acts. Critical discourses are constructed in response to encounters with particular works and audiences. If all the works we encounter are products of the same artistic tradition, and all the audiences we observe come from the same interpretive community, the resulting critical discourses will tend to feel rock-solid. They will explain most of our aesthetic experiences, and the few aesthetic experiences they don't explain will be easy for us to "other"—to explain away as wrong or bad or perverse.

For most of human history, meta-critical play has been difficult to achieve. In order to play with the tensions created between different critical systems, one must have enough competing critical systems at hand to make these tensions manifest. But before the advent of modern transportation and communication, everyone was much more tightly bound to the normative orbit of his or her immediate interpretive community. Within a community there might be arguments over different critical approaches ("Should we take the intent of the author into account or not?"), but the idea that the unfolding of this argument could itself be subject to critical analysis was unthinkable. There simply weren't enough examples of collisions between different critical systems to permit the formation of strategic constraints to explain the process. Critical analysis was treated as a way to explain experiences, not as an experience itself in need of explanation.

The twentieth century changed this state of affairs in a number of ways. Thanks to cheaper travel, a flood of different artistic traditions from around the world suddenly became available to previously isolated interpretive communities. Faster communication led to an acceleration of the tempo of critical thought—ideas could be shared and argued over at a previously unthinkable pace. Liberal economic policies produced popular works funded by the mass market that competed for attention with the patronage-driven high art of previous centuries. Advances in historical research led to a renewal of interest in works from lost traditions—for example, Baroque music and medieval literature.

As a result, critical certainty became much harder to achieve, and the contingent, provincial nature of all discourses became much harder to deny. There were simply too many competing critical systems, too many different types of works, too many different types of audiences. It is easy to write off works that lie outside the boundaries of your preferred discourse when such outliers are rare. But such an othering move becomes much more difficult when the number of "wrong" works exceeds the number of "right" ones.

It was the collapse of critical certainty in the twentieth century that opened up the possibility of meta-critical play. Deconstruction was the most significant product of this poststructuralist turn. First formulated by Jacques Derrida in the 1960s, deconstruction represents an attempt to grapple with the heterogeneity of twentieth-century culture. It is a critical discourse directed not at specific works of art or cultural practices, but at other discourses. It is a system of constraints that offers certain affordances, certain interpretive moves, when it is applied to a discourse. These moves are directed toward decentering and delegitimizing a discourse by undermining its foundational claims. The meta-critical play of deconstruction consists of exposing contradictions, uncovering perverse readings, and revealing the cultural tensions implicit in a discourse's structure.

Widespread deconstructive play has produced a universal decentering. The fragmentation of the critical landscape is repaired through a series of postmodern meta-critical moves that restore coherence by exploding contradictory truth claims. As part of this process, closure is deliberately avoided. Interpretive moves are chosen by prioritizing the indefinite deferral of meaning over convergence on any fixed terminal set of constraints. The goal in deconstructive play is not to seek a position that minimizes possible future interpretive moves. The goal is to halt play at the moment of maximum potentiality, when the urge to move toward closure is the strongest.

One of the strengths of deconstruction is that it can structure a satisfying meta-critical play space when applied to almost any discourse. It is a general-purpose toolkit for taking apart foundational claims in interesting and surprising ways. When we are inside deconstructive play, we experience it from moment to moment as a series of horizons. Each of these horizons lets us choose from a range of moves that reinterpret the discourse we are considering. The value of these interpretive moves is assessed through chains of anticipatory play: Does this reinterpretation lead toward or away from closure? Each reinterpretation opens up new (and sometimes unexpected) opportunities for increased reinterpretation. And because we are always working to defer closure, we always have new horizons to explore.

However, this indefinite deferral of meaning also reduces the satisfaction of deconstructive play. There is never a clean ending to deconstructive play, only an abandonment of the play space. Furthermore, since deconstructive play is always directed toward avoiding closure, it doesn't leave behind a portable set of interpretive constraints as a residue of the experience. We never arrive at a tidy terminal understanding (such as "*The Lord of the Rings* is about the power of the common man to resist evil"), because the whole point of deconstructive play is to make moves that oppose convergence on tidy terminal understandings.

What this means is that often the only residual understanding left behind after deconstructive play is a further strengthening of deconstruction's own foundational claims. Deconstruction winds up always being about deconstruction: "Here is a thing that I can do with a text, and I prove that here is a thing that I can do with a text by doing this thing with a text."

This is a criticism of deconstruction, but it's a mild one. The understanding that there are no privileged discourses is a useful understanding to have. And repeatedly demonstrating the validity of that understanding isn't a bad thing to do when the knowledge-generating algorithm of our brains drives us so relentlessly toward the normative satisfactions of truth. Furthermore, a critical stance that focuses our attention on the presence effects of being inside a moment of critical engagement isn't a bad thing in a culture that prioritizes interpretation over process. However, it does introduce a certain sameness to all deconstructive arguments. Once you understand the rules, you know how the deconstruction game is inevitably going to end, and so, although there might be some interest in the particular twists and turns you make along the way, the overall experience begins to feel flat and pointless. Deconstruction as a system of constraints has, for you, become played out.

However, there is another, deeper flaw that interferes with deconstruction's ability to function as a successful meta-critical play space. Deconstruction is a discourse that structures play spaces with other discourses, which suggests that it should be capable of structuring a play space with *itself*. It should be *recursive*. In other words, we should be able to deconstruct deconstruction—to use the constraints of deconstruction to structure a set of interpretive moves that explode deconstruction's own foundational claims.

Unfortunately, deconstruction doesn't structure a very satisfying recursive play space. Deconstruction normally works to reinforce its own foundational claims. But this generates a contradiction if the object of our play is to explode foundational claims. Coherence goes out the window, and we are left with a fragmentary jumble of competing constraints that collapse the play space. We can, of course, abandon coherence just as we abandoned closure and satisfy ourselves with gazing wistfully out over the wreckage, but there isn't much play to be had in this approach. It's a thing to do, but not a very useful or interesting thing to do.

My point here is not to "disprove" deconstruction. In fact, the ludic frame wouldn't be possible without the decentering groundwork laid by the deconstructive moves of the poststructuralist turn. My point is to use deconstruction as an example of how a meta-critical play space functions, and how it is possible for such a play space to fail. The fact that such failure is possible doesn't mean that deconstruction (or any other critical method) is useless. A set of constraints can be useful and interesting even if it doesn't structure an interesting play space in all possible circumstances. A set of rules need not account for every possible type of ball. Deconstruction can still be a useful tool, even if it has flaws as a meta-critical discourse.

Ludic criticism is itself both a critical and a meta-critical discourse. It is a way of analyzing sets of constraints and the presence effects that emerge when those sets of constraints are explored. But it is also designed to be general enough that it can be applied to a wide range of different sets of constraints, including the constraints that define other critical discourses. It's a way of analyzing experiences, but it's also a way of analyzing the experience of analyzing experiences. It's also (unlike deconstruction) explicitly designed to be recursive. It's a set of constraints that offers interesting interpretive moves when applied to its own practice. In other words, ludic criticism offers useful insights into the presence effects of ludic criticism.

So pause for a moment. Stop reading. And think about how you are engaging with this text. It's hard for me to predict exactly what you are experiencing, because I don't know what extratextual constraints you brought to this encounter. And I don't know the particular interpretive trajectory that you have followed to reach the point you're at now. But *you* know. You are immersed in a moment of critical engagement defined by the intersection of the words that you are currently reading with your extratextual constraints. If you pay close attention, you can sense the instinctive tug of coherence and closure. How are you working to situate and contain this book within your understanding of the world? How are you working to shut down your anticipatory chains and arrive at your settled understanding of what this book is trying to say?

If you have succeeded in doing that, pause again and consider the moment of *meta-critical* engagement you just experienced. What did it feel like to be inside that moment? How did the application of the ludic frame to your own receptive act itself create a moment that itself can be analyzed with the ludic frame? These are questions that I can't even begin to answer, because the words that I'm typing right now form a very, very small part of the constraints that define the meta-critical play space you just experienced (are still experiencing). The moves that you just made (are still making) are yours alone. The meaning that you just constructed (and are still constructing) is yours alone.

Concluding Thoughts

As I said in chapter 2, I have long believed that the most useful skill a game designer can have is the ability to look *through* the rules. By this I mean the ability to glimpse the experience the game will provide simply by analyzing its constraints. Until you can do this, until you can see the ramifications of different design choices without coding them up and trying them out, you are simply stumbling around in the dark, changing things at random to see what happens.

Furthermore, once you *can* look through the rules, you can work in the opposite direction. You can start with the particular experience you want to evoke, and then deliberately design a set of constraints to structure a playfield that will encourage it. The rules of the game become, like a painter's brushes, tools that can be used to produce particular aesthetic effects. You aren't merely splashing paint around, hoping that you will accidentally make a pretty pattern. You are making art.

I'm a game designer. I'm not a philosopher, or a neuroscientist, or a professor of English literature. And so, in trying to develop my own critical tools to think about play, I approached the problem as though it were a problem of game design.

There is a particular experience that I have tried to structure for you, the reader. Chapter by chapter I have laid out a set of constraints that bound a particular sort of playfield. From the very beginning, my definitions have been chosen systematically in order to invite convergence on a particular sort of understanding. I can't be certain that you have played the way I intended. After all, I don't have control over the extratextual constraints you brought to the encounter, or the specific interpretive moves you made along the way. What I have written may have intersected with your preexisting constraints in ways that I haven't anticipated. The meaning you take away from this book may be quite different from what I intended. It's an unavoidable consequence of what is required to reconcile your encounter with this book with your individual lived experience.

I'm fine with that. In fact, I hope for it. Once of the greatest pleasures one can have as a game designer is to see a player playing your game in a completely unexpected way.

With the broad focus of this final chapter, it may seem as though I'm claiming that ludic criticism is intended to be some sort of master narrative, some sort of totalizing discourse that subsumes all other discourses within itself. It certainly could be used that way. But doing so would run counter to the implicit decentering claims that are embedded within it. The aesthetic of play is merely a set of provisional constraints that allow us to make certain interpretive moves, nothing more. It makes no truth claims about itself, because making a truth claim is a forbidden move within the aesthetic.

All knowledge is provisional. We construct interpretive constraints to make sense of situations we find ourselves in, and then parsimoniously adjust those constraints as the world unfolds around us. We use anticipatory play to discover the ramifications of our interpretive frames and then modify our frames to accommodate the interpretive moves that we want to make. A critical theory is simply another set of constraints. It's a necessary simplification that we adopt to make engagement with the universe tractable. The understanding that it represents will always be a lessening and a distortion. It will leave some things unsaid, and say other things entirely out of proportion to their significance.

This book offers one way of looking at games, at art, at culture, at life, and at the world around us. It's a way that I find particularly useful and interesting. But *it isn't true*. Or, rather, it's true to exactly the same extent that all ways of looking at things are true: in the quality of the predictions it makes, in the quality of play it produces, in how portable it is. The aesthetic of play is (merely) a set of rules that (sometimes) can structure a particularly interesting sort of mental play space.

Now go play.

Bibliography

Aarseth, Espin J. 1997. *Cybertext: Perspectives on Ergodic Literature*. Johns Hopkins University Press.

Abrams, M. H. 1912. *Literature and Belief*. Columbia University Press.

Adams, Hazard, ed. 1971. *Critical Theory Since Plato*. Harcourt Brace Jovanovich.

Allis, Louis Victor. 1994. Searching for Solutions in Games and Artificial Intelligence (http://fragrieu.free.fr/SearchingForSolutions.pdf).

Aristotle. 1932. *The Poetics*. Harvard Unversity Press.

Austin, John L. 1975. *How to Do Things with Words*. Oxford University Press.

Bailey, Anthony. Zigzagging Through a Strange Universe. October 12, 1997 (http://speeddemosarchive.com/quake/qdq/articles/ZigZag/).

Bal, Mieke. 2009. *Narratology: Introduction to the Theory of Narrative*. University of Toronto Press.

Barthes, Roland. 1968. *Elements of Semiology*. Hill and Wang.

Barthes, Roland. 1977. *Image—Music—Text*. Hill and Wang.

Barthes, Roland. 1974. *S/Z*. Hill and Wang.

Barthes, Roland. 1975. *The Pleasure of the Text*. Hill and Wang.

Bateman, Chris, ed. 2009. *Beyond Game Design: Nine Steps Toward Creating Better Videogames*. Cengage.

Bateman, Chris. 2011. *Imaginary Games*. Zero Books.

Bekoff, Marc, and John A. Byers, eds. 1998. *Animal Play: Evolutionary, Comparative and Ecological Persepectives*. Cambridge University Press.

Belsey, Catherine. 2002. *Poststructuralism: A Very Short Introduction*. Oxford University Press.

Benjamin, Walter. 1969. *Illuminations: Essays and Reflections*, ed. H. Arendt. Schocken.

Blackmur, R. P. 1986. *Selected Essays of R. P. Blackmur*, ed. D. Donoghue. Ecco.

Bogost, Ian. 2011. *How to Do Things with Videogames*. University of Minnesota Press.

Bogost, Ian. 2006. *Unit Operations: An Approach to Videogame Criticism*. MIT Press.

Bor, Daniel. 2012. *The Ravenous Brain: How the New Science of Consciousness Explains Our Insatiable Search for Meaning*. Basic Books.

Bordwell, David. 1985. *Narration in the Fiction Film*. University of Wisconsin Press.

Botermans, Jack, Tony Burrett, Pieter van Delft, and Carla van Splunteren. 1989. *The World of Games: Their Origins and History, How to Play Them, and How to Make Them*. Facts On File.

Bromberg-Martin, Ethan S., Masayuki Matsumoto, and Okihide Hikosaka. 2010. Dopamine in Motivational Control: Rewarding, Aversive, and Alerting. *Neuron* 68, no. 5: 815–834.

Brown, Margaret Wise, and Clement Herd. 1947. *Goodnight Moon*. Harper.

Caillois, Roger. 2001. *Man, Play and Games*. University of Illinois Press.

Cannon, Claire Matson, and Richard D. Palmiter. 2003. Reward without Dopamine. *Journal of Neuroscience* 23, no. 34: 10827–10831.

Chaitin, Gregory. 2006. Epistemology as Information Theory: From Leibniz to Ω. Collapse 1: 26–51.

Chandler, Daniel. 2007. *Semiotics: The Basics*. Routledge.

Chatman, Seymour. 1978. *Story and Discourse: Narrative Structure in Fiction and Film*. Cornell University Press.

Church, Doug. Formal Abstract Design Tools. 1999. http://www.gamasutra .com/view/feature/3357/formal_abstract_design_tools.php (accessed November 1, 2013).

Cohen, Scott. 1984. *Zap! The Rise and Fall of Atari*. McGraw-Hill.

Consalvo, Mia. 2007. *Cheating: Gaining Advantage in Videogames*. MIT Press.

Costikyan, Greg. 1996. I Have No Words & I Must Design: Toward a Critical Vocabulary for Games (http://www.costik.com/nowords2002.pdf).

Costikyan, Greg, and Drew Davidson, eds. 2011. *Tabletop: Analog Game Design*. ETC.

Costikyan, Greg. 2013. *Uncertainty in Games*. MIT Press.

Crawford, Chris. 2005. *Chris Crawford on Interactive Storytelling*. New Riders.

Crawford, Chris. 2003. *Chris Crawford on Game Design*. New Riders.

Csikszentmihalyi, Mihaly. 2000. *Beyond Boredom and Anxiety: Experiencing Flow in Work and Play*. Jossey-Bass.

Csikszentmihalyi, Mihaly. 1990. *Flow: The Psychology of Optimal Experience*. Harper.

Csikszentmihalyi, Mihaly, and Rick E. Robinson. 1990. *The Art of Seeing: An Interpretation of the Aesthetic Encounter*. Getty.

Davidson, Paul R., and Daniel M. Wolpert. 2005. Widespread Access to Predictive Models in the Motor System: A Short Review. *Journal of Neural Engineering* 2, no. 3: S313–S319.

Deleuze, Gilles. 1994. *Difference and Repetition*. Columbia University Press.

Deleuze, Gilles, and Félix Guattari. 1987. *A Thousand Plateaus: Capitalism and Schizophrenia*. University of Minnesota Press.

Dennett, Daniel. 1987. *The Intentional Stance*. MIT Press.

Derrida, Jacques. 1997. *Of Grammatology*, corrected edition. Johns Hopkins University Press.

Derrida, Jacques. 1978. *Writing and Difference*. Routledge.

Dewey, John. 1998. *The Essential Dewey: Pragmatism, Education, Democracy*, volume 1, ed. L. Hickman and T. Alexander. Indiana University Press.

Dewey, John. 1998. *The Essential Dewey: Ethics, Logic, Psychology*, volume 2, ed. L. Hickman and T. Alexander. Indiana University Press.

Ebert, Roger. 2010. Video Games Can Never Be Art. *Chicago Sun-Times*, April 16.

Eco, Umberto. 1978. *A Theory of Semiotics*. Indiana University Press.

Eco, Umberto. 1990. *The Limits of Interpretation*. Indiana University Press.

Eco, Umberto. 1984. *The Role of the Reader: Explorations in the Semiotics of Texts*. Indiana Univerity Press.

Edelman, Shimon. 2008. *Computing the Mind: How the Mind Really Works*. Oxford University Press.

Edwards, Ron. 2003. Gamism: Step On Up (http://www.indie-rpgs.com/articles/21/).

Edwards, Ron. GNS and Other Matters of Role-Playing Theory. *The Forge: The Internet Home for Independent Role-Playing Games*. October 14, 2001. http://www.indie-rpgs.com/articles/1/ (accessed October 31, 2013).

Edwards, Ron. Narrativism: Story Now. *The Forge: The Internet Home for Independent Role-Playing Games*, January 29, 2004 (http://www.indie-rpgs.com/_articles/narr_essay.html) (accessed October 31, 2013).

Edwards, Ron. Simulationism: The Right to Dream. *The Forge: The Internet Home for Independent Role-Playing Games,* January 29, 2003 (http://www.indie-rpgs.com/articles/15/) (accessed October 31, 2013).

Fagen, Robert M. 1981. *Animal Play Behavior.* Oxford University Press.

Fein, Greta. 1981. Pretend Play in Childhood: An Integrative Review. *Child Development* 52, no. 4: 1095–1118.

Firth, Chris. 2007. *Making Up the Mind: How the Brain Creates Our Mental World.* Blackwell.

Fish, Stanley. 1980. *Is There A Text in This Class? The Authority of Interpretive Communities.* Harvard University Press.

Freytag, Gustav. 1900. *Technique of the Drama: A Exposition of Dramatic Composition and Art.* Scott Foresman.

Gadamer, Hans-Georg. 2004. *Truth and Method. Second, Revised.* Continuum.

Genette, Gérard. 1980. *Narrative Discourse: An Essay in Method.* Cornell University Press.

Genette, Gérard. 1997. *Paratexts: Thresholds of Interpretation.* Cambridge University Press.

Goldman, William. 1973. *The Princess Bride.* Ballantine.

Gumbrecht, Hans Ulrich. 2004. *Production of Presence: What Meaning Cannot Convey.* Stanford Unversity Press.

Harrigan, Kevin A., and Mike Dixon. PAR Sheets, Probabilities and Slot Machine Play: Implications for Problem and Non-Problem Gambling. *Journal of Gambling Issues,* no. 23 (June 2009).

Harrigan, Pat, and Noah Wardrip-Fruin, eds. 2007. *Second Person: Role-Playing and Story in Games and Playable Media.* MIT Press.

Heal, Jane. 2003. *Mind, Reason and Imagination: Selected Essays in Philosophy of Mind and Language.* Cambridge University Press.

Hebb, D. O. 1949. *The Organization of Behavior: A Neuropsychological Theory.* Wiley.

Hindmarch, Will, and Jeff Tidball. 2008. *Things We Think About Games.* Gameplaywright.

Hocking, Clint. 2007. Ludonarrative Dissonance in Bioshock (http://clicknothing.typepad.com/click_nothing/2007/10/ludonarrative-d.html).

Hopcroft, John E., and Jeffrey D. Ullman. 1979. *Introduction to Automata Theory, Languages and Computation.* Addison-Wesley.

Huizinga, Johan. 1955. *Homo Ludens: A Study of the Play Element in Human Culture*. Beacon.

Hunicke, Robin, Marc LeBlanc, and Robert Zubek. 2004. MDA: A Formal Approach to Game Design and Game Research (http://www.cs.northwestern.edu/~hunicke/MDA.pdf).

Huron, David. 2006. *Sweet Anticipation: Music and the Psychology of Expectation*. MIT Press.

Husserl, Edmund. 1964. *The Phenomenology of Internal Time-Consciousness*. Indiana University Press.

Iser, Wolfgang. 1978. *The Act of Reading: A Theory of Aesthetic Response*. Johns Hopkins University Press.

James, William. 2000. *Pragmatism and Other Writings*. Penguin.

Jauss, Hans Robert. 1982. *Toward and Aesthetic of Reception*. University of Minnesota Press.

Johnson, Mark. 1987. *The Body in the Mind: The Bodily Basis of Meaning, Imagination, and Reason*. University of Chicago Press.

Johnstone, Keith. 1981. *Impro: Improvisation and the Theater*. Routledge.

Juul, Jesper. 2005. *Half-Real: Video Games between Real Rules and Fictional Worlds*. MIT Press.

Juul, Jesper. 1998. A Clash Between Games and Narrative. Paper presented at DAC conference, Bergen, Norway (www.jesperjuul.net/text/clash_between_game_and_narrative.html).

Kandel, Eric R., James H. Schwartz, and Thomas M. Jessell. 2000. *Principles of Neuroscience*, fourth edition. McGraw-Hill.

Kemp, Gary. 2006. *Quine: A Guide for the Perplexed*. Continuum.

King, Brad, and John Borland. 2003. *Dungeons and Dreamers: The Rise of Computer Game Culture from Geek to Chic*. McGraw-Hill.

Koster, Raph. 2005. *A Theory of Fun for Game Design*. Paraglyph.

Kumparu, Kunio. 2005. *The Noh Theater: Principles and Perspectives*. Floating World Editions.

Laurel, Brenda. 1993. *Computers as Theatre*. Addison-Wesley.

Linden, David J. 2011. *The Compass of Pleasure: How Our Brains Make Fatty Foods, Orgasm, Exercise, Marijuana, Generosity, Vodka, Learning, and Gambling Feel So Good*. Penguin.

Mackay, Daniel. 2001. *The Fantasy Role-Playing Game: A New Performing Art*. McFarland.

Malaby, Thomas M. 2007. Beyond Play: A New Approach to Games. *Games and Culture* 2: 95–113.

Mar, Raymond A., and Keith Oatley. 2008. The Function of Fiction Is the Abstraction and Simulation of Social Experience. *Perspectives on Psychological Science* 3 (3): 173–192.

Maynard, Senko K. 1997. *Japanese Communication: Language and Thought in Context*. University of Hawai'i Press.

McGonigal, Jane. 2011. *Reality is Broken: Why Games Make Us Better and How They Can Change the World*. Penguin.

Meisner, Sanford, and Dennis Longwell. 1987. *Sanford Meisner on Acting*. Vintage.

Metzinger, Thomas. 2004. *Being No One: The Self-Model Theory of Subjectivity*. MIT Press.

Metzinger, Thomas. 2009. *The Ego Tunnel: The Science of the Mind and the Myth of the Self*. Basic Books.

Meyer, Leonard B. 1956. *Emotion and Meaning in Music*. University of Chicago Press.

Murray, Janet H. 1997. *Hamlet on the Holodeck: The Future of Narrative in Cyberspace*. Free Press.

Myers, David. 1992. Time, Symbol Transformations, and Computer Games. *Play & Culture* 5: 441–457.

Newman, James. 2002. The Myth of the Ergodic Video Game. *Game Studies* 2, no. 1 (http://www.gamestudies.org/0102/newman/)

Norris, Christopher. 1982. *Deconstruction: Theory and Practice*. Methuen.

Oatley, Keith. 1999. Why Fiction May Be Twice as True as Fact: Fiction as Cognitive and Emotional Simulation. *Review of General Psychology* 3 (2): 101–117.

Parlett, David. 2005. Rules OK or Hoyle on Troubled Waters (http://www.davpar.eu/gamester/rulesOK.html).

Parlett, David. 1999. *The Oxford History of Board Games*. Oxford University Press.

Peirce, Charles Sanders. 1992. *The Essential Peirce: Selected Philosophical Writings*, volume 1, ed. N. Houser and C. Kloesel. Indiana University Press.

Peirce, Charles Sanders. 1998. *The Essential Peirce: Selected Philosophical Writings*, volume 2, ed. Peirce Edition Project. Indiana University Press.

Pellis, Sergio, and Vivien Pellis. 2009. *The Playful Brain: Venturing to the Limits of Neuroscience*. Oneworld.

Peters, Gary. 2009. *The Philosophy of Improvisation*. University of Chicago Press.

Peterson, Jon. 2012. *Playing at the World: A History of Simulating Wars, People and Fantastic Adventures From Chess to Role-Playing Games*. Unreason Press.

Popper, Karl. 2002. *The Logic of Scientific Discovery*. Routledge Classics.

Quine, W. V. 1992. *Pursuit of Truth*, revised edition. Harvard University Press.

Quine, W. V. 2004. *Quintessence: Basic Readings from the Philosophy of W. V. Quine*, ed. R. Gibson Jr. Belknap.

Rayfield, Donald. 1998. *Anton Chekhov: A Life*. Northwestern University Press.

Riffaterre, Michael. 1984. *Semiotics of Poetry*. Indiana University Press.

Rorty, Richard. 1979. *Philosophy and the Mirror of Nature*. Princeton University Press.

Rorty, Richard. 1982. *The Consequences of Pragmatism*. University of Minnesota Press.

Rosenblatt, Louise M. 1995. *Literature as Exploration*, fifth edition. Modern Language Association of America.

Rosenblatt, Louise M. 2005. *Making Meaning with Texts: Selected Essays*. Heinemann.

Rosenblatt, Louise M. 1994. *The Reader, the Text, the Poem: The Transactional Theory of the Literary Work*. Southern Illinois Unversity Press.

Russell, Matheson. 2006. *Husserl: A Guide for the Perplexed*. Continuum.

Russin, Robin U., and William Missouri Downs. 2003. *Screenplay: Writing the Picture*. Silman-James.

Ryan, Marie-Laure. 2006. *Avatars of Story*. University of Minnesota Press.

Ryan, Marie-Laure. 2001. Beyond Myth and Metaphor: The Case of Narrative in Digital Media. *Game Studies* 1, no. 1.

Ryan, Marie-Laure. 2001. *Narrative as Virtual Reality*. Johns Hopkins University Press.

Salen, Katie, and Eric Zimmerman. 2004. *Rules of Play: Game Design Fundamentals*. MIT Press.

Sartre, Jean-Paul. 1988. *"What Is Literature?" and Other Essays*. Harvard University Press.

Saussure, Ferdinand de. 1983. *Course in General Linguistics*, ed. C. Bally and A. Sechehaye. Open Court.

Schechner, Richard. 2003. *Performance Theory*. Routledge.

Schell, Jesse. 2008. *The Art of Game Design: A Book of Lenses*. Morgan Kaufman.

Scruton, Robert. 1996. *Modern Philosophy: An Introduction and Survey*. Penguin.

Searle, John R. 1995. *The Construction of Social Reality*. Free Press.

Searle, John. 1969. *Speech Acts*. Cambridge University Press.

Sekuler, Robert, and Randolph Blake. 1994. *Perception*, third edition. McGraw-Hill.

Shannon, Claude E. 1950. Programming a Computer for Playing Chess. *Philosophical Magazine* 41 (314): 256–275.

Shea, Robert, and Robert Anton Wilson. 1975. *The Illuminatus Trilogy*. Dell.

Sicart, Miguel. 2009. *The Ethics of Computer Games*. MIT Press.

Singer, Dorothy G., and Jerome L. Singer. 1990. *The House of Make-Believe: Children's Play and the Developing Imagination*. Harvard University Press.

Sirlin, David. 2006. *Playing to Win: Becoming the Champion*. Lulu.com.

Sniderman, Stephen. 1999. Unwritten Rules (http://www.gamepuzzles.com/tlog/tlog2.htm).

Sontag, Susan. 1990. *Against Interpretation and Other Essays*. Picador.

Stanislavski, Constantin. 2003. *An Actor Prepares*. Routledge.

Strasberg, Lee. 1988. *A Dream of Passion: The Development of The Method*. Plume.

Suits, Bernard. 2005. *The Grasshopper: Games, Life and Utopia*. Broadview.

Sutton-Smith, Brian. 1997. *The Ambiguity of Play*. Harvard University Press.

Thurber, James. 1937. The Macbeth Murder Mystery. *The New Yorker*, October 2.

Turner, Victor. 1982. *From Ritual to Theatre: The Human Seriousness of Play*. PAJ.

Upton, Elizabeth Randell. 2013. *Music and Performance in the Later Middle Ages*. Palgrave Macmillan.

Vaihinger, Hans. 1925. *The Philosophy of "As If": A System of Theoretical, Practical and Religious Fictions of Mankind*. Harcourt, Brace.

Walton, Kendall L. 1990. *Mimesis as Make-Believe: On the Foundations of the Representational Arts*. Harvard University Press.

Wardrip-Fruin, Noah, and Pat Harrigan, eds. 2004. *First Person: New Media as Story, Performance, and Game*. MIT Press.

Wells, H. G. 1913. *Little Wars*. Frank Palmer.

Wilson, Douglas. and Sicart, Miguel. 2010. Now It's Personal: On Abusive Game Design. Paper presented at FuturePlay 2010, Vancouver.

Wilson, Edmund. 1945. Who Cares Who Killed Roger Ackroyd? *The New Yorker*, January 20.

Wolf, Mark J. P., and Bernard Perron. 2003. *The Video Game Theory Reader*. Routledge.

Wolpert, Daniel. 2011. The Real Reason for Brains. Presented at TED conference (http://www.ted.com/talks/daniel_wolpert_the_real_reason_for_brains.html).

Wolpert, Daniel, and J. Randall Flanagan. 2001. Motor Prediction. *Current Biology* 11, no. 18: R729–R732.

Zangeneh, Masood, Alex Blaszczynski, and Nigel E. Turner, eds. 2007. *In the Pursuit of Winning: Problem Gambling Theory, Research and Treatment*. Springer.

Ludography

4000 AD. Parker Brothers, 1972.

Anzio. Avalon Hill, 1969.

Asteroids. Atari, 1979.

Blitzkrieg. Avalon Hill, 1969.

Burnout. Criterion Games, 2001.

Call of Duty. Infinity Ward, 2003.

Canabalt. Adam Saltsman, 2009.

Candy Crush Saga (2012). King, 2012.

Candy Land. Milton Bradley, 1949.

Chainmail. Guidon Games, 1971.

Chess

Civilization V. Firaxis Games, 2010.

Computer Space. Nutting Associates, 1971.

Cosmic Encounter. Eon, 1977.

Dance Dance Revolution. Konami, 1998.

Dear Esther. The Chinese Room, 2012.

Diablo III. Blizzard Entertainment, 2012.

Divine Right. TSR, 1979.

Donkey Kong. Nintendo, 1981.

Doom. id Software, 1993.

Dragon's Lair. Advanced Microcomputer Systems. Cinematronics, 1983.

Dungeons & Dragons. TSR, 1974.

Fable II. Lionhead Studios, 2008.

Fat Princess. Titan Studios, 2009.

Flower. thatgamecompany, 2009.

FreeCell

Go

God of War. Sony Computer Entertainment, 2005.

Grand Theft Auto. Rockstar Games, 1997–2013.

Guitar Hero. Harmonix, 2005.

Ico. Team Ico, 2001.

Imperium. GDW Games, 1977.

Jedi Knight II: Jedi Outcast. Raven Software, 2002.

Journey. thatgamecompany, 2012.

Monopoly. Parker Brothers, 1935.

Myst. Cyan, 1993.

Night Driver. Micronetics, 1976.

Nine Men's Morris

Ogre. Metagaming Concepts, 1977.

Pole Position. Namco, 1982.

Pong. Atari, 1972.

Portal. Valve, 2007.

Quake. id Software, 1996.

Ridge Racer. Namco, 1993.

Rock Band. Harmonix, 2007.

Scrabble. Selchow and Righter, 1952.

Settlers of Catan. Mayfair Games, 1995.

Shadow of the Colossus. Team Ico, 2005.

SimCity. Maxis, 1989.

Síochán Leat. Brenda Romero, 2009.

Skies of Arcadia. Overworks, 2000.

Snakes & Ladders

Sorcery. The Workshop, 2012.

Split/Second. Black Rock, 2010.

Star Fleet Battles. Task Force Games, 1979.

Super Mario Bros. Nintendo, 1985.

Super Smash Bros. Hal Laboratory, 1999.

Tetris. Alexey Pajitnov, 1984.

The Game of Life. Milton Bradley, 1963.

The Legend of Zelda: Ocarina of Time. Nintendo, 1998.

The Sims. Maxis, 2000.

Thief: The Dark Project. Looking Glass, 1998.

Tom Clancy's Ghost Recon. Red Storm Entertainment, 2001.

Tom Clancy's Rainbow Six. Red Storm Entertainment 1998.

Train. Brenda Romero, 2009.

Trouble. Milton Bradley, 1965.

Uncharted: Drake's Fortune. Naughty Dog, 2007.

Waterloo. Avalon Hill, 1962.

World of Warcraft. Blizzard Entertainment, 2004.

Index